What Shakespeare Stole From Rome

What Shakespeare Stole From Rome

by Brian Arkins

Carysfort Press

A Carysfort Presss Book in association with Peter Lang
What Shakespeare Stole From Rome
by Brian Arkins

First published in Ireland in 2012 as a paperback original by
Carysfort Press, 58 Woodfield, Scholarstown Road
Dublin 16, Ireland

ISBN 978-1-78874-848-3
©2012 Copyright remains with the author

Typeset by Carysfort Press
Cover design: eprint limited

This publication was grant-aided by the Publication Fund of the
National University of Ireland, Galway

This book is published with the financial assistance of
The Arts Council (An Chomhairle Ealaíon) Dublin, Ireland

Caution: All rights reserved. No part of this book may be printed or reproduced
or utilized in any form or by any electronic, mechanical, or other means, now
known or hereafter invented including photocopying and recording, or in any
information storage or retrieval system without permission in writing from the
publishers.

for Clongowes Wood College

almae matri

Contents

Preliminaries	1
1 | Shakespeare's Knowledge of Classics	9
2 | Reading Roman History	19
3 | The Impact of Heavy Seneca	45
4 | The Impact of Light Plautus	63
5 | The Pervasive Presence of Ovid	77
6 | The Matter of Virgil	95
7 | The Uses of Latin	103
8 | Greek Themes in Shakespeare	113
Conclusion	131
Notes	133
Select Bibliography	153

Preliminaries

1

It is a given of Shakespeare criticism that the man cannot be pinned down, that the plays provide no easy answers, that they possess no didactic intent. Coleridge refers to 'the unfathomable depths of his oceanic mind'; Dryden asserts that 'He was the man who of all Moderns, and perhaps Ancient poets, had the largest and most comprehensive soul'. So Bloom explains that 'Shakespeare did not think one thought and one thought only; rather scandalously, he thought all thoughts, for all of us'. Accordingly, Berryman sees him as an 'encyclopaedic bastard'. This ensures that we cannot know the views of Shakespeare the man, that he engages in what Greenblatt nicely calls 'the brilliant practice of strategic opacity'[1].

Shakespeare's refusal to instruct can be contrasted with Shaw's persistent practice of writing plays that have designs upon us, that are didactic. Indeed Shaw provides Prefaces for his plays that explain what their message is (James Agate claimed that his plays 'are the price we pay for Shaw's prefaces')[2]. It is Shakespeare's failure to be at all didactic that led Shaw to make the extravagant and absurd claim that 'With the single exception of Homer, there is no eminent writer, not even Sir Walter Scott, whom I can despise so entirely as I despise Shakespeare when I measure my mind against his'[3].

Other dramatists such as Sophocles come somewhere in between in this spectrum. It is clear that in *Antigone* the young woman Antigone is right to insist on the burial of her brother Polyneices, and that the king Creon is wrong to prevent her doing so; *pace* Hegel, they are not both right. As the blind prophet Tiresias points out, the gods will not tolerate those who leave human bodies unburied. But in *King Oedipus*, there is no apparent message, since we never find out why Oedipus was fated to kill his father and to marry his mother; an example of general irony, as our expectation that the world makes sense is shattered. *King Lear* may be read in a similar way: ' "this is what we have to face, and we do not know, and we cannot quarrel with the dramatist for not telling us, how to face it"'[4].

Shakespeare's refusal to be dogmatic, his persistent scepticism, could derive from many situations and sources he met with during his life[5], and seems to be something consciously willed. Vicious disputes between Catholic and Protestant threw into doubt the nature of religious belief. The ancient ordering of society was changing with the advent of social mobility, and the practice of enclosure, the surrounding of common arable land to allow individual farmers to provide pasture for sheep. Montaigne answers the question 'What do I know?' with the simple negative 'Nothing'. Machiavelli called into question the nature of political power. Donne wrote 'And new philosophy calls all in doubt', referring to the scientific theories of Kepler, Copernicus and Galileo[6]. Meanwhile, in his own life Shakespeare had to contend with the death of his son Hamnet (or Hamlet) in 1596[7].

All that is enough to make any man sceptical. But there is something else: like a chameleon, Shakespeare could adopt every point of view, could *empathize* with every character, even villains like Richard III or Macbeth. De Quincey explains about the murderer: 'our sympathy must be with *him*; (of course I mean a sympathy of comprehension, a sympathy by which we enter into his feelings, and are made to understand them, - not a sympathy of pity or approbation)'[8]. It is Shakespeare's special gift to exhibit a sympathy of comprehension for a huge variety of women and men (not to mention the dog Crab).

Literary and dramatic genre offers a further way into the sceptical nature of Shakespeare[9]. Commending the versatility of the Players in *Hamlet* (2.2.333-5), Polonius adverts to the blurring of genre: 'The best actors in the world either for tragedy, comedy, history, pastoral, pastoral-comical, historical-pastoral, tragical-historical, tragical-comical-historical-pastoral'. Shakespeare's own practice exhibits this blurring of genre, because he very rarely writes pure tragedy, being, as Yeats said, 'always a writer of tragi-comedy'[10]. George Steiner concurs, and provides an authoritative gloss: 'He *knows*, overwhelmingly, that the facts of the world are hybrid, that desolation and joy, destruction and degeneration are simultaneous. The sum of the extant is never in one key, it is never one thing only'[11].

Some of the plays examined in this book are not one thing only. Certainly, plays such as *Richard III*, *Hamlet*, and *Macbeth* can be termed 'tragedies' (even if they are not wholly tragic). But the genre of the plays that deal with Roman history is more tricky: *Coriolanus*, *Julius Caesar*, *Antony and Cleopatra*, *Cymbeline*, *Titus Andronicus*. Are these plays histories, a term normally reserved for plays about English history, or a subgenre of 'histories' that deal with Roman history? Or are they 'tragedies' that relate the death of the hero: Coriolanus, Julius Caesar, Antony, Titus Andronicus? And is *Cymbeline* a 'history' that deals with both English and Roman history, or one of the late 'romances', as is often held? Whatever the answer to these questions, their existence again shows that Shakespeare does not come in neat categories with their attendant clarity.

So where does this leave the genre of *Troilus and Cressida*? The Epistle to the play classifies it as a 'comedy', but in the First Folio it was included in the 'tragedies'; it could also be viewed as a 'history', a 'Greek' play (as with the 'Roman' plays), a 'tragical satire'. *Troilus and Cressida* could, of course, be called a 'problem' play, so that uncertainty about its genre may relate to its sceptical approach to moral issues: 'What's aught, but as 'tis valued?' (2.2.5). In this play, as in *All's Well That Ends Well* and *Measure for Measure*, Shakespeare employs the tactic of making us unsure how to judge moral issues, unsure whether to come down on one side or another of a moral dilemma; that is akin to the concept of *aporia* in philosophy, where it is found impossible to give an answer to a particular problem[12]. Of *Troilus and Cressida*, there can be no single correct reading, nor of *Coriolanus*, as Hawkes explains: 'It isn't that it can be "read" in a number of ways. It is that it can't be coherently read in any single way'[13].

In terms of the present, this scepticism of Shakespeare can be linked to the thought of postmodernism. A central feature of postmodernism is its rejection of master narratives, totalizing theories that seek to account for everything, whether in politics, or religion, or science (such narratives are often held by the nation-state). What replaces them is various versions of relativism and scepticism – a scepticism exhibited by Shakespeare in regard to the English nation-state and its Protestant religion, if also to revolution against that state and Catholicism. Whitman's oft-quoted dictum seems specially apt: 'Do I contradict myself? / Very well then I contradict myself. / (I am large, I contain multitudes')[14].

Keats saw that Shakespearean multitudes are a type of power: 'at once it struck me, what quality went to form a Man of achievement especially in literature & which Shakespeare possessed so enormously – I mean *Negative Capability*, that is when man is capable of being in uncertainties, Mysteries, doubts, without any irritable reaching after fact & reason'[15]. But it is too easy to stress in this formula the merely negative, and to fail to give due weight to its endorsement of scepticism as a form of power. To be precise: a dramatist and poet like Shakespeare offers a *form of knowledge*, set out in an artistic medium, play or poem, that differs not only from scientific knowledge (so much prized in our time), but also from the discursive knowledge of theology or philosophy. So Walsh asserts that successful literary art 'provides knowledge in the form of realization: the realization of what anything might come to as a form of lived experience'[16] (a view that would be strengthened if Aristotle's much disputed term 'catharsis' means 'intellectual clarification')[17]. *King Lear* may serve as an example: 'to encounter *Lear* fully is to have made a major advance in self-knowledge and in knowledge of the world'. Hence Calvino writes that 'the classics help us understand who we are and the point we have reached'[18].

One vital aspect of such understanding is that Shakespeare in his plays was responsible for a much enlarged portrayal of human character, a position argued for by Harold Bloom in his book *Shakespeare : The Invention of the Human*, and anticipated by Yeats in *A Vision*: 'I see in Shakespeare a man in whom human personality, hitherto restrained by its dependence upon Christendom or by its own need for self-control, burst like a shell'[19]. So in reading Shakespeare's plays, we must set aside Aristotle's argument for the primacy of plot in drama, and give due weight to character.[20]

2

This book is a contribution to Reception Studies[21], the analysis of how Greek and Roman material is used in later eras (such a process already took place in the Greco-Roman world, as with Virgil's use of Homer). It is vital to analyse the use by Shakespeare of Roman material by means of a coherent theory. In Renaissance England, the doctrine that writers should practice literary imitation (*imitatio*)

– already advocated in the Greco-Roman world by critics such as Longinus – was a given, almost mandatory.[23] Such imitation was not to be contrived or slavish, but natural and creative. So it is necessary to bring into question a number of terms that are often used to describe it. These terms describe a *passive* process, in which the later author simply allows Greek and Roman themes flow into her or his work. Consider the following definitions from the *Oxford English Dictionary*:

heritage: 'That which has been or may be inherited'
legacy: 'Anything handed down by an ancestor or predecessor'
tradition: 'The action of handing over something material to another'
influence: 'The action or fact of flowing in'

Other terms now prevalent are also inadequate. The much used term 'intertextuality' posits a relationship between two literary works, but fails to indicate that a relationship of appropriation is involved. Equally well, the currently dominant term 'reception' is open to similar objections: ' "reception" is too blunt, too *passive* a term for the dynamics of resistance and appropriation, recognition and self-aggrandisement that make up this drama of cultural identity'[24].

What we need are terms that clearly show that for the later writer the process of using an earlier writer is *active*. Eliot in his essay on Massinger provides one such term, 'to steal': 'Immature poets imitate; mature poets steal; bad poets deface what they take and good poets make it into something better, or at least something different'. The Irish dramatist Marina Carr concurs: 'It seems that you are allowed to steal what you need while learning the craft and that there is no crime in that'. She cites Shakespeare as an example: he 'took from everywhere, but look what he did with his plunder'[25]. If the verb 'steal' is felt to be too familiar, then the verb 'appropriate' meaning 'To make over to any one as his own' (OED) seems apt.

A further term that is useful here and that derives from postcolonial theory is the Brazilian concept of 'cannibalism': colonized people *devour* material from the colonists in a new and energized form that meets their needs. A view already envisaged by Du Bellay as early as 1549: in dealing with Greek and Roman writers, it is necessary for modern writers to 'transform themselves into them, devour them, and after properly digesting them, turn them into blood and sustenance'[26]. So the colonized Caliban in *The Tempest* says to his colonizer Prospero and his daughter Miranda

'You gave me language, and my profit on't / Is, I know how to curse' (1.2.362-3).

Such appropriation by Shakespeare of Greek and Latin authors has nothing about it of what Harold Bloom calls 'the anxiety of influence'[27]. This theory holds that the new poet is always looking over his (sic) shoulder at the immense achievement of his predecessors, that his belated state causes him anxiety, that he finds it difficult to write. On the contrary, Shakespeare is an excellent example whose sources are for him a type of freedom; Dryden's statement about Ben Jonson can be applied to him: 'what would be theft in other poets is only victory in him'[28]. In so far as Shakespeare did exhibit the anxiety of influence, this was never in relation to Roman or to Greek writers, but to his exact contemporary Christopher Marlowe (1564-93). Shakespeare had to meet the challenge of *Tamburlaine*, *Dr. Faustus* and *The Jew of Malta*, and, by the time of Marlowe's murder in 1593, his achievement – probably the three *Henry VI* plays, *Two Gentlemen of Verona*, *The Taming of the Shrew* – was not obviously superior to that of his rival.[29]

Not everyone was enamoured of Shakespeare's cavalier way with the work of other writers. In 1592, Robert Greene, who was a graduate of both Oxford and Cambridge, but of dubious morals, launched a famous attack on Shakespeare in his prose work *A Groatsworth of Wit*: 'there is an upstart crow, beautified with our feathers that with his *Tygers heart wrapt in a Players hyde*, supposed he is as well able to bombast out a blanke verse as the best of you: and being an absolute *Johannes Factotum*, is in his own conceit the only Shake-scene in a counterey'.[30]

The meaning of some of Greene's attack seems clear. The charge of being a Jack of All Trades (*Johannes Factotum*) relates to the fact that a mere player like Shakespeare has seen fit to become a dramatist. The phrase 'with his tiger's heart wrapped in a Player's hide' – which adapts the line 'O tiger's heart wrapped in a woman's hide' from *3 Henry VI* (1.4.138), and is spoken by the Duke of York to the bloodthirsty Queen Margaret – may attack Shakespeare's character or his religion or his rhetoric. More opaque is the phrase 'beautified with our feathers' (referring to expensive head-dresses worn by players), but it is likely to allude to Shakespeare's practice of appropriating material from other dramatists such as Marlowe: 'an alarming ability to plunder, appropriate, and absorb'[31]. In that case, Greene is referring to the little crow in Horace, *Epistles* 1.3, which steals the hues from other birds, and is then stripped of them.

Shakespeare was to have his revenge upon Greene. In *Hamlet* (2.2.109-10), Polonius views Hamlet's phrase 'the beautified Ophelia' as 'an ill phrase, a vile phrase, "beautified" is a vile phrase'. But Shakespeare used Greene's prose romance *Pandosto* as the main source for *The Winter's Tale*. While in an ambivalent move, he partly based the great comic character of Falstaff on Green's raffish life[32].

1 | Shakespeare's Knowledge Of Classics

1

Shakespeare's friend and critic Ben Jonson stated that 'He was not of an age, but for all time'. Yeats is more accurate: 'A great piece of literature is entirely of its own locality and yet infinitely transferable'[1]. So the second part of Jonson's assertion is true: Shakespeare has become universal, honoured across centuries and continents. But the first part of Jonson's statement is not true, since Shakespeare, like every one else, is very much the product of his own time, of Elizabethan and Jacobean England. Consider, for example, his multiple roles in the heady world of London theatre: actor, dramatist, shareholder in a theatre company (the Lord Chamberlain's Men, later the King's Men), lease-holder of a theatre (the Globe, Blackfriars).

Indeed Shakespeare has become an inseparable part of what we call the Renaissance[2], which began in Padua in the second half of the thirteenth century, and reached its heydey from about 1420 to 1620. This Renaissance, the rebirth of the world of Greece and Rome involved, in particular, a fresh appropriation of Greek and Latin authors on a massive scale. So in Elizabethan England, knowledge of Greco-Roman antiquity, and especially of Latin language and literature, was a form of what Bourdieu calls 'cultural capital'; a body of acquired knowledge that marked out its possessor as a serious player among the educated elite[3]. Such capital was gained in England mostly through education at the grammar schools and through private reading (a small number attended the universities of Oxford and Cambridge). Indeed in Shakespeare's day, learning Latin functioned as a Renaissance *rite de passage*, a kind of puberty rite that allowed young boys entry to a competitive male elite by learning a language that was not spoken at home, and that was linked to the concept of becoming physically hardy[4]. Hence Montaigne's statement that 'We are ever ready to ask *Hath he any skill in the Greek and Latin tongue?*'[5]

2

Shakespeare began his schooling in Stratford at the age of about 5 at the elementary of 'petty' school, which taught English reading and writing, and religion. In 1571 at the age of 7, Shakespeare enrolled in the grammar school[6], the King's New School on Church St, where he attended six days a week for almost all of the year, beginning at 6 or 7 in the morning, and continuing until about 5 or 6 in the afternoon. The central, the dominant subject of instruction was Latin, which had by this time an immense prestige in Elizabethan England; in 1571, the bishops asked British schoolmasters to teach books 'whereby the fulness and fineness of the Latin and Greeke toung may be learned'[7].

The teaching of Latin placed great stress on grammar, on translation, on rhetoric, on memory work. The intricate grammar of Latin, which, unlike English, is a highly inflected language – the basic verb *amare*, 'to love', has close to fifty different forms – was relentlessly pursued by means of William Lily's *A Short Introduction to Grammar* (in English), and of his *Brevissima Institutio* (in Latin). Translation involved a double process: first, from Latin to English; second, when the Latin text was removed, from English back to Latin. Prized in the Renaissance as it was in the Greco-Roman world, rhetoric dealt with the very many figures of speech (such as metaphor, alliteration, assonance), with the use of moral aphorisms (*sententiae*), with arguing on two sides of a proposition (*controversiae*). Key texts in rhetoric were the *Rhetorica and Herennium*, the first Latin work to deal with style, parts of Quintilian's long work on the education of the orator, and the *De Copia* of Erasmus that finds innumerable ways of saying the same thing in Latin. In all of this, boys were required to make use of their *memory*, what the schoolmaster Holofernes calls 'the ventricle of memory' (*Love's Labour's Lost* 4.2.69).

This regime in the grammar school ensured that Shakespeare 'had as good a formal literary training as had any of his contemporaries'; and 'had at least as good a knowledge of Latin language and literature as a modern graduate in the classics'[8]. So we can disregard Ben Jonson's notorious slur that Shakespeare had 'small Latin', which has had a success in the world that is wholly undeserved. The question of whether Shakespeare knew any Greek is more complex: does Jonson's further assertion that he had 'less Greek' connote 'some Greek' or 'no Greek?' Baldwin feels it very probable that Shakespeare got as far as the simplified (*koiné*) Greek of the New Testament, but there is no evidence for this. What seems to militate against it is the fact that Shakespeare's dealings with the Greek world are so very *indirect* (see Chapter 8). Whatever the merits of education in Latin for the bulk of pupils, it had, for an actor and writer of plays like Shakespeare, the great advantage of privileging language, the ability to present two sides of an argument, the memorizing of material, the verbal manipulation of sources.

Based on what was available in other Elizabethan grammar schools, the following curriculum in Latin was very probably followed by Shakespeare. In Latin drama, then prized as the model to follow, the comedies of Plautus and especially Terence (seen as a writer of pure Latin), and the tragedies of Seneca. Latin epic was represented in a major way by the *Metamorphoses* of Ovid, and by Virgil's *Aeneid*; two other works of Ovid that featured were the love letters of the *Heroides*, and the poems of exile, *Tristia*, plus some *Satires* by Juvenal. In Latin prose, we have the self-serving *Commentaries* of Julius Caesar, the historical monographs of Sallust, parts of Livy's massive *History of Rome*. For philosophy, there was Cicero's work *De Officiis, On Duties*, which expounded Greek philosophical ideas. Translated into Latin, the animal fables of the Greek writer Aesop were also studied. Included too were Neolatin works: the pastoral poetry of Mantuan, nickname of Baptista Spagnoli (1448-1516), which appears in *Love's Labour's Lost* (4.2.93-9), and a compendium by Palingenius called *Zodiacus Vitae*.

What must be remembered in all of this is that the practice of keeping commonplace books, in which excerpts from various writers were gathered together, and used at will, allowed the inference that people had read more than they had. Indeed Shakespeare probably had access at school to two collections of maxims in Latin, the *Disticha Moralia* ascribed to Cato, and Culmannus' *Sententiae Pueriles*.

There may be more to Shakespeare's knowledge of Latin than this. In his *Brief Lives*, John Aubrey asserted of Shakespeare that 'he understood Latin pretty well, for he had been in his younger years a schoolmaster in the country'[9]. This statement appears to be authentic, since Aubrey's informant was William Beeston, whose father Christopher had been a member of Shakespeare's company. But where 'in the country' did Shakespeare teach Latin? The Catholic Hoghton family of Hoghton Tower in Lancashire has a tradition that Shakespeare spent two years – 1580 and 1581 – with them, and recent scholarship has tended to accept this[10]. How this came about has been plausibly explained as follows.

After Elizabeth's accession to the throne in 1558, Protestantism was re-established as the state religion. Warwickshire remained a bastion of Catholic recusants, and Shakespeare's father was a Catholic: he was persecuted for not attending Protestant church services, and appears to have owned a copy of the *Spiritual Testament* of Carlo Borromeo, Archbishop of Milan and a leading figure in the Counter-Reformation. This document was brought to England in 1580 by Edmund Campion, the Jesuit martyr, who visited Warwickshire before going to Lancashire. A brother of Campion's fellow-martyr Thomas Cottam named John taught in the grammar school at Stratford in the years 1579-81, and the Cottams were relatives and tenants of the intensely Catholic family of the Hoghtons in Lancashire. So it is thought that John Cottam arranged for Shakespeare to work for the Hoghtons as a schoolmaster, as a teacher of Latin, and, since they maintained players, of drama. What was involved is indicated in *The Taming of the Shrew* by the gentleman Baptista about the education of his daughter Bianca, who knows Latin (1.1.92-95): 'And for I know she taketh most delight / In music, instruments, and poetry, / Schoolmasters will I keep within my house, / Fit to instruct her youth'.

3

As it happens, Shakespeare has left us a comic portrayal of what a class in Latin grammar might have been like. In Act 4, scene 1 of *The Merry Wives of Windsor*, the Welsh parson Sir Hugh Evans, who bases himself on Lily's Grammar, asks the schoolboy William (a significant name?) about the meaning of Latin words, and the declension of the demonstrative pronoun 'this'. Comedy is provided by Mistress Quickly's finding of false, mainly sexual meaning in the Latin words[11]. But the stern Evans notes that, if William forgets his pronouns, he will receive a whipping. Evans proceeds in a mechanical way, requiring William to translate not just from Latin into English, but back again to Latin:

EVANS What is *lapis*, William?
WILLIAM A stone.
EVANS And what is 'a stone', William?
WILLIAM A pebble.
EVANS No, it is *lapis*. I pray you remember in your prain.
WILLIAM *Lapis.*

Evans then moves on to the demonstrative pronoun 'this'. William gets the nominative singular right (*hic, haec, hoc*), but is wrong about the accusative singular masculine, offering *hinc* meaning 'from here' instead of the correct *hunc*. When Evans tries to trick William by asking for the vocative case of 'this', which he pronounces as 'focative', and which does not exist (*caret*), a series of sexual innuendoes follows: Evans 'focative' suggests 'fuck'; William's tentative reply 'O – vocativo – O' suggests the vagina; Quickly takes Latin *caret* to be English 'carrot' that suggests the penis. Quickly continues in this vein after William supplies the genitive plural of 'this' (*horum, harum, horum*) by referring to another term for the vagina 'case', and by finding English 'whore' in the Latin. She also finds a sexual meaning in Latin forms of 'this' such as *hic* and *hac*: 'He teaches him to hick and to hock, which they'll do fast enough of themselves'.

This mode of teaching Latin grammar remained much the same for more than 400 years. In his autobiographical novel *A Portrait of the Artist as a Young man*, Joyce describes a Latin class in the Jesuit boarding school of Clongowes Wood College (which he attended from 1888 to 1891). When Father Arnall asks Jack Lawton to decline the noun *mare* meaning 'the sea', the pupil gets as far as the end of the singular, but is unable to provide the plural. Another pupil – Fleming – ventures the view that the word has no plural (it has), and receives from Father Dolan the physical punishment envisaged by Evans. But Joyce, like Shakespeare can have fun with the demonstrative pronoun *hic, haec, hoc*: 'hicky hecky hock, huges huges huges, hughy, hughy, hughy'[11a]

4

For Shakespeare, further knowledge about Rome and about Greece comes from his reading of translations into English of works by Latin and by Greek authors, for a huge industry of translation came into being in Elizabethan England, suggesting the truth of Pound's dictum that 'A great literature is perhaps always a great age of translation'[12]. Like so many writers, Shakespeare used these translations of Greek and Latin authors at will. In the case of Latin authors, he used translations into English to supplement reading a text in the original; in the case of Greek authors, he relied entirely on translations because he did not know Greek[13].

The most important translation from Latin for Shakespeare was Arthur Golding's *Metamorphoses* of Ovid (1567), which provided an almost limitless store of Greek myths. Also important was the translation by a number of authors of Seneca's *Tenne Tragedies* (1581), which Thomas Nashe saw as a source for English writers: English Seneca 'will afford you whole *Hamlets*'[14]. Further translations from Latin include William Adlington's *The Golden Ass* by Apuleius (1566), Philemon Holland's *History of Rome* by Livy (1600), and Philemon Holland's *Pliny the Elder* (1601).

The key translation from Greek for Shakespeare is Plutarch's *Lives* by Sir Thomas North (1579), an English version of Amyot's French translation from the Greek of Plutarch. These *Lives* became the major source for three plays about Roman history: *Coriolanus*, *Julius Caesar*, and *Antony and Cleopatra*. Shakespeare also read George Chapman's partial translation of the *Iliad* of Homer, which is one of the sources for the play *Troilus and Cressida*.

5

Shakespeare uses various methods to appropriate and to outdo his Greek and Roman sources. So it is not only the case that these sources make an impact on Shakespeare, but it is also the case that, in the light of his reading of them, we may look at the Roman and Greek material in a different way. As Eliot said, the past is 'altered by the present as much as the present is directed by the past'; hence 'it is not merely that Ovid influenced Shakespeare, Shakespeare has also changed the way Ovid is read'[15].

An early play of Shakespeare that uses material from Latin literature may seek to establish a marker, *Titus Andronicus* for tragedy, *The Comedy of Errors* for comedy. In the vast accumulation of horrors in *Titus Andronicus*, Shakespeare not only showing his contemporaries Marlowe and Kyd how to write a revenge tragedy, but is also surpassing the cannibal feast of Seneca's tragedy *Thyestes* and of Ovid's *Metamorphoses*; as Titus says (5.2.195), 'worse then Procne I will be revenged'. In *The Comedy of Errors*, Shakespeare makes use not just of one play by Plautus, the main source *Menaechmi*, but a second play by him *Amphitruo* (a practice previously employed by Plautus' fellow writer of comedies,

Terence). This blending of two Latin plays allowed Shakespeare to introduce a *second* set of twins, and so to vastly increase the instances of mistaken identity.

Ovid is the Latin author who enjoys the most pervasive presence in Shakespeare.[16] For the Elizabethans in general and Shakespeare in particular, Ovid's great epic poem *Metamorphoses* that contains an encyclopaedic account of Greek myths was the work of Ovid that mattered most; Shakespeare garnered about 80% of his references to Greek mythology from it. A number of vital aspects of *Metamorphoses* impinged on Shakespeare: the pointed brilliance of Ovid's rhetoric in an age itself obsessed with verbal ingenuity; the theme found in Shakespeare's early work of difficult love, as in the miniature epic *The Rape of Lucrece*, where he vastly expands the account of the Rape from Ovid's 132 lines to 1,855; the landscape of mysterious deities that suggests the fairy world of *A Midsummer Night's Dream*; not least the steely determination of Ovid's Medea, who provides one aspect of Lady Macbeth.

Shakespeare may develop what is already present in the source. From Plutarch's *Lives*, he takes on board the stress on the individual person, together with that person's inner divisions, but goes beyond it to produce, from *Julius Caesar* in 1599 on, a more complex type of character, a more complex type of clash, than had appeared in his plays up to that time[17]. Shakespeare also expands the role of women in the plays based on Plutarch such as Portia in *Julius Caesar* and Cleopatra in *Antony and Cleopatra*. At the same time, a play about Roman history such as *Julius Caesar* might relate not only to the past, but also to the present: the topic of murdering a ruler had a contemporary analogue, because, in the months before the writing of *Julius Caesar*, there had been several attempts on Elizabeth's life by those who supported the Catholic cause[18].

Sometimes the Greek or Roman source may exhibit Shakespeare's refusal to be pinned down, his opacity. In *Coriolanus*, it is notoriously hard to come down on the side of either the aristocracy (patricians) or the ordinary people (plebeians)[19]. For Shakespeare, ancient Rome is no more transparent than Jacobean England.

More complex still is the famous duet between Lorenzo and Jessica at the end of *The Merchant of Venice* (5.1.1-74):

> **LORENZO** The moon shines bright. In such a night as this,
> When the sweet wind did gently kiss the trees
> And they did make no noise, in such a night

Troilus methinks mounted the Trojan walls
And sighed his soul towards the Grecian tents,
Where Cressid lay that night.

JESSICA Did Thisbe fearfully o'ertrip the dew
And sow the lion's shadow ere himself
And ran dismayed away.

LORENZO In such a night
Stood Dido with a willow in her hand
Upon the wild sea banks and waft for her love
To come again to Carthage.

JESSICA In such a night
Medea gathered the enchanted herbs
That did renew old Aeson.

Complexities of source, of mythological system, of relationships between the lovers, and between the characters and the audience ensure that this passage cannot be labelled as ironic or as romantic, but remains enigmatic, ambivalent, diffuse[20]. The main sources are Ovid, Virgil and Chaucer; the mythological systems are Greek, Roman and mediaeval. The lovers speak of passionate love between Troilus and Cressida, Pyramus and Thisbe, Aeneas and Dido, Jason and Medea. They also speak of the disastrous ending of that love in the deaths of Pyramus and Thisbe, and of Dido. But there is also renewal of life, when Medea rejuvenates Jason's father Aeson. Over all this Shakespeare presides, and an Elizabethan audience listens. One thing they would certainly hear is the way in which the contemporary lovers are intoxicated with their own rhetoric, with the procedure of capping what the other says (as seen in the fourfold repetition of the phrase 'In such a night'). This stress on language for its own sake, together with the ambivalence of the content, renders the duet impossible to pin down to a single meaning. Eliot wrote that words 'Decay with imprecision';[21] Shakespeare's words may be imprecise, but they bloom, glitter, coruscate.

7

Shakespeare's modes of appropriation of Roman and Greek material have not been to everyone's taste, to those who insist that such treatment must be neoclassical in tone. For the term 'neoclassical' does not mean simply the use of Greek and Roman themes, but a use that exhibits special characteristics: the belief that art should instruct as well as please; keeping to the so-called unities of action, place and time in drama; making genius and/or nature subordinate to art; observing, above all, *decorum*, what is judged right and proper. A.E. Housman finds that Milton is neoclassical, and so to be preferred to Shakespeare who is not. The qualities he ascribes to Milton that Shakespeare lacks are 'The dignity, the sanity, the unfaltering elevation of style, the just subordination of detail, the due adaptation of means to ends, the high respect of the craftsman for his craft and for himself' (But even Milton could sometimes set decorum aside: his writing in English is chaste, but he could be obscene when writing in Latin)[22].

For what Shakespeare brings to the use of Roman and Greek material is the 'open' play[23], anathema to such people as Housman; and to his contemporaries Sidney and Jonson: tragedy and comedy coalesce; language can be elevated, but also colloquial and sexual; the unities are largely ignored, and sub-plots are frequent; respect for the craft does not involve pedantry; there is no attempt at crude instruction.

Nor is it the case that Greek and Latin authors always exhibit decorum. Aristophanes is full of drink and sex (often in obscene language), and of scandalous jokes about politicians. In Latin literature, there is a subversive stream that focuses on sexual love and sex: Catullus, the Elegists, Petronius, Martial. And even early Horace, an author seen as wholly 'classical', has some obscenity: *dum futuo*, 'while I'm fucking her' (*Satires* 1.2.127).

There is something of a paradox about Shakespeare's use of the Roman and Greek classics: he has, to a great extent, replaced them, but to fully understand his work a knowledge of the Greco-Roman world is necessary.[24] The following seven chapters aim to provide that knowledge.

2 | Reading Roman History

1

For the Renaissance, Roman history was not simply one past among many, but the most important past. In Rome, vitally important men controlled politics, the military, the law and government, and provided a source of political enlightenment for the present (Greece was largely unknown). This view matches that of the historian Livy who said of the record of human experience that 'you can find for yourself and your country both examples and warnings'[1]. This general stress on Roman history explains why Shakespeare chose to write five plays about it, ranging in time from the early Republic (*Coriolanus*) to the end of the Republic (*Julius Caesar, Antony and Cleopatra*) to the early Empire (*Cymbeline*) to the later Empire (*Titus Andronicus*). But Shakespeare's approach to historical drama will be much more nuanced then the moralizing of Livy.

There is a paradox about how the very ancient history of Rome related to the English present. While Shakespeare's numerous plays about English history (a type very popular in Elizabethan England) might be constrained in referring to contemporary events, plays about Rome could tackle important political issues more freely because of the *distancing* effect: since they are set in a remote past, they can, without seeming to, deal with issues important to the Elizabethan and Jacobean eras. Hence the director Trevor Nunn said that Shakespeare used Roman settings 'to conduct' a less inhibited examination of political motives and social organization than was possible when he was dealing with English history'[2].

Analysis of Shakespeare's plays about Roman history may begin by invoking the formalist approach of Hayden White to the problem of historical knowledge[3]. Seeking to discover the structural elements in the writing of history, White finds this writing has plots based on literary genres such as Tragedy, Comedy, Romance and Satire. This process can usefully be transferred from historical writing to literary works. So the kind of plot Shakespeare employs in *Titus Andronicus*, and in the plays of Roman history inspired by the Greek writer Plutarch – *Coriolanus, Julius Caesar, Antony and Cleopatra* – is that of Tragedy, while the plot of *Cymbeline* is that of Romance. This stress or genre ensures that there can be no question of Shakespeare writing about history in a way that provides us with what Ranke saw as the task of the historian: 'to show how it really was' (*wie es eigentlich gewesen*). Indeed the writing of history in general involves, in a crucial way, the perspective of the later historian.

These considerations must inform comment on two aspects of Shakespeare's Roman plays, anachronism and metatheatrical speeches. When Shakespeare writes of Coriolanus' *hat* (2.3.98) and of the *striking clock* in *Julius Caesar* (2.1.192), he draws attention to the fact that he is writing about Roman history from the perspective of the Jacobean and Elizabethan eras, not as some wholly detached observer, but as a writer concerned with bringing the past to life. Similarly, when characters in these Roman plays point, in a metatheatrical way, to their own dramatic status, we must recall that this is a *play* about history, that it will reflect the point of view of the dramatist, if not also the actors. So soon after the murder of Julius Caesar, the conspirator Cassius imagines future eras enacting this deed in new countries and new languages, such as this performance of *Julius Caesar* in England in 1599 and in English (3.1.111-3):

> How many ages hence
> Shall this our lofty scene be acted over
> In states unborn and accents yet unknown!

If Cassius envisages future tragedies, Cleopatra thinks of actors staging low comedy, in which Antony is drunk, and she is a prostitute, and in which her part is played by a boy, as in Shakespeare's play (5.2.218-21):

>   Antony
> Shall be brought drunken forth, and I shall see
> Some squeaking Cleopatra boy my greatness
> I'th posture of a whore.

2

By far the most important source used by Shakespeare for his Roman plays was the *Lives* of Plutarch[4] (about 46 to about 120 A. D.), who engaged in the idiosyncratic project of writing twenty-three pairs of biographies, in which a Greek military or political leader is compared to a Roman one. In these, the subject of the life is centre-stage, abstracted from political and military history, and becomes exemplary (as in Livy): he is a man who is good and successful (Julius Caesar), or, rarely, bad and subject to misfortune (Antony). Naturally, this crude moralizing is foreign to the strategic opacity of Shakespeare, who transforms Plutarch into something rich and strange.

Plutarch's *Lives* were accurately translated from Greek into French by Jacques Amyot in 1559, and into English in 1579 by Sir Thomas North; a revised and expanded version was published in 1595 by Shakespeare's friend from Stratford, Richard Field[5]. Since Shakespeare did not know Greek, he used North's translation, so that his source for *Coriolanus*, *Julius Caesar* and *Antony and Cleopatra* was an English translation, itself based on a French one, of a Greek text about Roman history. Plutarch provided Shakespeare with a general view of aspects of the Roman Republic, so that, as Eliot says, he 'acquired more essential history from Plutarch than most men could from the British Museum'[6]. But Shakespeare also derived from Plutarch something that is both more specific and more important: the ability to portray the interior nature of a character in a new and subtle way, and to focus on the process of making decisions, as he had not done before[7]. These facts are first seen in 1599 in the character of Henry in *Henry V* (note too Fluellen's comparison of Henry V to Alexander the Great; 4.7.25-51), and in the character of Brutus in *Julius Caesar*. Hamlet was soon to follow.

3

Three of Shakespeare's plays about Roman history – *Coriolanus*, *Julius Caesar*, *Antony and Cleopatra* – form a loose trilogy dealing with major issues in Rome such as whether the government should be of the few or of one man, whether power should be aristocratic (patrician) or democratic (plebeian), together with the role played by great men in these clashes[8].

In terms of the chronology of Roman history, Shakespeare's first Roman play is *Coriolanus*, although it was written in 1608 after *Julius Caesar* (1599) and *Antony and Cleopatra* (1606/7). Figures like Caesar and Antony were well known in Shakespeare's day, Coriolanus much less so, so that Spencer notes that 'To write *Coriolanus* was one of the great facts of historical imagination in Renaissance Europe'[9]. This tragedy focuses on two political themes. One is the clash in Rome between the aristocrats led by Coriolanus and the common people led by their tribunes, who defended them from violence and aggression. The second theme is the war between Rome and the Volscians, who lived south of Rome and were led by Aufidius; the name 'Rome' is used 86 times in *Coriolanus*, nearly always by aristocrats. Modern productions of *Coriolanus* often adopt a particular political stance – right-wing or left-wing – but, as so often with Shakespeare, it is not possible to view the play as supporting one side or the other of the two political issues, leading Coleridge to say that *Coriolanus* shows 'the wonderful philosophic impartiality of Shakespeare's politics'[10].

The main source for *Coriolanus* is Plutarch's *Life* of *Coriolanus*, a semi-legendary figure, who took his name from the capture of the Volscian town of Corioli in 493 B.C. Plutarch supplied the basic narrative of the tragedy, but Shakespeare greatly expanded the roles of Coriolanus' mother Volumnia, his friend Menenius (given a much more elaborate version of the fable of the belly), the tribunes of the people, and the Volscian general Aufidius;[11] on the other hand, Shakespeare suppresses the thirty day truce between Rome and the Volscians.

Coriolanus opens with public violence by mutinous citizens, whose representative nature is stressed by the fact that they are not given individual names; such an opening is unique in plays of this period. Shakespeare conflates a single rising of riots about debt in 494 B.C. and riots about the lack of corn in 491 B.C. into a rising about corn (this reflects uprisings in England in 1607/08 about the practice of enclosure, the conversion of arable land into pasture for sheep, and about lack of food). The people feel that the aristocrats are hoarding grain, and do not care about the hunger of ordinary people, indicating the fact that from the earliest times Romans thought it the duty of the State to supply corn to the people at a reasonable price. Menenius produces the stock response of conservative politicians that the famine is an act of God, not of humans: 'For the dearth, / The gods, not the patricians, make it'

(1.1.71-2). To bolster his position, Menenius cites the 'pretty tale' of the belly (1.1; found in Livy and Plutarch): the belly gives life to the members of the body by distributing the food it ingests, but these members may rebel. Menenius applies this to Rome, stating that 'The senators of Rome are this good belly, / And you the mutinous members' (1.1.146-7).

But the First Citizen knows, like all radical politicians, that these disasters are presided over by men for their own purposes, often private gain (1.1.78-85):

> They ne'er cared
> for us yet. Suffer us to famish, and their store –
> houses crammed with grain; make edicts for usury,
> to support usurers; repeal daily any wholesome act
> established against the rich, and provide more
> piercing statutes daily, to chain up and restrain
> the poor. If the wars eat us not up, they will; and
> there's all the love they bear us.

Indeed when the tribune Sicinius asks the rhetorical question 'What is the city but the people?' the answer is clearly 'nothing' (3.1.197). But Coriolanus has a very different view of the people, viewing them as fickle: 'With every minute you do change a mind' (1.1.181), supported in a later era by Horace's reference to 'the mob of fickle citizens' (*Odes* 1.1.7). For though as individual men they are acceptable, as a group they are irrational and changeable.

The complex nature of the general Coriolanus, who is of distinguished ancestry, is central to Shakespeare's play. Indeed the adjective 'noble' and its cognates occur 85 times. It is clear that he is the supreme embodiment of Roman *virtus*, a major part of which was military success, since he has defeated the Volscians in battle; as the general Cominius says, 'It is held / That valour is the chiefest virtue and / Most dignifies the haver' (2.2.83-5). The honour due to Coriolanus is stressed by the virtual litany of his names in Act 2, scene 1 – 'With fame a name to Martius Caius. These / In honour follows Coriolanus' (163-4) – and by the granting to him of an *ovatio*, a lesser form of military triumph, which began outside the city of Rome and ended at the Capitol.

But it becomes obvious that Coriolanus' military prowess is not enough: he is unable to bring about the transition from the army to politics. Contentious debate was always vital in Roman politics, but the fighter Coriolanus cannot talk (2.2.73): 'When blows have made me stay, I fled from words' (this is not in Plutarch). If the crowd is fickle, Coriolanus' problem is the opposite one of being very inflexible; as his mother Volumnia says, 'You are too absolute' (3.2.39). So he is quick to anger, lacks imagination, is given no soliloquy in the play. So his violence against the Volscians is similar to his violence against the people of Rome. Worse: this unbending warrior is seen to be aiming at absolute control: 'he affect tyrannical power', says the tribune Brutus (3.3.2).

Events in Rome after Coriolanus' military success against the Volscians very clearly establish his inflexible nature. The tribunes object to making Coriolanus consul, the chief political office of the Roman state, and accuse him of treason. Instead of attempting to placate the people, he rants against them. As a result, he is banished from Rome, and goes to the Volscian town of Antium. Coriolanus thus becomes a paradigm of a person whose love can easily turn to hate: 'My birthplace hate I, and my love's upon this enemy town' (4.4.23-4). But matters are not so simple for a Roman aristocrat in exile, since he now feels he has no identity: Coriolanus 'forbade all names: / He was a kind of nothing, titleless' (5.1.11-3). Equally well, Aufidius calls him 'Martius' and refuses to dignify him with the name 'Coriolanus', when he goes back on his promise to attack Rome: 'Dost thou think / I'll grace thee with that robbery, thy stolen name / Coriolanus in Corioles?' (5.6.88-90). Coriolanus by any other name is not the same man.

The reason Coriolanus does not, in the end, attack Rome is because his mother Volumnia persuades him not to. Coriolanus, she argues, will either be paraded through the streets as a foreign enemy, or else he will bring about his country's ruin, killing his wife and children. But by destroying Rome, Coriolanus will lose his reputation as a warrior, and will become anathema to future ages. So although Volumnia engages in the archetypically feminine activity of sewing (spinning in Rome), she exemplifies the fact that Roman women often exercised important behind-the-scenes roles in politics[12]. Indeed such women could be bloodthirsty: Volumnia posits a startling analogy between milk coming from a woman's breasts and blood coming from a wounded man's head: 'The breasts of Hecuba, / When she did suckle Hector, looked not lovelier / Than Hector's forehead when it spit forth blood / At Grecian sword contemning' (1.3.40-2)[13]. Of two liquids that give life, one fulfils its proper peaceful function, the other no longer does because of war. So Volumnia's assertion is that the purpose of life is violent war, her motto make war, not love. And when Volumnia prevails over her son, political power passes to her. She has always, of course, exercised emotional power over Coriolanus, who is dominated by her, and so has an intense, homosocial relationship with Aufidius, enemy and friend.

Coriolanus undergoes an ignoble death (Livy is agnostic about this), in which his excesses are punished, and he becomes a scapegoat for the city of Rome, a man on whose body Aufidius stands. The mood is summed up by the Second Lord's fatalistic urging 'Let's make the best of it' (5.6.147), suggesting that Aufidius' closing speech that lauds Coriolanus and the funeral march played for him should be viewed as ironic. This death is not tragic, as are those of Brutus and Cassius in *Julius Caesar*, and of Antony and Cleopatra in *Antony and Cleopatra*. By 1608, Shakespeare's view of politics had become very bleak.

4

Shakespeare's plays *Julius Caesar* and *Antony and Cleopatra* deal with the history of Rome at the time of the Late Republic in the first century B.C. Rome was then governed by an oligarchy that consisted mostly of old aristocratic families, who were divided, to use broad terms, between conservatives (*optimates*) and radicals (*populares*)[14]. This unstable situation, which was exacerbated by the demands of Rome's growing Empire, ensured that a succession of military leaders competed with each other for power in a series of civil wars: Sulla versus Marius, Caesar versus Pompey, Octavian versus Antony. After Julius Caesar defeated Pompey at the battle of Pharsulus in 49 B.C., and after he overcame Pompey's sons in Spain at the battle of Munda in 45 B.C., he was proclaimed *dictator* for life in February 44 B.C.; this position, which conferred supreme military and judicial authority, was originally meant to be held for a very limited time (such as six months) during a major crisis. Caesar's new position not only involved one-man rule in Rome, but for some raised the spectre of kingship, a concept anathema to the Romans since the expulsion of the kings in 510 B.C.

Shakespeare's play *Julius Caesar* (1599)[15] – both a Roman play and a tragedy – deals with the killing of Caesar[16] on the Ides (15) of March 44 B.C. by Brutus, Cassius and others, who supported the Republican system of government, and with the resulting clash between the conspirators and the Caesarian party led by Mark Antony and Octavius (the future Emperor Augustus). This violent act could be viewed in two entirely different ways: Dante condemns

Brutus and dispatches him to the lowest circle of Hell; the French Revolution praises him as a liberator. The ethical issue at stake is how to assess Caesar's killing: was this a justified assassination of a man who wanted to rule as a despot? or was this an unjustified murder of a man who had legally been granted absolute power? As Syme puts it in his seminal work *The Roman Revolution*, 'Liberty or stable government: that was the question confronting the Romans themselves'[17]. Shakespeare, true to form, does not come down on one side or the other; as though exemplifying Hegel's view that tragedy like *Antigone* can portray a clash between two positions that are equally valid.

In 1599, these issues in *Julius Caesar* have contemporary resonances.[18] The murder of Caesar, later deified, mirrors conspiracies against the aging god-like Elizabeth, who had a bust of Caesar in her palace in Greenwich. Since the Chorus in *Henry V* (also of 1599) notes that Roman crowds welcoming Caesar home can be compared to London crowds sending Essex off to Ireland, the ambition of Caesar might mirror that of Essex. The stripping of Caesar's statues could reflect the removal of Catholic images by Protestant England. More definitely and more mundanely, a variety of Elizabethan places, buildings, dress, clothes and books implies a basic similarity between the world of Rome and the world of England.

The central enabling source for *Julius Caesar* was Plutarch, especially the *Lives* of Brutus and of Caesar (the latter quarter). Plutarch provides the general historical plot based around the killing of Caesar, as well as many details. But Shakespeare added much material of his own[19]. This includes the boy Lucius, and the full treatment of the conspirator Casca and the poet Cinna; the famous speeches in the Forum after Caesar's death by Antony and Brutus (as well as the latter's soliloquy at Act 2, scene 6). Then *Julius Caesar* brings about the telescoping of time, so that the events of three years become a story of five eventful days. So Shakespeare manipulated Plutarch to fashion his first great tragedy, a new kind of play, a short political thriller. It is proper here to speak of the freedom of influence.

Gaius Julius Caesar, who came from an aristocratic family, was a hugely complex person. He was an astute politician, a military genius, a gifted writer. He showed great brutality in killing hundreds of thousands in Gaul (France), but striking clemency towards his former Roman enemies (including Brutus and Cassius). He was arrogant and, according to some, tyrannical: 'for always I am Caesar' (1.2.211). This speaking by Caesar of himself in the third person – there are nearly 20 instances in the play – stresses both authority and a brand name (as the titles Kaizer and Czar were to show). As Cassius realizes, when he asks 'what should be in that "Caesar"?' (1.2.140)

Caesar's absolute power is recognized by Antony – 'When Caesar says, "Do this", it is perform'd' – and by Cassius, who compares him to one of the Seven Wonders of the Greco-Roman world, the giant bronze statue of Helios, the sun god, on the island of Rhodes, the Colossus (1.2.133-6). A sinister exercise of Caesar's power is seen in his treatment of the tribunes of the people Flavius and Marullus, who are hostile to him, remove crowns from his statues, and are 'put to silence' (1.2.283), that is deprived of their office. With power goes bravado and arrogance. Caesar's bravado is seen in his statement about going to the Senate: 'Caesar shall go forth' (2.2.10). His arrogance becomes clear, when he coldly rebukes Metellus Cimber (properly Tillius Cimber) for seeking to petition him on the part of his banished brother Publius. Caesar justifies this action by heavily stressing his inflexible nature and his unique position among men: 'I am constant as the northern star... I do know but one / That unassailable holds on his rank' (3.1.60, 68-9).

But Shakespeare's Caesar is also a man, subject to the infirmities of the flesh. As was well-known in Rome, he suffered from epilepsy, and has a fit here in public (1.2). But Shakespeare invents two other weaknesses for Caesar: he is deaf (does he listen?) and he is a weak swimmer. Shakespeare also invents the infertility of Caesar's wife Calpurnia, through whom he is vulnerable: he commands Antony to touch her at the fertility rite of the Lupercalia in order for her to become pregnant. Like all mortals Caesar will die, and Hamlet knows that the body of Caesar that 'kept the world in awe' will 'patch a wall t'expel the water's flow' (5.1.204-5).

And yet Caesar's death in Act 3, scene 1 in no way removes him from the action: his spirit, indeed his Ghost, dominate the second half of the play (in which the name Caesar occurs 211 times). Here the main action takes place in the political vacuum caused by Caesar's death that must be filled either by his supporters Antony, Octavian and Lepidus, or by the conspirators against him led by Brutus and Cassius. Such dominance by the dead Caesar was adumbrated by the portents that preceded his murder such as a lion giving birth in the street, and the dead arising from their tombs; as

Calpurnia says, 'When beggars die, there are no comets seen; / The heavens themselves blaze forth the death of princes' (2.2.30-1). Language reflects the way Caesar presides over the action, as we encounter the constant, almost talismanic use of the name 'Caesar'. The high point of this relentless stress on Caesar is the appearance of his Ghost to Brutus on two occasions, at Sardis in Lydia (modern Turkey) and at Philippi (in northern Greece), where the final battle between the opposing groups was fought, bringing the Roman Republic to an end. At Sardis, the Ghost of Caesar is brief, but chilling: asked who he is, he replies 'Thy evil spirit, Brutus'; asked if Brutus will see him again, he replies 'Ay, at Philippi'.

When the Ghost does indeed appear to Brutus at Philippi, he takes it as a sign he will die: 'I know my hour is come'. No wonder, then, that Brutus regards Caesar as causing the deaths of his soldiers at Philippi, as a still potent figure: 'O Julius Caesar, thou art mighty yet! / Thy spirit walks abroad, and turns our swords / In our own proper entrails' (4.3.281,284; 5.5.20; 5.3.94).

For Theodore Mommsen, the greatest historian of Rome in the nineteenth century, Caesar was the most admirable man who ever lived. A view accepted by Shaw in his play *Caesar and Cleopatra*: 'My Caesar is Mommsen's Caesar dramatized'. Whatever we make of Shakespeare's Caesar, certainty about him eludes us; Shaw teaches us about a great man in the most explicit possible way. Shaw preaches, Shakespeare remains invisible.[20]

Chief among the conspirators is Marcus Junius Brutus, who has by far the largest number of lines in the play, and who stresses *honour* in his dealings with Caesar; in 44 B.C. he was *praetor urbanus*, the official responsible for the administration of justice between Roman citizens. Brutus' script is already written, since he is the distant descendent of Junius Brutus who was (supposedly) responsible for killing the tyrannical last king of Rome, Tarquinius Superbus, in 510 B.C. As Cassius, who was married to Brutus' sister, reminds him: 'There was a Brutus once that would have brooked / Th'eternal devil to keep his state in Rome / As easily as a king' (1.2.158-60). So it is Cassius who must urge the initially reluctant Brutus to act against Caesar, but once he agrees to take part in the conspiracy, he becomes its natural leader.

The conspirators believe that Caesar wants to be king; although he rejects the crown offered three times by Antony, Casca thinks that 'he was very loath to lay his fingers off it' (1.2.239-40). In reality, Caesar as *dictator* for life needed no extra powers. But in politics perception is all, and conspirators like Brutus believe 'He would be crown'd' (2.1.12).

Accordingly, for Brutus there must be a premptive strike: 'Then lest he may, prevent' (2.1.28). Previously, Brutus (whose name in Latin connotes 'dull', 'insensible') asserted 'I am not gamesome: I do lack some part / Of that quick spirit that is in Antony'(1.2.27-28). Now his inactivity and his inner conflict have given way to a decision to act.

Caesar's impending death is preceded not merely by portants, but also by the famous warning of the soothsayer Spurinna to him to 'Beware the Ides of March', and by his wife Calpurnia's dream, during which she cries out three times 'Help, ho! They murder Caesar' (1.2.18; 2.2.3). As Caesar is attacked by multiple assassins at the Capitol (where Shakespeare places the Senate house), his dying words to Brutus, which require the answer 'yes', are significant. Whereas Suetonius[21] records them in Greek as 'you too, son', Shakespeare's *'Et tu, Brute?'* – 'you too, Brutus' – is the only Latin in the plays of Roman history based on Plutarch, and draws attention in striking fashion to the fact that, in this pivotal moment, we are situated in the city of Rome. The justification for this violent act is found in the slogan of Lucius Cornelius Cinna: 'Liberty! Freedom! Tyranny is dead' (3.1.78).

Anxious not to appear bloodthirsty (despite bathing in Caesar's blood), the conspirators spare Antony (a big mistake), allow him to bring Caesar's body to the Forum, allow him to speak at his funeral. There the speeches of Brutus and of Antony show Shakespeare using his rhetorical skills to the utmost[22]. Brutus employs brief, pointed prose that appeals to reason, suggesting both the Spartan habit of laconic speech and the style of Seneca's *Letters*. But he displays a lack of political purpose, is not ready for decisions. Noted for the florid type of oratory known as Asianist, Antony speaks at three times the length of Brutus in verse that is passionate and exuberant; he appeals to passion in a devious way, knows that he wants to avenge Caesar, is out for the conspirators' blood.

Both Brutus and Antony make extensive use of the numerous rhetorical devices known to the Elizabethans, with Antony employing more than fifty of these. One such is irony. Brutus had stressed his own 'honour'; to undermine him, Antony uses the catchphrase 'Brutus is an honourable man' four times in 35 lines to increasingly ironic effect ('a plain blunt man' indeed, 3.2.220). Central in all of this is the reaction of the common people of Rome, plebeians whose lack of personal names stresses their mob-like character. Initially, they accept Brutus' claims, but, after Antony speaks, they change completely: they All say, 'Revenge! – About! – Seek! –Burn! – Fire! – Kill! – Slay! – Let not a traitor live' (3.2.206-7).

The mob is further inflamed when Antony eventually reads Caesar's will, in which he gave each Roman citizen the substantial sum of 75 silver drachmas (Brutus gave his soldiers 2,000 drachmas each), and he bestowed his ample gardens by the river Tiber upon the populace 'To walk abroad and recreate yourselves'. The first plebeian proposes that they will 'fire the traitors' houses' (3.2.253, 257). Juvenal (10.81) famously claimed that what the mob wanted was *panem et circenses*, 'bread and games'; Antony has provided it with versions of both.

Among the immediate casualties of the mob's desire for revenge against the conspirators was Gaius Helvius Cinna, an innocent poet, the friend of Catullus, and ironically a supporter of Caesar (3.3). He is mistaken by the mob for the conspirator Lucius Cornelius Cinna, so that, when he says his name is Cinna, they say 'Tear him to pieces! He's a conspirator'. But when Cinna proclaims his true identity as the poet, the cry is still 'Tear him', but now because of 'his bad verses'. Cinna's imminent death shows Shakespeare reflecting on the impotence of poetry in the face of brute power; as Virgil has the poet Moeris say, 'our songs, Lycidas, have such power among the weapons of Mars as they say Chaonian doves have when the eagle comes' (*Eclogues* 9.11-3). Here we have the stark answer to Brutus' rhetorical question about the poet (Marcus Phaonius) who affects Cynic philosophy, and tries to intervene in the quarrel between himself and Cassius: 'What should the wars do with these jigging fools?' (4.3.136); That answer is 'kill them'.

Following complex political manoeuvres after Caesar's death, the triumvirate of Octavian, Antony and Lepidus was set up in November 43 B.C. to govern Rome for five years. But Italy and the eastern provinces of the Empire endured massive destruction and disruption, with Italy also suffering famine. In a magnificent speech, Antony prophesies what will happen in this ghastly new world, when the Greek principle of destruction Ate leaves the Underworld for earth (3.1.263-75):

> Domestic fury and fierce civil strife
> Shall cumber all the ports of Italy;
> Blood and destruction shall be so in use,

> And dreadful objects so familiar,
> That mothers shall but smile when they behold
> Their infants quartered with the hands of war,
> All pity chok'd with custom of fell deeds;
> And Caesar's spirit, ranging for revenge,
> With Ate by his side come hot from hell,
> Shall in these confines with a monarch's voice
> Cry havoc and let slip the dogs of war,
> That this foul deed shall smell above the earth
> With carrion men, groaning for burial.

Among the first acts of the triumvirs was the issuing of lists of men to be killed because of their politics or wealth, the proscriptions. A grisly exchange ensured that Lepidus' brother and Antony's nephew must die, (4.1.1-6). In the conspirators' camp, there is some confusion about the number of senators proscribed: Messala reports it as 'one hundred senators, Brutus' letters as seventy senators; the actual number was 130 (4.3.171-7). Among those proscribed was Cicero, who was generally opposed to Caesar, but tended to vacillate. It is this trimming that Casca refers to in his account of Cicero's speech when Antony offered Caesar the crown. Casca notes that he 'spoke Greek' and that 'it was Greek to me' (1.2.275,281). Since educated Romans knew Greek, and since Plutarch says Casca spoke in Greek[23], this does not mean that Casca was literally unable to understand Cicero, but that he was unable to parse, to decipher what he might mean. But after Caesar's death, Cicero became one of the main supporters of the conspirators, and so had to die; his head and hands were cut off and brought to Antony, whom he had violently attacked in a series of speeches, and then fixed to the speaking platform in the Forum, from where he had so often addressed the people.

Highly praised in the seventeenth century, the quarrel scene between Brutus and Cassius shows that they, like Caesar, are not just committed politicians, but are also human with human weaknesses: Brutus is arrogant, Cassius hot-tempered. The issue between the two men is money, specifically bribery, for which Roman politicians were notorious: Brutus accuses Cassius of having 'an itching palm' (4.3.10); Cassius angrily denies this. Furious exchanges between the two – the reverse of their normal homosocial links – end at last in reconciliation.

In the battle of Philippi, both sides developed massive numbers of troops: the conspirators had about 80,000 men, the triumvirs somewhat more than that. Brutus ensures that the Republican forces fight at Philippi against the better judgement of Cassius, who abandons his Epicurean rejection of portents to view the fall of two mighty eagles as a bad omen. When the triumvirs win, both Cassius and Brutus commit suicide in Stoic fashion.

In Stoic philosophy, the individual person is permitted to commit suicide[23a] if the circumstances of his life become intolerable; living under a tyrant is a good example of that. Such self-killing may be regarded as the only genuinely free act a person does. The paradigm here is the unbending Stoic Cato the Younger, who killed himself in 46 B.C. rather than be subject to the perceived tyranny of Julius Caesar. Wrongly accused of plotting against Nero, Seneca also committed suicide, staging his death as a dramatic performance in which he dictated a treatise, and spoke to his wife and friends; as he said, 'it is an excellent thing to learn how to die'. A lesson Cawdor in *Macbeth* had certainly learnt, as Malcolm tells us: 'He died / As one that had been studied in his death'. Contemplating suicide, Horatio knows that such a death is Roman: 'I am more an antique Roman than a Dane'[23b].

Cassius kills himself with the sword that also killed Caesar, who is therefore the ultimate cause of Cassius' death: 'Caesar, thou art reveng'd, / Even with the sword that kill'd thee' (5.3.45-6). Brutus lauds his dead companion as 'The last of all the Romans', it being 'impossible that ever Rome / Should breed thy fellow' (5.3.99-101). Brutus used to condemn suicide when he was a Platonist – 'I did blame Cato for the death / Which he did give himself' – but now gets his servant Strato to hold his sword, so that 'He runs on his sword and dies' (5.5.52).

Antony, who mocked Brutus in his funeral speech, now pays him a striking tribute as 'the noblest Roman of them all', who acted for the 'common good' in killing Caesar, and who sums him up (5.5.68-75):

> His life was gentle, and the elements
> So mix'd in him, that Nature might stand up
> And say to all the world, 'This was a man!'

The world of *Julius Caesar* is a world of men. But women in *Julius Caesar* have an important role to play. A point adumbrated by Servilia, mother of Brutus and Cassius (by different men), who was deeply involved in the close network of oligarchic families: in 43 B.C., she dominated a meeting with Casca, Cicero and others, when the question was whether Brutus should bring back his army from Greece to Italy[24]. Brutus' wife Portia, daughter of the Stoic hero

Cato, feels that her ancestry and her marriage to a leading politician entitle her to know what is on Brutus' mind; indeed she states that 'I have a man's mind' (2.4.8). To further her case, Portia gives herself a voluntary wound in the thigh. This shows that she exhibits the constancy and virtue of a man, anticipating the suicides of Brutus and of Cassius, but also hints at a genital wound, and the lack of a phallus, symbol of power in a patriarchal society[25]. But Portia does seem to become aware of the conspiracy against Caesar, and to act as a true Republican. The situation after Caesar's death, in which Brutus is absent in the East and the triumvirs ever stronger, is not to her liking, and she too commits suicide, by swallowing fire. The daughter of Cato indeed.

Less prominent is Caesar's wife Calpurnia. Frightened by portents, she is firm with her husband – 'you shall not stir out of your house to-day' – and Caesar initially accepts her view: 'for thy humour I will stay at home' (2.2.9,56). But Caesar then decides that he will not be ruled by a woman, and decides to go to the Senate.

The tragedy *Julius Caesar*, the tragedy of Caesar, of Brutus, of Rome itself, ends with Antony lauding Brutus and with Octavian looking after his burial. But the performance seen by a Swiss visitor, Thomas Platter, at the Globe Theatre in September 1599 did not conclude with that ending. He notes that four of the actors 'after the play, according to their custom... did a most elegant and curious dance, two dressed in men's clothes, and two in women's'. This is a toned-down version of the famous 'jig', a comic ballad accompanied by energetic dancing that provided relief after the main play. The jig corresponds in Athenian drama to the satyr-play, put on after three tragedies, that dealt with the comic or grotesque aspects of Greek myth. In *Julius Caesar*, unlike *Macbeth* and *King Lear*, there is no comedy; relief must wait until the end.

5

Shakespeare continues his version of Roman history with *Antony and Cleopatra* (1606/7)[26], in which two of the triumvirs – Octavian and Antony vie with each other for control of the Roman Empire (the third, Lepidus, is sidelined). The action of *Antony and Cleopatra* covers the years 40-30 B.C.: the treaty of Misenum between the triumvirs and a major opponent Sextus Pompey; the defeat of the Parthians by Antony's general Ventidius; the Senate's declaration of war on Cleopatra in 32 B.C., and the battle of Actium in 31 B.C., in which Octavian defeated Antony and Cleopatra, and became the sole ruler of the Roman world. That world in the play is specially vast, moving between Egypt, Rome, Misenum on the Bay of Naples, Athens, Actium in northern Greece, Syria; as the fluidity of the Jacobean stage allowed, Shakespeare ignores the unities of time and place to produce a play that is specially fast-moving, making use of many short scenes in the manner of cinema. *Antony and Cleopatra* is also a play of youth: at the opening, Octavian is 23, and his sister Octavia, who marries Antony, about 30; Antony himself is 42 and Cleopatra 29; Sextus Pompey is about 27 (only Lepidus at about 50 could be seen as old).

There is, of course, another vital element in the power struggle between Antony and Octavian: Antony's sexual relationship with Cleopatra. This is often misunderstood. Both of these people exercised great power, and sought to consolidate it through sex, in order that they could rule the whole world together. As Foucauld says, 'Pleasure and power do not cancel or turn back against one another; they seek out, overlap, and reinforce one another'[27]. Antony and Cleopatra knew what they were doing: was there not a precedent in Julius Caesar's relationship with Cleopatra, by whom she allegedly had a child Caesarion: 'He ploughed her and she cropp'd' (2.2.234)? The constant denigration of Antony's private life by other Romans must be seen against the background of Roman invective in which violent attacks on a person's lifestyle were mandatory: sex, drink, gambling, debt. Indeed Antony is already accused of all of these in 44 B.C. in Cicero's *Second Phillippic*. But he went on to win at Philippi.

Shakespeare's main source for *Antony and Cleopatra* was again Plutarch, now the *Life* of Antony, the largest of the *Lives*. As with *Julius Caesar*, Plutarch supplied the general historical background, together with much detail, but Shakespeare also makes substantial changes. These include: a vastly expanded role for Enobarbus as a detached, satiric commentator; a reduced role for Octavia, and no mention of her children by Antony; the virtual omission of the campaigns against Parthia; an invented scene (2.5) about Cleopatra's jealousy of Octavia; a sense of transcendence at the end of the lives of Antony and Cleopatra (her last words are not in Plutarch)[28].

Not long after the formation of the triumvirate in 43 B.C., relationships between Octavian and Antony were strained. When Antony was in the East, his wife Fulvia and his brother Lucius fought against Octavian in Italy in the Perusine War (41-40 B.C.), but lost, and Fulvia had to flee to Greece. Fulvia is another very potent example of a Roman woman involved in politics, aiming, says Plutarch, to 'command him that commanded legions and great armies'; hearing of her death, Antony says 'There's a great spirit gone' (1.2.122)[29].

Antony and Octavian then meet in Rome to patch up their differences, a major element of this reconciliation being the marriage of Antony to Octavian's sister Octavia; a spectacular example of how the Roman oligarchy cemented political alliances by means of marriage. In 37 B.C., Octavia's skilled diplomacy helped bring about the Treaty of Tarentum that was designed to keep together Octavian and Antony for a further five years. But Antony went back to Cleopatra in Egypt, and he divorced Octavia in 32 B.C.; since by then her person had been declared sacrosanct, her treatment by Antony furnished a cause of war[29a]. Meanwhile, Antony was intent on consolidating and extending Cleopatra's successful rule: in public on a throne in Alexandria 'Unto her / He gave the stablishment of Egypt; made her / Of lower Syria, Cyprus, Lydia, / Absolute queen (3.3-6.8-11).

Octavian and Antony had also to deal with Sextus Pompey, son of Pompey the Great, who controlled 'the empire of the sea' (1.2.192), and was preventing food supplies reaching Italy. The triumvirs come to an agreement with Pompey, whose follower Menas suggests to him that he should kill all three; Pompey refuses. The ineffectual Lepidus (deferred to by Plutarch) had also to be dealt with, and is forced by Octavian to retire into private life; that he is unsuitable is shown by his drunkenness: 'The third part then he is drunk' (2.7.92). With Lepidus gone, Enobarbus astutely remarks of Octavia and Antony 'They'll grind the one the other' (3.5.14).

And so it proves: Antony and Cleopatra join battle with Octavian at Actium in north-west Greece on September 2, 31 B.C. This battle was by no means the glorious affair of later propaganda by Octavian and his followers, but was, as Syme says, 'a shabby affair'[30] conducted at sea, in which Cleopatra and Antony fled to southern Greece; their absolute defeat did not occur until a week later when Antony's land army surrendered. Nevertheless, Antony feels that he has lost: 'I am so hated in the world that I / Have lost my way for ever' (3.11.3-4). Yet neither he nor Cleopatra are dead, and there is still a great deal – some 1250 lines – of *Antony and Cleopatra* to follow.

Cleopatra (whose name in Greek means 'glory to the father') was the last of the Greek dynasty of the Ptolemies, who first came to power in Egypt after the death of Alexander the Great in 323 B.C.: she is 'descended of so many royal kings' (5.2.231). Cleopatra was clever, ambitious and manipulative, using her sexuality to ally herself with powerful Roman leaders such as Julius Caesar and Antony in order to pursue her political ends. She held not that the world is well lost for love, but that the political world can be better won through love. All of which justifies the performance of Cleopatra in the late twentieth century as 'a thoroughly modern woman, spiky rather than soft, intelligent and calculating rather than consumed by sexual passions, they explore sensuality as power'[31]. No wonder, then, that Rome feared Cleopatra as no woman before.

A central feature of Cleopatra, as of *Antony and Cleopatra*, is extravagance, excess, hyperbole that is the play's main stylistic feature; this alternates with a simple, direct style. Enobarbus feels that Cleopatra is a paradox to be described as hyperbole (2.2.242-7):

> Age cannot wither her, nor custom stale
> Her infinite variety; other women cloy
> The appetites hey feed, but she makes hungry
> Where most she satisfies; for vilest things
> Become themselves in her, that the holy priests
> Bless her when she is riggish.

Bacon held that 'hyperbole is comely in nothing but love'[32], and it is found in the relationship between Antony and Cleopatra, which involved unconditional acceptance of each other, right from the beginning of the play. When she asks Antony how much he loves her, his reply states that there is no end to love: 'There's beggary in the love that can be reckoned' (1.1.15). This aphorism finds an analogue in the persona of the love poet Propertius (thought to be modelled on Antony)[33]: *verus amor nullum novit habere modum*, 'true love does not recognize any boundary' (2.15.30). Indeed Cleopatra enjoys multiple orgasms: 'I have seen her die twenty times' (1.2.140-1; 'die' is slang for 'orgasm'). The love of Cleopatra and Antony has also a comic, if not camp, aspect: Antony suggests that the two should in Alexandria 'wander through the streets, and note / The qualities of people' (1.2.55-6); Enobarbus says 'I saw her once / Hop forty paces through the public street' (2.2.235-6).

The classic instance of hyperbole in regard to Cleopatra is the description of her on the barge at Tarsus on the river Cydnus in

Cilicia (south east Turkey) in 41 B.C. She had been summoned by Antony (who knew her before this) to answer (false) charges of helping the Republicans Brutus and Cassius, but stage-managed the occasion for her own advantage in ways that are political, economic, religious and sexual. The description gains force because it is spoken by the normally ironic Enobarbus to pragmatic Romans, and shows Shakespeare transmuting Plutarch, whom he follows closely, into great poetry (2.2.198-212):

> The barge she sat in, like a burnished throne
> Burned on the water; the poop was beaten gold,
> Purple the sails, and so perfumèd that
> The winds were lovesick with them; the oars were silver,
> Which to the tune of flutes kept stroke, and made
> As amorous of their strokes. For her own person,
> It beggared all description: she did lie
> In her pavilion – cloth-of-gold of tissue –
> O'er picturing that Venus where we see
> The fancy out-work nature; on each side her
> Stood pretty, dimpled boys, like smiling Cupids,
> With divers-coloured fans, whose wind did seem
> To glow the delicate cheeks which they did cool,
> And what they undid did.

Here we have the opulence of precious metals, gold and silver, the royal colour purple, the elements of fire, water and air, all colluding in the extravagant description of the barge and its occupant in forms of personification. Love is suggested when the water, beaten by oars, becomes 'amorous', and when the sails of the barge makes the winds 'lovesick'. Then Cleopatra is not just compared to the goddess of love, Venus, but outdoes her, with Venus herself moving beyond anything in nature; the queen is attended by handsome boys who resemble Cupid, the god of love and son of Venus. This comparison of Cleopatra to Venus brings to mind the fact that, in accordance with Egyptian custom, she sees herself as the embodiment of the goddess Isis (linked to Aphrodite / Venus), who is the principle of Nature and of water, presides over love affairs, and was by now a central divinity in the Greco-Roman world. So Octavian is aggrieved that 'She / In th'habiliments of the goddess Isis / That day appeared and often gave audience, / As 'tis reported, so' (3.6.16-9).

While Antony liked the good life, he was by no means neglectful of political matters. Octavian himself notes that, in the campaign's after Julius Caesar's death, Antony fought against famine 'like a soldier' by eating berries and drinking horses' urine (1.4.56-70). Cleopatra states that 'He was disposed to mirth, but on the sudden / A Roman thought had struck him' (1.2.87-8). After Antony's death, Cleopatra pays him a striking tribute, asserting that he transcended normal human life: he dominated the world like the Colossus of Rhodes; he provided bounty like a perpetual autumn; he rose above the pleasures that were his element as a dolphin leaps from the sea; his retinue included kings and princes; he disposed of territories like silver coins (5.2.81-91). Once more extravagance is the order of the day.

Even more extravagant is Antony's view that he was the embodiment of the Greco-Roman hero Hercules, who became a god after his death, and from whom he claimed descent[34]. Since Antony dressed like Hercules and tried to look like him, Cleopatra sees him as a 'Herculean Roman' (1.3.85). But when Antony is close to his final defeat, supernatural music indicates that Hercules abandoned him: 'Tis the god Hercules whom Antony loved / Now leaves him' (4.3.21-2). Cavafy's poem 'The God Abandons Antony' captures this moment, and advocates a resigned approach: [35]

> When suddenly at midnight you hear
> an invisible company pass
> with exquisite music, voices –
> do not lament your luck that now gives out, your work
> that has failed, schemes of your life
> all proved to be false – do not lament that uselessly.
> Like one for long prepared, like a courageous man,
> Say good-bye to her, to the Alexandria who is leaving.

But when Antony envisages his death in terms of Hercules' (4.13.43-7), he is far from resigned, and seeks revenge for Cleopatra's supposed betrayal. Hercules' wife Deianeira sent a poisoned shirt (got from the centaur Nessus) through her servant Lichas to Hercules, thinking it a love potion; in fact it killed him, and he hurled Lichas into the sea before he died:

> The shirt of Nessus is upon me – teach me
> Alcides, thou mine ancestor, thy rage:
> Let me lodge Lichas on the horns o'th'moon,
> And with these hands that grasped the heaviest club,
> Subdue my worthiest self. The witch shall die!'

Finally, the cross-dressing of Antony and Cleopatra (2.5.22-3) could suggest the way Hercules is subject to the Queen of Lydia Omphale, so that she wears his lion skin and club, he dresses in her clothes. But it is better viewed as another element of camp (Omphale is used in Octavia's propaganda against Antony).

Both Antony and Cleopatra commit suicide, but there is a big difference between the two cases. Antony's death cannot be compared with that of the classic Stoic hero Cato, or with those of Brutus and Cassius, all of whom fought for the Roman Republic against the perceived monarchical tendencies of Julius Caesar. But Antony is *not* fighting for the Republic: the issue is which *autocrat* will rule the Roman Empire. So the fact that he makes a mess of his suicide could be seen as passing ironic comment on his position. Indeed Octavian notes that 'The breaking of so great a thing should make a greater crack' (5.1.14-5).

On the other hand, Cleopatra's suicide (which takes place nine days later) is done 'after the high Roman fashion' (4.5.91), and is a triumph. The mode of this is unknown, but Shakespeare's view that it is achieved by poisonous asps fits with the fact that the asp is linked to the goddess Isis, with whom Cleopatra identified. There is a transcendent element to Cleopatra's death: dressed in royal robes, she recalls her first meeting with Antony: 'I am again for Cydnus / To meet Mark Antony'; she exclaims 'Husband, I come'; and she admits to 'immortal longings', that deny death, *mors* (5.2.227-8, 286, 280).

This triumphant aspect of Cleopatra's death is brilliantly captured by Horace (*Odes* 1. 37.25-32). In the first part of his poem, Horace retails Octavian's propaganda against Cleopatra, but, in the second part, he ennobles her, and lauds her death that resembles that of a male Roman Stoic:

> She is fiercer than ever in her chosen death,
> denying clearly to the savage Liburnian ships
> to be led as a private citizen,
> no humble woman in a proud triumph.

So instead of a live Cleopatra for his triumph in Rome, Octavian had to be content with an ersatz substitute, an effigy of the queen (Propertius 3.11.53-4). Here there are two triumphs.

Shakespeare's play *Antony and Cleopatra* shows what can be done with the intermingling of sex and power; Shaw's play *Caesar and Cleopatra* is seriously flawed because that theme is omitted. Shaw refuses to allow a sexual relationship between Caesar and Cleopatra, since he disliked such themes in contemporary melodrama, and since he had a non-sexual marriage (whatever that is). But this misses the point that Cleopatra, an adult woman not an adolescent, uses sex to promote her political aims. O'Connor sums up: 'In Shaw's *Caesar and Cleopatra* she is desexualized, infantilized and mocked. It is difficult to forgive him for that'.[35a] Precisely.

6

Roman history is the sole theme in *Coriolanus, Julius Caesar* and *Antony and Cleopatra*; it plays a much lesser role in *Cymbeline* (1610), for this highly theatrical play yokes together the troubled love story of Posthumus and the princess Innogen (including a wager about her chastity that comes from Bocaccio's *Decameron);* the loss and restoration of Guiderius and Arviragus, sons of the king Cymbeline; the plot of the Queen to kill Innogen and Cymbeline; the role of Milford Haven in Wales in the establishment of the Tudor monarchy;[36] and relations between Britain and Rome at the time of the Emperor Augustus (31 B.C.–14 A.D.). Connections exist between some of these themes: the collapse and restoration of the relationship between Innogen and Posthumus mirrors that between Britain and Rome; the Roman general Caius Lucius takes Innogen, disguised as the page Fidele, into his service.

In *Cymbeline*, Britain and Rome are depicted with a mixture of fact and fantasy that involves a mingling of historical periods, and that draws on Holinshed's *Chronicles*, itself partly based on Julius Caesar's *Gallic War*. During the reign of Cassibelan (properly Cassivelaunus), who controlled much of the south east of England, Britain submitted without conditions to Julius Caesar, and agreed to pay tribute. But in his expeditions to Britain in the years 55 and 54 B.C., Caesar lost a large number of ships, because of Roman ignorance of tides in the English Channel;[37] as the Queen says (3.1.24-9):

> With shame –
> The first that ever touched him – he was carried
> From off our coast, twice beaten; and his shipping,
> Poor ignorant baubles, on our terrible seas
> Like eggshells moved upon their surges, cracked
> As easily 'gainst our rocks...

So Caesar could not in Britain make the boast he made after the battle of Zela ' "Came and saw and overcame"'.

At the centre of *Cymbeline's* account of the relationship between Britain and Rome is the issue of tribute: Britain has refused to pay, and Lucius, the Roman ambassador, demands its restoration

(Augustus may have presided over negotiations to re-establish it). When Britain refuses this demand, Lucius states that Rome is now at war with Britain: 'War and confusion / In Caesar's name pronounce I 'against thee' (3.1.64-5). Although Rome is preoccupied with campaigns (6-9 A.D.) in Dalmatia on the east coast of the Adriatic, and in Pannonia, a Roman province south and west of the Danube, Lucius is made a general, and required to take on the British in a fictitious battle at Milford Haven. In the battle, the Britons at first flee, but then win and capture Lucius due to the efforts of the banished lord Belisarius, and the king's two sons, Guiderius and Arviragus. Despite this victory, Cymbeline agrees to pay tribute to Rome – 'we submit to Caesar / And to the Roman empire, promising / To pay our wanted tribute' (5.4.461-3) – and proposes a partnership between the two countries: 'Let / A Roman and a British ensign wave / Friendly together' (5.4.480-2). In reality, Britain was conquered by the Emperor Claudius in 43 A.D., but the positive ending of *Cymbeline* is determined both by the requirements of tragicomedy and/or romance, and a need to posit a worthy predecessor for the British monarchy.

There is a further important Roman element in the play, the appearance of Jupiter, king of the gods, as a *deus ex machina*, who descends in thunder and lightning, sitting on an eagle, his special bird. Though elusive, Jupiter asserts his power, telling the ghosts of Posthumus' father, Sicilius Leonatus, and his two brothers to back off. As befits the genres of tragicomedy and romance, Jupiter points out that success and happiness come after trials, and therefore states that Posthumus will enjoy his marriage to Innogen. So Jupiter's role is to pave the way for the numerous forms of restoration that come at the end of the play. This importance of Jupiter was stressed in Peter Hall's production at the Olivier theatre in 1988: 'in a *coup de theatre* matching that of the text, the circular heavens tilted behind Jupiter so that he and his now three-dimensional eagle appeared at the centre of a universe of brilliantly illuminated stars and planets'[38].

7

The four plays just analysed deal with *particular* moments in Roman history: in *Coriolanus*, the story of Coriolanus in the fifth century B.C.; in *Julius Caesar*, the murder of Julius Caesar in 44 B.C. and its aftermath; in *Antony and Cleopatra*, the subsequent struggle for control of the Roman world between Octavian (the future Augustus) and Antony that ended in 31 B.C.; in *Cymbeline*, the Roman Empire in the first century A.D. But *Titus Andronicus* presents a very different case: although it was published in 1594 as a 'Most Lamentable Romaine Tragedie', and although the setting is, in a vague way, that of the late Roman Empire, it cannot be pinned down to a particular moment in the history of Rome (this is complicated by the facts that George Peele probably wrote significant parts of the play[39], and that both Senecan revenge tragedy and Ovid's *Metamorphoses* contribute greatly to it).

Rather, *Titus Andronicus* presents a conglomeration of various facets of Roman history that is fictional and that appears to have no main source: the harsh Emperor Saturninus and, at the end, the new Emperor Lucius; the senators of the aristocracy and the tribunes of the people; ceremonies such as the election of an Emperor and the entrance of Titus in a chariot; barbarians in the shape of Goths such as Tamora and Moors such as Aaron. Spencer explains: 'The play does not assume a political situation known to Roman history; it is, rather, a summary of Roman politics. It is not so much that any particular set of political institutions is assumed in *Titus*, but rather that it includes *all* the political institutions Rome ever had. The author seems anxious, not to get it all right, but to get it all in'[40]. This eclectic version of the whole of Roman history proved very congenial, not only to its initial Elizabethan audience of 1594, but also, as Ben Jonson laments, to a Jacobean audience twenty years or more later: 'He that will swear *Jeronimo* (Kyd's *The Spanish Tragedy*) or *Andronicus* are the best plays yet, shall pass unexcepted at here as a man whose judgement shows it is constant, and hath stood still these five and twenty or thirty years'.[40a]

8

The Roman plays – *Coriolanus, Julius Caesar, Antony and Cleopatra* – are among Shakespeare's finest drama. Eliot concurs: '*Coriolanus* may not be as "interesting" as *Hamlet*, but it is, with *Antony and Cleopatra*, Shakespeare's most assured artistic success'[41]. Trevor Nunn directed the Roman plays (including *Titus Andronicus*) for the Royal Shakespeare Company in 1972 because they seemed 'to me to have the most meaning and the most point and the most relevance'. One reason for this is that discussion of political issues in drama gains much for being set not in the contemporary world where perspective is hard to achieve, but at some time in the past that allows for a *distancing* effect.

Contemporary politics can therefore be refracted through the lens of another time, and will be forcibly addressed because of that. As the case of Sophocles' *Antigone* shows in spectacular fashion in recent times: the tragedy is seen, over and over again, to mirror contemporary clashes between the State and the individual person[42].

3 | The Impact Of Heavy Seneca

1

The First Folio designates eleven plays by Shakespeare as 'tragedies'; these are, in order of printing, Coriolanus, Titus Andronicus, Romeo and Juliet, Timon of Athens, Julius Caesar, Macbeth, Hamlet, King Lear, Othello, Antony and Cleopatra, Cymbeline. (Other labels are possible for some of these plays: Coriolanus, Julius Caesar and Antony and Cleopatra can be classified as 'Roman' plays, Cymbeline as 'romance'). Central to these tragedies is an element of disastrous suffering; as Schopenhauer says, 'the presentation of a great misfortune is alone essential'[1] to tragedy. Violent death is central to tragedy – Byron held that 'All tragedies end in a death'[2] – so that Hamlet concludes with the decease of Hamlet, Laertes, Gertrude and Claudius. But Shakespeare's tragedies do not always end on a note of unrelieved gloom: in Hamlet, Fortinbras will rule in Denmark; in Macbeth, the new king Malcolm invites people to attend his coronation: 'So thanks to all at once, and to each one, / Whom we invite to see us crowned at Scone' (5.7.104-5). While such positive notes do not wipe out the awful events that have already taken place, their existence in Shakespeare leads George Steiner (who has a very austere concept of tragedy) to claim that only Timon of Athens and possibly King Lear should be claimed as tragedies[3]. A less narrow view of Shakespearean tragedy would regard all the remaining nine plays listed in the First Folio as 'tragedies', with the exception of Cymbeline that has the happy ending of 'romance'.

Shakespeare's tragedies deal with the upper class of rulers and nobles, but do not because of that provide support for the Establishment of his day. Already in fifth century Athens, where tragedies were performed as part of a civic and religious festival in honour of the god Dionysus, the issues raised by the tragic dramatists, and especially by Euripides, rendered problematic aspects of Athenian society: war (*The Trojan Women*), feminism (*Medea*), the religion of Dionysus himself (*Bacchae*). As Croally says of the Greeks, 'tragedy questions ideology'[4]. A dictum that fits Shakespeare equally well, because his tragedies enact a clash between differing points of view, in which one idea is pitted against another, without either of them being necessarily privileged. So *Henry V* leaves open the question of whether the king is a glorious ruler or a hypocritical militarist[5].

2

As Eliot saw, the model for tragedy in Shakespeare's era was not the Greeks, but Seneca: 'No author exercised a wider or deeper influence upon the Elizabethan mind or upon the Elizabethan form of tragedy than did Seneca'[6]. So a useful prolegomenon to an analysis of the impact of Seneca on Shakespeare is a brief account of his tragedies.

Born about 1 B.C. in Cordoba in southern Spain, Lucius Annaeus Seneca[7] was soon brought to Rome, where he was educated in Greek and Latin literature, in rhetoric and in philosophy (he became an adherent of Stoicism). Seneca pursued a political career, and, in 48 A.D., Agrippina, wife of the Emperor Claudius, had him made tutor to her son Nero, the future Emperor (54-68 A.D.). As a chief advisor, Seneca tried to restrain the excesses of Nero's reign, but ultimately could not control the Emperor, and was forced to commit suicide in 65 A.D. All this ensured that Seneca 'was to experience, as few major writers in the history of the world have ever experienced, the nature and effects of unlimited political power'[8].

Seneca's eight[9] tragedies ostensibly deal with themes from Greek mythology: *Agamemnon, Thyestes, Oedipus, Hercules Furens, Medea, Phaedra, Trojan Women, Phoenician Women*. But the subtext of these tragedies is the violence of Imperial Rome, and, in particular, the theme of evil: evil is material, takes root in the human soul, becomes most potent in the soul of the ruler. This concept of Seneca helped shape the characters of Titus Andronicus, Hamlet, Richard III, Macbeth. The evil male ruler is a constant reality in Seneca, the paradigm being Atreus, king of Mycenae, who serves his brother Thyestes the flesh of his own children; here evil is closely linked to revenge, since Thyestes had seduced Atreus' wife

Aerope. Evil may also exist in women, notably in Medea who kills her own children (who are also killed in *Thyestes, Hercules Furens, Trojan Women*).

The violence of Imperial Rome, and especially the popular contests between gladiators, who fought and killed each other in venues such as the Colosseum, mirrored the violence of Shakespeare's England, in which judicial executions involved the hanging, drawing and quartering of a human body, with its severed head being publicly displayed. Benjamin's celebrated dictum seems apt: 'There is no document of civilization which is not at the same time a document of barbarism'[10]. In both Rome and London there was bear-baiting, which might have curious links to the theatre. Horace asserts that the wretched common people (*plebecula*) demand 'either a bear or boxers' during stage performances'; the tragic actor Edward Alleyn was made Master of the Bears, and the Hope Theatre that opened in 1614 was designed for *both* bear-baiting *and* stage plays[11]. All of which suggests that the tragedies of Imperial Rome and of Elizabethan and Jacobean England come under the rubric of the Theatre of Cruelty advocated by Artaud[12]. Significantly, Artaud held that Seneca is 'the greatest tragic writer in history'[13].

Relevant here is the massive violence of the ruler in the twentieth century – Hitler, Stalin, Mao Zedong, Truman (for Hiroshima) – that gave, from mid century on, Senecan tragedy an appeal, an edge that it had not had for about 150 years, that enables us to see more clearly how the writers of the Renaissance, including Shakespeare, responded to violent Senecan rulers. Seneca is no longer a third-rate Greek tragedian, rather a major tragic writer for our times; just as he was for Shakespeare.

Brief mention must be made of two other aspects of Seneca's tragedies, Stoic philosophy and Latin rhetoric. Stoicism[14] originated in the Hellenistic period of ancient history (323 to 31 B.C.), and, like that era in general, concentrated on the individual person, on how a man should live a good life. This stress on ethics demanded a rational therapy of the soul that privileges virtue, transforms a person's life – regardless of external circumstances – leads to proper types of behaviour, and so ensures happiness. Hence the aim of the wise man is to acquiesce in whatever comes his way; giving us the colloquial English adjective 'stoic'. Seneca is by far the most important Stoic philosopher whose works are extant, works that provide what Queen Elizabeth called 'wholesome advisings'. But while Seneca's prose work expound Stoic doctrine without reservation, his tragedies make use of Stoic concepts without at all endorsing those concepts. The writing of 'Stoic' tragedy (or 'Christian' tragedy) may be impossible since the theme of redemption undermines the whole point of tragedy.

The rhetoric that is central to Seneca's tragic style (and that owes much to Ovid) provides a series of shocks that greatly exaggerate the facts (hyperbole), that linger on scenes of horrific realism, that employ numerous moral aphorisms (*sententiae*). Another feature is vigorous line-for-line exchanges between two characters (*stichomythia*), as seen in the case of Hamlet and his mother (3.4.7-15). Senecan rhetoric was a major enabling force for Elizabethan and Jacobean dramatists, not least for Shakespeare; it provided the *verbal* equivalent of the customary violence on the stage, so as to produce what Marlowe famously called 'high astounding terms' (*Tamburlaine* Prologue 5).

3

The tragic drama of Elizabethan and Jacobean England is inconceivable without Seneca. The roll-call of playwrights who appropriate Seneca's tragedies includes Marlowe, Kyd, Marston, Middleton, Webster and, not least, Shakespeare[15]. Seneca was indeed in the Elizabethan air. Already in 1551, Seneca's play *The Trojan Women* was performed at Cambridge, and productions of *Medea* and *Oedipus* followed. Then the first English tragedy *Gordobuc*, performed in 1562, was praised by Sidney (despite his reservations) as 'climbing to the height of Seneca his style'. Meanwhile, Seneca was being translated into English between 1559 and 1567 by several authors, who were scholars, fellows of the universities, clergymen, and who used a line of 14 syllables: Jasper Heywood, Alexander Neville, John Studley. These plays were published in collected form by Thomas Newton in 1581, and have, writes Eliot, 'considerable political charm and quite academic accuracy, with occasional flashes of real beauty'[15a]. So Shakespeare could read Seneca both in the original Latin and in English translation.

Shakespeares's debt to Seneca[16] was spotted by Francis Menes in 1598: 'As Plautus and Seneca are accounted the best for Comedy and Tragedy among the Latins; so Shakespeare among the English is the most excellent in both kinds for the stage'[17]. But Shakespeare himself regarded Seneca as a touchtone in drama: 'Seneca cannot be too heavy nor Plautus too light' (*Hamlet* 2.2.336-7). Shakespeare's appropriation of Seneca lies mainly in his stress on the theme of evil in the ruler, evil that manifests itself in revenge – *Titus Andronicus*, *Hamlet* – or in ambition: *Richard III*, *Macbeth*. But there are a number of lesser elements he takes from Seneca: the motif of the Stoic suicide; a character's metatheatrical stress on her or his position in the play; the use of moralizing aphorisms (*sententiae*).

4

The four plays of Shakespeare that clearly appropriate Seneca's tragedies are concerned with two types of power: the revenge plays *Titus Andronicus* and *Hamlet* are about a refusal to be *overpowered*; the plays of ambition *Richard III* and *Macbeth* are about the will to *superior power*[17].

Revenge typically involves the commission in the past by A of an injury such as murder that B will, after anticipation, avenge in a private way; such an act has no legal status, and is famously labelled by Bacon as 'wild justice'. But the imperative for revenge remains. In Aeschylus' tragedy *The Libation Bearers*, the Chorus assert 'It is the law: when blood of slaughter / wets the ground it wants more blood'. Antonio in Marston's tragedy *Antonio's Revenge* says 'Blood cries for blood, and murder murder'. Macbeth concurs with a proverb after the murder of Banquo: 'It will have blood, they say: blood will have blood'[18].

Revenge is central to Seneca's tragedies: in *Agamemnon*, Clytemnestra takes revenge for the sacrifice of her daughter Iphigeneia by killing her husband Agamemnon; in *Medea*, Medea takes revenge on Jason for abandoning her by killing her rival and her own children by Jason; in *Thyestes*, Atreus takes revenge on Thyestes for seducing his wife by killing his children and making him eat them.

The prototype of the English revenge play is Kyd's *The Spanish Tragedy* (about 1587), soon to be followed by Marlowe's *The Jew of Malta* (about 1590); here personal grievances result in violent revenge. Indeed *The Spanish Tragedy* begins with not just the ghost of the murdered Don Andrea, but also with the figure of Revenge (both remain present throughout the play). Kyd and Marlowe are followed by Marston (*Antonio's Revenge*), Middleton (*The Revenger's Tragedy*), Webster (*The Duchess of Malfi*) and, not least, by Shakespeare in *Titus Andronicus*[19] and *Hamlet*. Among the central features of these plays is delay in acting on the part of the avenger, that person's real or feigned madness, his death at the end of the play in a scenario where perpetrator and victim are both destroyed. Revenge tragedy is therefore about murder – an initial private killing to be followed by a further private one – and so differs from the detective story, in which the initial private murder is dealt with by public law. Accordingly, P. D. James asserts that 'What the detective story is about is not murder but the restoration of order'[20]. And yet, despite private vengeance, a form of order may also appear in revenge tragedy: in *Titus Andronicus*, Lucius will become Emperor in Rome; in *Hamlet*, Fortinbras will rule over Denmark.

5

Dating from 1593 or earlier, *Titus Andronicus* was an immensely popular early play of Shakespeare (partly written by George Peele)[21] that sought to outdo the revenge tragedies of Seneca, Kyd and Marlowe by means of its enormous catalogue of horrors. Consider this list:

> Titus Andronicus, Roman general, sacrifices Alarbus, the eldest son of Tamora, queen of the Goths.
>
> Titus kills his defiant son Mutius.
>
> Demetrius and Chiron, sons of Tamora, kill Bassianus, brother of the Emperor Saturninus and husband of Titus' daughter, Lavinia.
>
> Demetrius and Chiron rape Lavinia, and cut off her hands and tongue (this is off-stage, as in Greek tragedies).
>
> Saturninus executes Martius and Quintus, sons of Titus.
>
> Titus cuts off his hand to appease Saturninus.
>
> Aaron the Moor, lover of Tamora, kills the Nurse.
>
> Titus kills Demetrius and Chiron, and Lavinia.
>
> Titus feeds Tamora with the flesh of Demetrius and Chiron, and then kills her.
>
> Saturninus kills Titus, whose son Lucius kills Saturninus.

All this is summed up by Aaron, the embodiment of evil (5.1.63-5):

> For I must talk of murders, rapes and massacres,
> Acts of black night, abominable deeds,
> Conplots of mischief, treason, villiancies.

These horrors result from the fact that *Titus Andronicus* is a revenge tragedy like those of Seneca, as several characters affirm. Titus asks 'which way shall I find Revenge's cake?' Aaron states that 'Blood and revenge are hammering in my head'. And Tamora is metamorphosed into Revenge itself: 'I am Revenge'[22].

The shocking nature of *Titus Andronicus* and its links to Seneca and other Latin authors (such as Ovid and Horace) led Muir to assert that 'It is a nice irony that Shakespeare's most shocking play should be closest in spirit to the classics'[23]. But this is very misleading, because Greek and Latin literature was itself *already very shocking*. In Euripides' *Hecuba*, the Trojan queen Hecuba sees her daughter Polyxena sacrificed on the tomb of Achilles, and her youngest son Polydorus killed by the Thracian king Polymestor; in revenge, Hecuba's women put out the king's eyes, and kill his sons. In Seneca's *The Trojan Women*, he deals not only with the grisly sacrifice of Polyxena, but also with the gruesome murder of Astynax, son of Hector and Andromache. And Seneca (as well as Ovid) provides an analogue for the feast of human flesh that Titus prepares: in Thyestes, Atreus kills the children of his brother Thyestes, and serves them up to him; in Ovid, when Tereus, husband of Procne, rapes her sister Philomela and cuts off her tongue, Procne kills their son Itys and serves him to Tereus.

Still, the horror in Shakespeare is greater: Demetrius and Chiron cut off not only Lavinia's tongue, but also her hands; Titus makes her receive the rapists' blood, grinds their bones to powder before baking their heads. As Titus says, 'For worse than Philomel you used my daughter /And worse than Procne I will be revenged' (5.2.194-5). Marlowe spoke of 'high astounding terms'; Shakespeare goes one better with relentless astounding horrors that here surpass those of Seneca and Ovid. The comment we need is found at the end of Conrad's novel *Heart of Darkness* (1902), when the dying Kurtz recognizes the reality of evil: 'The horror! The horror!'

The horrors of *Titus Andronicus* have often failed to appeal; Eliot called it 'one of the stupidest and most uninspired plays ever written'[23a]. But since Peter Brook's landmark production at Stratford in 1955, the play's merits and its relevance to the modern world have become clear: as Brook says, 'The real appeal of *Titus* (over theoretically "greater" plays like *Hamlet* and *Lear*) was that abstract – stylized – Roman classical though it appeared to be, it was obviously for everyone in the audience about the most modern of emotions – about violence, hatred, cruelty, pain – in a form that *because unrealistic* transcended the anecdote and became for each audience *quite abstract and thus totally real*'[24]. Significantly, the rehabilitation of Seneca as a dramatist began soon after Brook's production: the violence of life and of drama in Nero's Rome, Elizabeth's England, the twentieth century, coalesce. Indeed Rome becomes an eternal 'wilderness of tigers' (3.1.54) under Nero, Saturninus, Mussolini[25].

6

Analysis of Seneca's impact upon *Hamlet* (about 1600) must start with Doran: '*Hamlet* is certainly not much like any play of Seneca's one can name, but Seneca is undoubtedly one of the effective ingredients in the emotional charge of *Hamlet*. *Hamlet* without Seneca is inconceivable'[26]. For like a number of Seneca's tragedies, *Hamlet* is a revenge play, in which Hamlet is required to kill his uncle Claudius, who murdered his father, and then married the widow Gertrude, Hamlet's mother. So what Thomas Lodge remembers of the lost play, the *Ur – Hamlet*, is the ghost of the murdered man crying 'so miserably at the Theatre, like an oyster wife, "Hamlet, revenge"'[27]. Indeed when Hamlet says 'Now could I drink hot blood, / And do such bitter business as the day / Would quake to look on', Caryl Churchill, translator of Seneca's revenge play *Thyestes*, states that 'He wants to be a hero in a Senecan play'[28].

The translations of Seneca into English (1581) also have an impact here, as Thomas Nashe noted in 1589, when he criticizes upstart dramatists who do not know Latin, but can make use of these translations: [29] 'Yet English *Seneca* read by candlelight yields many good sentences, as *Blood is a beggar* and so forth; and if you entreat him fair to a frosty morning, he will afford you whole Hamlets – I should say handfuls of tragic speeches'. Nashe refers to rhetoric as in 'To be or not to be'; to striking aphorisms, of which *Hamlet* is full; to bloody acts as listed by Horatio (5.2.365-7): 'of carnal, bloody and unnatural acts, / Of accidental judgements, casual slaughters, / Of death put by cunning and forced cause'. For it is not merely the case that corpses pile up at the end of *Hamlet*, but that death is the central theme of the play: as Hamlet says, 'That's the end' (4.3.24)[30].

For all that, Shakespeare makes major changes to the revenge play. The most obvious of these is the striking way in which *Hamlet* contains many elements[31] not essential to the genre: the political relationship between Denmark and Norway; the marriage of Claudius and Gertrude; relationships of Hamlet with Horatio and with Ophelia (together with her songs); the subplot of Rosencrantz and Guildenstern; the scheming, but tedious courtier Polonius; the philosophizing about life, especially by Hamlet; the introduction of a large number of new words (about 600). The sheer scale of all of this – *Hamlet* in the Second Quarto runs to over 3,500 lines – offers one reason for the much-debated slowness of Hamlet to avenge his father's death. A slowness adumbrated in miniature by the hesitation of the Greek warrior Pyrrhus in killing the Trojan princess Polyxena in Seneca's tragedy *The Trojan Women*, and by the hesitation in *Hamlet* itself of the same warrior in killing king Priam[32]. Yet Hamlet does act: he murders Polonius, has Rosencrantz and Guildenstern killed, jumps into Ophelia's grave.

The problematic Ghost in *Hamlet* is also different from other such Ghosts in revenge tragedy. Unlike the Ghost of Don Andrea in Kyd's *The Spanish Tragedy*, he fails to appear at the end of the play. Then this Ghost limits Hamlet's revenge by declaring his mother exempt: 'nor let thy soul contrive / Against thy mother aught' (1.5.85-6); Hamlet obeys, stating that he will not copy the Emperor Nero in killing his mother Agrippina (who had him made Emperor): 'Let not ever / The soul of Nero enter this firm bosom' (3.2.383-4)[33].

Hamlet, however dilatory, is an avenger subject to the passion of anger; such passions were condemned by Stoics like Seneca, who wrote a treatise on the nature, futility and cure of Anger (*De Ira*). But when Hamlet praises his ideal friend Horatio, he notes that this man has the qualities of the Stoic sage, who is not affected by external circumstances, not given to passion: 'A man that Fortune's buffets and rewards / Hast ta'en with equal thanks'; a man 'That is not passion's slave' (3.2.63-4, 68). Still, towards the end of the play, Hamlet too turns Stoic in his acceptance of death ('it'): 'If it be, 'tis not to come. If it be not to come, it will be now. If it be not now, yet it will come' (5.2.198-200). Here the Senecan avenger has become the Senecan sage.

7

Both *Richard III* and *Macbeth* deal with the Senecan theme of evil in the ruler, evil that derives from the ambition to be king. While ambition to get on in life was a potent force amid the rapid social, economic, and religious changes of Elizabethan England, it was also a theme exemplified by the usurping king of Thebes in Seneca's tragedy *Hercules Furens*. Both Richard and Macbeth are responsible for several murders (including the murder of children), but there is a difference between them: whereas Macbeth's evil deeds result directly from his ambition, those of Richard seem to be indulged in for their own sake[34].

Schiller held that *Richard III* (about 1591/2) is 'one of the noblest tragedies I know... No Shakespearean play has so much reminded me of Greek tragedy'[35]. Such a link must be general in nature: both Aeschylus' *Oresteia* and *Richard III* end when a vicious vendetta – that of the House of Atreus, that of the Houses of York and Lancaster – is replaced by a new order. But *Richard III* owes much more specific debts to Seneca, so that Muir calls it 'The most Senecan of Shakespeare's plays'[36]. So the figure of Richard – gloomy, introspective, brutal, witty – resembles ruthless leaders from Seneca's tragedies such as Atreus, Pyrrhus and Lycus (if also the mediaeval Vice, the Renaissance Machiavel, the anti-Christ)[37]. Indeed he achieves mythical status as he commits a spectacular series of crimes (*scelera*) that surpass those of any villain in Greek or Roman tragedy (a star role for Richard Burbage).

There are further, more precise Senecan elements in *Richard III* that are not found in the chronicles of Hall and Holinshed that Shakespeare used as a source[38]. The most remarkable of these is found in the scene (1.2) where Richard wooes Anne, whose father Henry VI, and husband Edward he has killed; a scene called by Kott 'one of the greatest scenes written by Shakespeare, and one of the greatest ever written'[39]. In Seneca's *Hercules Furens*, the usurping monarch Lycus seeks to strengthen his rule by forcing marriage on the wife of the absent hero Hercules; in *Richard III*, Richard seeks to persuade Anne to marry him by using devices of Senecan rhetoric such as repetition, antithesis and line (or half line) for line exchanges (stichomythia). In a further tragedy of Seneca, *Phaedra*, Hippolytus prepares to use his sword on Phaedra, who illicitly loves him, and, in a variant of that, Richard suggests to Anne that she kill him with his sword. Faced with a sexualization of the situation – sword equals penis – both Hippolytus and Anne drop the sword.

Another scene in *Richard III*, that of the mourning queens (4.4), relates to Seneca's tragedy *The Trojan Women*. In that play, after the Greek capture of Troy, the Trojan women, who are to be assigned as slaves to various Greek leaders, bemoan their fate, especially Hecuba, widow of King Priam, and Andromache, widow of Hector; this is a feminized community, whose men have been killed. In *Richard III* there is also a feminized community, one of women who have lost their children at Richard's hand: old Queen Margaret, who is an outsider like Helen; Anne corresponds to Polyxena because they undergo a marriage that means death; Queen Elizabeth, who resembles Andromache; and the Duchess of York, who is like Hecuba, because they have both given birth to disastrous sons: Paris cause of the Trojan War, Richard cause of a new war in England.

8

Richard III owes a good deal to Seneca, but *Macbeth* (1606) is rightly called by Paul 'the most Senecan of all Shakespeare's plays'. In terms of length, it is one of his shortest dramas at about 2,000 lines, and so suggests the much greater brevity of a tragedy by Seneca such as *Thyestes* that runs to just over 1,100 lines.

A powerful chief (thane) in Scotland, Macbeth is consumed with vaulting ambition, the lust to become king, and so exemplifies once more the Senecan theme of evil in the ruler; his wife, Lady Macbeth, is, at one stage, even more evil. Indeed *Macbeth*, much of which is set in darkness, involves a war between evil (dark) and virtue (light). But Macbeth differs from Richard III: whereas Richard is the villain as hero, Macbeth is a hero who becomes a villain[41]. So he first murders Duncan, then Banquo, then Macduff's wife and children, murders that affect the whole world. The linguistic analogue for this sense of evil is Shakespeare's heightened rhetoric that derives from, but surpasses that of Seneca; as seen, in spectacular fashion, in this soliloquy of Macbeth (1.7.1-28):

> If it were done when 'tis done, then 'twere well
> It were done quickly; if th'assassination
> Could trammel up the consequence and catch
> With his surcease, success, that but this blow
> Might be the be-all and the end-all-here,
> But here, upon this bank and shoal of time
> We'd jump the life to come. But in these cases
> We still have judgement here, that we but teach
> Bloody instructions, which being taught, return
> To plague th'inventor. This even-handed justice
> Commends th'ingredience of our poisoned chalice
> To our own lips. He's here in double trust:

> First, as I am his kinsman, and his subject,
> Strong both against the deed; then, as his host
> Who should against his murderer shut the door,
> Nor bear the knife myself. Besides, this Duncan
> Hath borne his faculties so meek, hath been
> So clear in his great office, that his virtues
> Will plead like angels, trumpet-tongues against
> The deep damnation of his taking-off;
> And pity, like a naked new-born babe,
> Striding the blast, or Heaven's cherubim, horsed
> Upon the sightless couriers of the air,
> Shall blow the horrid deed in every eye
> That tears shall drown the wind. I have no spur
> To prick the sides of my intent, but only
> Vaulting ambition, which o'er leaps itself
> And falls on th'other –

The tragedy of Seneca that has a major impact on *Macbeth* is *Hercules Furens* (*The Madness of Hercules*), in which the Greek hero Hercules kills not only the usurper Lycus, but also, while mad, his wife Megara and his three children. Macbeth is also a usurper, who is killed at the end of the play, and he murders children (though not his own); madness is found, but in Lady Macbeth, not her husband. Macbeth's reflections on Sleep (2.2.38-43) appropriate the views of the Chorus on Sleep in Seneca's tragedy (1065-81), with both passages using an intricate cluster of phrases in opposition[43]. Among the phrases used by Seneca are 'the conqueror of ills', 'rest of the mind', 'rest of day and companion of the night'. Macbeth's reflections derive from the fact that he believes that, having murdered the sleeping Duncan, he 'does murder sleep' (2.2.35-9):

> the innocent sleep,
> Sleep that knits up the ravelled sleeve of care,
> The death of each day's life, sore labour's both,
> Balm of hurt minds, great nature's second course,
> Chief nourisher in life's feast.

Like Hercules after the killing of his children, Macbeth is aware of his guilt after the murder of Duncan; both men feel that no amount of water will wash away their crimes, both stress the unclean hand (*Hercules Furens* 1323-29; *Macbeth* 2.2.59-62):

> What Tanais or what Nile or what Tigris
> raging with Persian water or what fierce Rhine
> or Tagus flowing swollen with the golden sand of Spain
> will cleanse this hand? If cold Crimea poured its icy sea,
> if all great Neptune's ocean rinsed my hands, the deep set stains

would cling incarnadine.
Will all great Neptune's ocean wash this blood
Clean from my hand? No, this my hand will rather
The multitudinous seas incarnadine,
Making the green one red.

To which should be contrasted Lady Macbeth's pithy rejoinder 'A little water clears us of this deed' (2.2.66).

Seneca's tragedy *The Madness of Hercules* provides an even more striking source for *Macbeth*, when both Hercules and Macbeth reflect on the ruin of their lives (*Hercules Furens* 1258-62; *Macbeth* 5.3.22-6):

There is no reason for me to hold, to delay my life
longer in this light; I have lost all my advantages,
mind, arms, fame, wife, children
even my madness. No one can be cured of a
polluted mind; crime must be cured by death.

I have lived long enough: my way of life
Is fall'n into the sere, the yellow leaf;
And that which should accompany old age,
As honour, love, obedience, troops of friends
I must not look to have...

But Macbeth now sees the polluted mind as belonging to Lady Macbeth, when he asks the Doctor 'Canst thou not minister to a mind diseas'd?' Finally, Macbeth's nihilistic account of human life towards the end of the play also owes something to Seneca. Writing as a Roman Stoic, Seneca speaks of 'this drama of human life, in which we are assigned the parts we are to play so badly'; Macbeth asserts 'Life's but a walking shadow, a poor player'[45]. But Macbeth has no plans for a Stoic suicide: 'why should I play the Roman fool and die on mine own sword?' (5.8.12). Female characters in *Macbeth* also relate to Seneca. As a paradigm of atrocious masculine daring, Lady MacBeth, the fiend-like queen, resembles the bloodthirsty Medea in his tragedy *Medea*[46]. Both women invoke powerful divine forces, as they seek a gender change that will turn them into violent men: Medea's self-rebuke to 'Exile all foolish female fear and pity from thy mind' (Studley) becomes Lady Macbeth's appeal to the murdering spirits to 'unsex me here / And fill me from the crown to the toe topfull / Of direst cruelty'. Medea is, of course, a child-killer, but Lady Macbeth sees herself as a *potential* killer of her baby: if a murderous action needs to be advanced, 'I would, while it was smiling in my face, / Have plucked my nipple from his boneless gums / And dashed the brains out' (1.7.56-9).

The Weird Sisters appear more akin to the Furies of Greek mythology then to the Fates. Even though the adjective 'weird' here connotes 'having the power to control the fate or destiny of men' (OED), the Sister do not have such power, which is that of the Fates. As they seek Macbeth's damnation, they resemble, rather, the avenging Fury of Seneca's revenge tragedy *Thyestes*. But they are dealing with Macbeth's future murders, not past ones. Linked to the Weird Sisters is the figure of Hecate (introduced into a revision of the play by Shakespeare or Middleton). She is an ancient chthonic goddess who enjoys very considerable power, being associated with the uncanny, ghosts, black magic. In Act 3, scene 5, Hecate rebukes the Weird Sisters for being involved with Macbeth, a matter she thinks should be reserved for herself; nevertheless, she instructs them to meet him again with their spells and charms. When they prepare for this, Hecate commends them.

9

Seneca makes use of a form of metatheatricality in which a character is aware that she or he is in a play, and usually announces their own name. The paradigm here is Medea in Seneca's tragedy *Medea*, who, as Wilamowitz said, 'has read Euripides'[47]. Medea employs this device on three separate occasions (lines 166, 171, 910):

Medea superest, 'Medea exists still';
Medea..fiam, 'I will become Medea';
Medea nunc sum, 'Now I am Medea'.

A striking later appropriation of this self-dramatization of Medea comes in Corneille's *Medáe* (1635), when the Nurse Nérine asks of her: 'Votre pays vous hait, votre époux est sans foi: / Dans un si grand revers que vous reste-t-il?' 'Your country hates you, your husband is faithless: / In such a great misfortune what remains for you?' Medea replies 'Moi, moi, dis-je et c'est assez', 'Me, me, I say, and it's enough'.[48]

This form of self-dramatization and the naming by a character of her or his self is frequent on the Elizabethan and Jacobean stage. In Kyd's *The Spanish Tragedy*, we have 'Know I am Hieronimo'. In Middleton's *The Revenger's Tragedy*, we have "Tis I, 'tis Vindice, 'tis I'. In Webster's *The Duchess of Malfi*, we have 'I am Duchess of Malfi still'. This device is found in early Shakespeare in *3 Henry VI*, when Gloucester, the future Richard III, says 'I am myself alone'. In laying claim to the throne of Denmark at Ophelia's grave, Hamlet announces 'This is I, / Hamlet the Dane'. Both Antony and Cleopatra also employ this device in the same scene: 'I am / Antony yet'; 'I will be Cleopatra'. The assertions of Seneca's Medea were to have a long history[49].

10

Seneca had a genius for moral aphorisms (*sententiae*) that are found throughout his prose and, in the more compressed form of a single line, the tragedies; as the Roman critic Quintilian said, 'There are many brilliant *sententiae* in him' (10.1.130). These pithy sayings appealed greatly to Shakespeare and his contemporaries. Two that deal in a similar way with the theme of 'crime' (*scelus*) – a word that occurs more than 200 times in Seneca's plays – were specially popular. At *Agamemnon* 115, Clytemnestra says *per scelera semper sceleribus tutum est iter*, 'the safe path through crimes is always by more crime'. At *Thyestes* 195-6, Atreus, who proposes to kill Thyestes' children and serve them up to him, states *scelera non ulcisceris, nisi vincis*, 'you will not have avenged crimes, unless you better them'.

Jonson in *Catiline* offers a rather prosaic version of the first of these that takes more than one line: 'The ills that I have done cannot be safe / But by attempting greater'. Marston in *The Malcontent* is better: 'Black deed only through black deed safely flies' (Seneca's line from *Agamemnon* is then quoted). Shakespeare has a number of versions of these Senecan aphorisms. After the murder of Duncan and his planning of the murder of Banquo and Fleance, Macbeth says 'Things bad begun make strong themselves by ill'. Later, when he is contemplating further crimes, Macbeth revises Seneca to say there is no going back: 'I am in blood / stepp'ed so far, that, should I wade no more, / Returning were as tedious as go o'er'. When Richard III reflects on his previous murder of Clarence and his present organizing of the murder of the princes in the Tower, he is closer to Seneca: 'But I am in / So far in blood that sin will pluck on sin'; 'sin' may be glossed as *scelus*, 'crime'. Related to all this is Hamlet's refusing to kill Claudius at prayer, so as to kill him while he is at some more disrespectful activity: 'Up sword, and know thou a more horrid hent' (an occasion to be grasped). For aphorisms about crime, sin and blood Seneca is the exemplar[50].

11

As we see in *A Midsummer Night's Dream*. Seneca may also be used by Shakespeare in comedy[51]. When Quince and his company propose to stage a play with the parodic title 'The most lamentable comedy and most cruel death of Pyramus', they establish links between comedy and tragedy. So the comic boaster Bottom – 'I could play Ercles rarely' (Hercules) – parodies[52] two passages from John Studley's translation of the tragedy *Hercules Oetaeus*, then thought to be by Seneca; this work of 1581 was written in a style that by now, in 1595-96, seemed outdated:

> O lord of ghosts, whose fiery flash
> That forth they had doth shake
> Doth cause the trembling lodges twain
> Of Phoebus' cer to quake...

> The roaring rocks have quaking stirred
> And none thereat have pushed;
> Hell gloomy gates I have burst ope
> Where grisly ghosts all hushed
> Have stood...

Shakespeare's parody works by means of excessive, ludicrous use of rhyme and alliteration (1.2.31-38):

> The raging rocks
> And shivering shocks
> Shall break the locks
> Of prison gates,
> And Phibbus' car
> Shall shine from far
> And make and mar
> The foolish Fates.

12

George Steiner asserted, in a brief and accurate way, that 'The Elizabethan and Jacobean dramatists ransacked Seneca'[53]. Not least Shakespeare, who found Seneca's tragedies to be a liberating, an enabling force in the writing of his own tragic dramas; just as the Latin plays are among 'The great homicidal classics'[54], so too are *Titus Andronicus, Hamlet, Richard III* and *Macbeth*. But Shakespeare makes use of Seneca in order to move beyond him: *Titus Andronicus* presents more horrors than Seneca ever did; *Hamlet* greatly expands the delay of the avenger; the protagonist in

Richard III is not just criminal, but also witty; Macbeth is wholly sane when he commits murders.

We need no longer regard Elizabethan and Jacobean interest in Seneca's tragedies as strange: they can be, and are being performed. Two notable examples in London have been Peter Brook's direction of *Oedipus* in a version by Ted Hughes, James Macdonald's direction of *Thyestes* in a translation by Caryl Churchill. The mills of God grind slowly, but they grind exceeding small[55].

4 | The Impact of Light Plautus

1

In evaluating the dramatic genres of comedy[1] and tragedy, critics have often maintained that tragedy is superior. Such privileging of tragedy is based, in part, on the fact that it stresses the spirit, while comedy stresses the body. Bodily functions are anathema to tragedy, but characters in comedy may eat and drink, may use obscene language and gestures (in Aristophanes). For all that, comedy often deals with serious issues by using a light touch. A further way of differentiating comedy and tragedy lies in their generally distinct endings: comedy tends to have a happy ending that stresses social order by means of a marriage or other celebration (the Greek noun *komoidia*) comes from *komos*, 'a celebration', and *oide*, 'a song'); tragedy tends to have a sad ending that involves the death of one or more characters. As Byron wrote in *Don Juan*, 'All tragedies are ended by a death, / all comedies are ended by a marriage'[2]. So *Hamlet* concludes with four deaths, *As You Like It* with four marriages.

Ultimately, the question of whether tragedy or comedy is the superior form may be unanswerable. When Beckett (who termed *Waiting for Godot* a 'tragicomedy') was asked by the poet Desmond Egan to adjudicate between the two genres, he declined to come down on one side or the other: [3]

> Sorry I can't help with yr. problem.
> Democritus laughed at Heraclitus
> weeping + H. wept at D. laughing.
> Pick yr. Fancy.

Indeed Socrates maintained that the same man should be able to write both tragedy and comedy;[4] here Shakespeare is exemplary.

2

In the Old Comedy of fifth century Athens, Aristophanes (about 445-385 B.C.) wrote nine plays that explore in a satirical, argumentative, but fantastic way the large public themes of war (*Acharnians, Peace, Lysistrata*), philosophy (*Clouds*), politics (*Knights*), the legal system (*Wasps*). In New Comedy that exemplifies the stress on the individual person in the Hellenistic era, Menander (342 – about 292 B.C.) abandons public themes in favour of the private life of the person, with special reference to the theme of sexual love, of boy meets girl. Freud sees this stress on sexual love as both physical and comic: 'the spheres of sexuality and obscenity offer the amplest occasions for obtaining comic pleasure... for they show human beings in their dependence on bodily needs... or they can reveal the physical demands lying behind the claim of mental love'[5].

Aristophanes' mode of comedy was never successfully transplanted to another society because it was too deeply implicated in the affairs of the unique city-state (*polis*) of Athens. Instead, the New Comedy of Menander and others was adopted and adapted in Rome by the comic dramatists Plautus (about 250-184 B.C.) and Terence (died about 160 B.C.)[6]; to become the basis for European comedy, in Jonson, Molière and Wilde among many others, and, in part, in Shakespeare. This early success in comedy highlights Rome's stress on laughter as found in other literary genres such as satire and epigram, and as found in social customs such as the ridicule of a general celebrating a military triumph in Rome. As Bakhtin said, 'It was Rome that taught European culture how to laugh and ridicule'[7].

While the comedies of Plautus and Terence are more various, more imaginative, more amusing than is often thought, in more than 20 of the 27 plays, the plot runs as follows: a young man desires a young woman (who is a slave or a courtesan), but is frustrated in his pursuit of her by the blocking character of his father (*senex*), until the woman is discovered to be freeborn, and the two then get married.

This plot involves 'the exchange of women'[8] between families, when a woman leaves her father's house to go to the house of her husband, with the marriage seen as a triumph of social integration.

Conversely, blocking characters such as the miser and the braggart soldier, who tend to be one-dimensional and to lack self-knowledge, are defeated and are removed from society. So Malvolio in *Twelfth Night* leaves for self-appointed exile. The comedies of Plautus do not always conform to the type of plot just outlined: the main source of Shakespeare's play *The Comedy of Errors* is the quite different *Menaechmi* that focuses on mistaken identity involving twins. But it is true that Roman comedy tends to make use of stock characters, listed by Terence as the running slave, good wives, bad courtesans, greedy spongers, the braggart soldier[9].

In the Renaissance, the comedies of Plautus and of Terence were played at Ferrara, the birthplace of modern theatre, at the court of Duke Ercole de l'Este (1431-1505). As he belittles the views of the common people, Yeats notes that this playing of Plautus at Ferrara paved the way for the learned comedy (*commedia erudita*) of Ariosto (1473-1533), a form that, at times, mediated Roman comedy to Shakespeare[10]:

> What cared Duke Ercole, that bid
> His mummers to the market-place,
> What th'onion-sellers thought or did
> So that his Plautus set the pace
> For the Italian comedies?

So in 1508, Ariosto's play *La Cassaria*, which was written in Italian, became the first original comedy to be produced in Europe. A further comedy by Ariosto called *I Suppositi*, which appropriates the deceits of Plautus' *Captivi* and Terence's *Eunuchus*, which was translated into English as *Supposes* by George Gascoigne in 1573, and became the source for the sub-plot of Bianca and her suitors in Shakespeare's early comedy *The Taming of the Shrew*. Indeed this sub-plot of *Shrew* replicates several features of Roman comedy: Lucentio is the young man (*adulescens*) in pursuit of a girl Bianca (*puella*), with a harsh father Baptista (*durus pater*) who is a blocking character.

There is also, of course, an English background to Shakespeare's comedies, that of the drama of folk ritual, in which life triumphs over the waste land of winter. Shakespeare depicts what Frye calls 'the drama of the green world', in which a comedy starts in a normal world, moves into the green world (such as the forest), and then returns to the normal world. As happens in *The Two Gentlemen of Verona*, where the eventual unions of Proteus and Julia, and of Valentine and Silvia, typical of New Comedy, are engineered in the forest.[11] The social analogue for this in Elizabethan England lies in the holidays that involve the release of social controls – what Rosalind in *As You Like It* calls 'holiday humour' – such as Mayday, Midsummer Eve, and the twelve days of the Christmas festival (*The Comedy of Errors* was performed at Christmas 1594).

3

Shakespeare made extensive use of the basic plots and characters found in Plautus and Terence. For Polonius in *Hamlet*, a play much concerned with the nature of drama, Plautus is the paradigm of comedy: 'Seneca cannot be too heavy, nor Plautus too light' (2.2.400-01). Indeed Shakespeare becomes, for Francis Meres, a contemporary version of Plautus: 'As Plautus and Seneca are accounted the best for Comedy and Tragedy among the Latines: so Shakespeare among the English is the most excellent in both kinds for the stage'[12]. Shakespeare preferred Plautus to Terence because Plautus added to Greek New Comedy a broad Italian humour and virtuoso use of language that matched his own practice (Julius Caesar said that Terence's style lacked vigour (*vis*)).

Such exuberance in Plautus and in Shakespeare left them open to criticism: Horace felt that Plautus' dramaturgy was slipshod; Jonson held that Shakespeare 'lacked art'. But Plautus' humour is described by Cicero as 'elegant, urbane, clever, witty'[14]; terms that suit the author of *As You Like It* and *Twelfth Night*.

4

Shakespeare's most obvious appropriation of Plautus is found in his early play *The Comedy of Errors* (between 1590 and 1594) that is based on *Menaechmi* (with further material from *Amphitruo*)[15]. Performances of *Menaechmi* were significant events in the Renaissance – in 1502 it was played before Pope Alexander VI – and it is possible that Shakespeare translated this comedy as a schoolmaster[16]. He certainly read Plautus' play in Latin rather than in the translation into English by William Warner that was not published until 1595[17]. *The Comedy or Errors* was performed at Grey's Inn on 28 December, 1594 (Holy Innocents' Day) in a carnivalesque atmosphere, where the confusions of the play were mirrored by disturbances due to overcrowding, so that it was called ever after *The Night of Errors*. At 1787 lines, *The Comedy of Errors* is Shakespeare's shortest play, and it observes the so called unities of place and time.

Coleridge held that *The Comedy of Errors* is 'a legitimate farce in exactest consonance with the philosophical principles and character of farce, as distinguished from comedy and from other entertainments'[18]. But Shakespeare gives his play the title 'comedy', so that, while the constant theme of mistaken identity is that of farce, it also deals with issues of marriage and courtship with the definition of the self, with the discord of death and violence (including the beating of servants), with Christian themes. Indeed *Errors* has significant elements of romance[19], whose narrative mode is illustrated by the long narrative exposition by Egeon at the beginning of the play. The subplot of Egeon's separation from his wife Emilia derives from the Latin story of Apollonius of Tyre, which is probably based on a Greek romantic novel of the second or third century A.D. The motif of Egeon's sentence to death may reflect the tyranny in Syracuse under Dionysus I (405-367 B.C.), as well as hostile relations between England and Spain. Central to the theme of romance in *Errors* (as in Shakespeare's late romances such as *Pericles*) is the way in which separated families – husband Egeon and wife Emilia, their two sons Antipholus, the two Dromios – are reunited and reborn after great hardship; as the Abbess and wife Emilia says, 'After so long grief, such 'nativity'' (5.1.406).

Not one of his best plays, the *Menaechmi* of Plautus is a much more basic drama than *Errors*, being essentially a farce. But it does exhibit a basic duality between the real world of business and hard work, and the comic dream of food, sex and money[20]. The core of the plot is the pursuit of Menaechmus of Syracuse (1) in Sicily of his twin Menaechmus of Epidamnus (2) in Illyria, who was separated from him when they were young, and the mistaken identities that then arise in Epidamnus between those two brothers; Menaechmus I is mistaken for Menaechmus 2 by almost all the important characters in turn.

Shakespeare makes extensive changes to Plautus' *Menaechmi*. While maintaining the exotic Mediterranean setting, he moves the action from Epidamnus on the coast of Illyria to Ephesus on the coast of Asia Minor, and introduces the story of the shipwreck of Egeon and his family to stress the themes of chaos and loss of identity. Adopting the practice of using two source plays (as exemplified and defended by Terence), Shakespeare (who had twins himself), adds to the twins of *Menaechmi* a second pair of twins from Plautus' mythological travesty *Amphitruo*, the Dromios (this name suggests the Greek root *drom* meaning 'to run', and so the endlessly busy Plautine slave (*servus currens*)). As Antipholus and Dromio of Syracuse are confused with Antipholus and Dromio of Ephesus, the incidents of error are increased by Shakespeare from 17 to 50[21]. And while Plautus concentrates on the local twin of Epidamnus, Shakespeare concentrates on the visiting twin of Syracuse, who has six soliloquys as against one for the twin of Ephesus.

Shakespeare stresses the importance of marriage by the fact that, unlike Plautus, he gives the wife of Antipholus of Ephesus a name, Adriana, while his mistress, who in Plautus has the suggestive name of Erotium (from Greek *erós* meaning sexual love), is simply called a 'courtesan'. Adriana appears to replicate a scene in *Amphitruo*, in which a husband (Amphitruo) is locked out of his house, while his wife (Alcmena) receives a lover (Jupiter) in the guise of her husband. But Adriana does *not* commit adultery with Antipholus of Syracuse. In another Shakespearean innovation, that Antipholus woos the sister-in-law of his brother, Luciana, who is an invented character. As is the peculiar Dr Pinch, quite unlike the conventional doctor in Plautus.

A major addition by Shakespeare in *Errors* to Plautus is a series of religious themes; as Levin says, 'Shakespeare's characters move, as usual, in a Christian ethos'[22]. In Ephesus, there is both true and false religion: the false exorcists of *Acts* 19 ensure that the city is seen to be the home of sorcerers and witches; but Ephesus is also seen by the author of the *Ephesians* (4.24) to be the potential centre of 'a spiritual revolution'. That theme of a new beginning permeates the massive recognition scene (*anagnorisis*) at the end of *Errors*. Not only is order and identity restored, not only is harmony established, but there is to be a baptismal feast for the families, members of which are redeemed through the holistic religion of the Abbess and her Priory, as opposed to the false religion of Pinch, and of the famous temple of Diana of the Ephesians, one of the seven wonders of the Greco-Roman world. But both the Abbess and Adriana, two strong women, may reflect the legend that Ephesus was founded by the Amazons, powerful warriors who always fought on horseback[22a].

What is noteworthy in all this is that Shakespeare appears to reflect the view that a Christian theme underlies the comedies of Plautus; as Frye says[23], 'the crudest Plautine comedy formula has much the same *structure* as the central Christian myth itself, with its divine son appeasing the wrath of a father and redeeming what is at once a society and a bride'. No wonder, then, that A. W. Schlegel held that *Errors* is 'perhaps the best of all written or possible Menaechmi'[24].

5

A number of other Shakespearean comedies have links to Roman comedy. Already in Shakespeare's day, *Twelfth Night* was linked to Plautus' *Menaechmi* by the young law student John Manningham, who saw a performance of the play at Middle Temple on February 2, 1602 (the feast of Candlemas): 'At our feast we had a play called 'Twelve Night, or What You Will', much like and neare to that in Italian called *Inganni*'[25]. The link to Plautus lies in the twins Viola and Sebastian, who are shipwrecked, separated and later united, and who cause confusion when Viola pretends to be the boy Cesario, identical to Sebastian. But Manningham's *Inganni*, which is in reality the anonymous *Gl'Ingannati, The Deceivers* – available to Shakespeare in a prose version by Barnabe Rich – is the source of the main plot.

Yet Roman comedy also features in important ways in *Twelfth Night*. Such as the traditional setting of two houses, in which Orsino and Olivia confine themselves, suggesting their self-absorbed state. Sir Tony Belch, lover of pleasure, famous purveyor of cakes and ale, resembles the parasite, ever eager for food, but sometimes excluded from it; like some parasites, Belch is an intriguer against Malvolio (Shakespeare's invention). Having a name that suggests 'malevolent' and attitudes that suit approaching Lent in 1602, Malvolio is a sour, puritanical figure who does not laugh (agelast) – like Lydus in Plautus' *Bacchides* – and excludes himself from the resolution at the end of the play. The clever slave of New Comedy also has a role to play in *Twelfth Night*: Orsino employs Viola like a slave to further his romance with Olivia; Maria forges a letter from Olivia to trick Malvolio into thinking his mistress is in love with him.

But Shakespearean comedy can move far beyond the relatively simple sexual situation of New Comedy, when a girl's assumption of male identity involves a complex exploration of gender roles, both heterosexual and homosexual[26]. In *Twelfth Night*, the witty, eloquent character Viola, who is played by a boy, is disguised as a boy named Cesario, and so imitates her twin brother Sebastian. Olivia falls in love with Cesario, as does Orsino, while Sebastian is adored by his friend Antonio. Gender confusion multiplies: Antonio mistakes Viola for Sebastian, Olivia takes Sebastian for Cesario. In a metatheatrical moment, Viola points out that she lacks 'a little thing', that is a penis, but of course the boy actor in question does not (3.4.255). This very complex exploration of gender roles ensures that the marriages at the end of the play – those of Orsino and Viola, and of Olivia and Sebastian – are not at all the idyllic unions of New Comedy, but have been rendered problematical by the questioning of rigid hierarchies in regard to male and female roles in society.

A broadly similar situation exists in *As You Like It* (1599). Rosalind, who speaks one quarter of the comedy's lines, is sexually ambivalent: she is played by a boy, and, uniquely, draws attention to this in the Epilogue; she crossdresses as a man with the name Ganymede, the catamite of Zeus; she falls in love with the slow-witted Orlando; she is emotionally attracted to the woman Celia; and she becomes emotionally attractive to the woman Phoebe. So Rosalind is a liberated woman, who exhibits 'masculine pride, verve, and cool aristocratic control'[27]. But she also resembles a heroine from New Comedy, who accepts the institution of marriage, a theme heavily stressed at the end of the play by the spectacular appearance, the theophany of the god of marriage Hymen. Jonson's masque *Hymenaei* (1606) shows what might be done with the presentation of this divine being: he is clothed like a Roman bride with yellow veil and sandals, and with marjoram in the hair. In *As You Like It*, Shakespeare stresses the honour due to Hymen, the theme of laughter, the topic of harmony between the four couples who are to be married: Rosalind and Orlando; Oliver and Celia; Silvius and Phoebe; Touchstone and Audrey. But, as in *Twelfth Night*, this emphasis on marriage has been partly undercut by what has preceded it.

There is further use of Roman comedy in *The Taming of the Shrew*. Plautus' *Mostellaria* provides the names of the clever slave Tranio – which suggests 'keen-witted' – and of the beaten slave Grumio. In both comedies, Tranio is a splendid example of the astute servant who is able to trick an old man, when that father – Theopropides or Vincentio – charges him with the care of his son, Philolaches or Lucentio. Tranio fails in his duty by helping the young man to live in an expensive way and to pursue women, and, when the father returns, locks him out and tells him lies. Both fathers discover the truth in the end, are reunited with their erring sons, pardon the deceitful servant.

Furthermore, the Plautine basics for the sub-plot of Lucentio and Bianca interacts with the main plot, deriving from the oral tradition of folktale, of Petruchio and Katerina. This complex construction aroused Dr. Johnson's admiration: 'Of this play the two plots are so well united that they can hardly be called two without injury to the art with which they are interwoven'[28]. So Plautus plays an important role in *Shrew*. But it remains unclear whether the depiction of Katherina is to be viewed as serious and therefore anti-women, or as ironic and therefore anti-patriarchal[29].

6

Shakespeare can use New Comedy in history plays (1 and 2 *Henry IV*), in romance (*The Tempest*), and even in tragedy (*Othello, King Lear*).

Appearing in two history plays *1 and 1 Henry IV*, as well as the comedy *The Merry Wives of Windsor*, Falstaff takes his place with the greatest of comic characters such as Lysistrata, Trimalchio, Don Quijote, Christy Mahon. Probably played by the famous comic actor Will Kemp, Falstaff is a universal figure, suggesting, *inter alia*, the mediaeval Vice, the Prodigal Son, the Lord of Misrule, tavern wit. Since Falstaff is such an extravagant figure, he defies most categories of praise and blame; as Dr. Johnson asked 'But Falstaff unimitated, unimitable Falstaff, how shall I describe thee? Thou compound of sense and vice; of sense which may be admired but not esteemed, of vice which may be despised, but hardly detested'[30]. Part of the polyphony of Falstaff's character is to be found in a number of stock characters from Roman comedy.

In *1 and 2 Henry IV*, the contrast between two worlds found in Plautus' *Menaechmi* is greatly intensified: on the one hand, we have Falstaff's comic world of the Boar's Head Tavern in Eastcheap that is portrayed in prose; on the other hand, we have the serious world of politics and soldiering inhabited by King Henry that is portrayed in verse. Falstaff's world enacts a Saturnalia, an overthrow of the everyday norm, which champions a comic stress on the body, and in which Falstaff is the Lord of Misrule (*Saturnalicius princeps*). Hence Falstaff becomes a most exuberant version of the parasite of New Comedy, one always eager to indulge in the reckless consumption of expensive food and wine. When he sexually pursues Mrs. Page and Mrs. Ford in *The Merry Wives of Windsor*, Falstaff exacts another role from Roman comedy, that of an old man who chases after a woman (*senex amans*) – like the lecherous Lysidamus in Plautus' *Casina*. Indeed Falstaff justifies his sexual desire by referring to the fact that Chaerea in Terence's *Eunuchus* applies the seduction of Danae by Jupiter to his own case: 'Couldn't a mere man like me do the same?' becomes 'When gods have hot backs, what shall poor men do?'[32]

Falstaff's relation to the braggart soldier of Roman comedy is more complex. When he is in love, he resembles such soldiers in Plautus and Terence: in Plautus' comedy *Miles Gloriosus*, Pyrgopolynices carries off the girl Philocomasium; in Terence's comedy *Eunuchus*, Traso (who gives Shakespeare the adjective 'thrasonical')[33] is in love with the courtesan Thais. Like these characters, Falstaff is well able to boast about his military prowess, overvaluing himself and undervaluing others, especially women. He equates himself with the greatest of Greek heroes Hercules – 'I am as valiant as Hercules' – and ludicrously applies to himself the famous boast of the military genius Julius Caesar about the battle of Zela in 47 B.C.: 'I came, saw, and overcame' (1 *Henry IV* 2.4.261; 2 *Henry IV* 5.5.46). In reality, Falstaff is a coward who runs away at Gad's Hill (even if he can produce a reasoned rejection of the concept of 'honour').

In the end of the day, Falstaff's alternative world of comedy must yield to the inexorable demands of History[34], the timeless activities of the carefree to the recorded time of the ruler: 'I know thee not, old man', says the newly crowned Henry V. (2 *Henry IV* 5.5.46). There is no room for Falstaff in the Palace; instead, he will go to Prison, to the Fleet. Such humiliation will accord with the generic demands of a history play like 2 *Henry IV*, but in *The Merry Wives of Windsor*, a comedy, Falstaff is humiliated even more: he is locked in a laundry basket, beaten in women's clothes, thrown into the Thames, has his finger burnt, and is pinched for his lechery by 'fairies'.

What is happening in all of this is that Falstaff has become a scapegoat (*pharmakos*), who appears in ritual in the Greek festival of the Thargelia (May-June), and in tragedy in Sophocles' *King Oedipus*. Such a man is expelled from the city in order to expiate its sins – here those not only of Falstaff, but also of Prince Hal in his past – so that the city may then prosper again; put in seasonal terms, winter is deflected and summer comes in. Here Shakespeare drastically overturns generic convention, as his greatest comic character becomes the main victim in getting rid of winter and ushering in summer. And yet the end of *The Merry Wives of*

Windsor preserves something of the usual comic resolution because Falstaff, like the slave of Roman comedy, is forgiven, laughs, and does not die. That death is reserved for another history play, *Henry V*, a drama about war alien to Falstaff's real interests.

Another Shakespearean character who combines New Comedy roles is Parolles in *All's Well That Ends Well* (he is an addition to the main source in Boccaccio, and was held by Charles I to be the chief attraction of the play). Nicholas Rowe noted that 'The Parasite and the Vain-glorious in Parolles, in *All's Well That Ends Well*, is as good as anything of that kind in *Plautus* or *Terence*'[35]. so Parolles is a soldier who boasts of wounding Captain Spurio (apt name), and who retreats from battle like a coward; stripped of his clothes and his vanity, he resembles Pyrgopolynices in Plautus. Then by Act 5, scene 2, Parolles has become a beggar and so a parasite eager to eat; as the old Lord Lafew says, 'though you are a fool and a knave, you shall eat' (5.2.50).

7

The Tempest is a far more complex play than any by Plautus or Terence, but elements in it relate to aspects of New Comedy[36]. So the hierarchy of free-born and of slave, central to the comedies of Plautus and Terence, is replicated when the irritable old man Prospero (*senex iratus*) owns the slaves Ariel and Caliban. Ariel is at first compliant: 'I come to answer thy last pleasure'; then rebels and asks for 'My libertie'; then like a clever slave (*servus callidus*) in Plautus, furthers the romance of Ferdinand and Miranda; and finally is promised freedom by Prospero (1.2.189-90, 245). Caliban has strong affinities with Plautine slaves: he curses like Toxilus in *Persa*; he is drunk like the slaves in *Miles Gloriosus*; he is sullen like Sceparnio in *Rudens*. Then Ferdinand is a free man who has been forcibly enslaved to Prospero, but is willingly enslaved to Miranda, a slave of love (*servus amoris*) like Propertius in Latin elegy; paradoxically, this latter state causes Prospero to free him.

Plautus' romantic comedy *Rudens* (which Scaliger felt should be called *Tempestas*) functions as a more specific subtext for *The Tempest*. Both plays open with a storm that causes shipwreck; the exiled old men Daemones and Prospero seek to protect their daughters Palaestra and Miranda from sexual assault by the pimp Labrax and by Caliban, a grotesque version of the young lover; Stephano fantasizes about freedom and power like the slave Gripus in *Rudens*. But the solutions found at the end of *Rudens* are rendered problematical in *The Tempest*. Certainly, Alonso gets back his son Ferdinand. But although Prospero renounces the intrigues and deception of comedy, he makes no new discovery about the other characters, who remain unredeemed; Prospero and his brother Antonio are still enemies. Equally well, the marriage of Ferdinand and Miranda is less than ideal: she finds him cheating at chess, and is prepared to accept that.

8

On two occasions, Shakespeare makes use of the conventions of Roman Comedy within the genre of tragedy to heighten the tragic effect: *Othello* and *King Lear*.

Several characters in *Othello* can be analysed in the light of stock characters in Roman Comedy[37]. Take, for example, Brabantio the father of Desdemona, an invention of Shakespeare not found in his Italian source Giraldi Cinthio: he is a blocking old man (*senex*), who is exercised about the unsuitable marriage of his daughter to Othello. Othello himself exhibits certain characteristics of the braggart soldier (*miles gloriosus*). While Othello is not boastful, he is in love with Desdemona and is sexually jealous of her, because, in a gullible way, he trusts his very clever subordinate Iago (*servus callidus*). Iago directs his master (as well as Desdemona's suitor Roderigo), skilfully improvises plots, falsely suggests to Othello that Desdemona has committed adultery with Cassio, his second-in-command. Here, as opposed to comedy, the result is tragic: Othello kills Desdemona – who is not a comic character, and whose name suggests in Greek 'The Unfortunate One' – and then himself.

In his last speech but one (5.2.337-55), Othello echoes both Ovid and Pliny the Elder to express his love for Desdemona. When he says 'then must you speak / Of one that loved not wisely, but too well', this echoes (whether intentionally or not) the deserted woman Phyllis in Ovid's *Heroides* (2.27): *Dic mihi, quid feci, nisi non sapienter amavi*, 'Tell me, what I have done, except that I loved not wisely'. Though a man, Othello has felt equally deserted and seeks to justify himself. And he is not beyond crying, dropping tears like resin, dropping them 'as fast as the Arabian trees / Their medicinable gum' (Pliny, *Natural History* 12.15).

Comedy usually ends in marriage. Even when the man suspects the woman he loves of infidelity – as Claudio and Hero in *Much Ado About Nothing*, as Leontes and Hermione in *The Winter's Tale* – the woman forgives the man, and they get married in the end. But

Othello begins with the marriage of Desdemona and Othello, ends with the *death* of the married couple on the marriage-bed in a grotesquely literal version of lovers' death (*Liebestod*). This is a great tragedy, even if there are some comic elements.

In *King Lear*, the subplot of Gloucester and his two sons, the bastard Edmund and the legitimate Edgar, makes use of motifs from the Roman Comedy of Plautus and Terence[38]. Indeed Edmund refers to the climax of New Comedy when Edgar enters: 'Pat! he comes like the catastrophe of the old comedy' (1.2.134). Gloucester is an example of the gullible old man (*senex*) who is duped about land by a clever unprincipled son Edmund, at once the young man (*adulescens*) and the clever slave (*servus callidus*). For Edmund's use of a forged letter recalls a similar deceitful letter in comedies by Plautus such as *Pseudolus* (it is not found in Shakespeare's sources for *King Lear*); and Edmund's staged dual with Edgar recalls the one in Terence's *Andria* between the slave Davos and the maid Mysis. Edgar too has comic aspects: he feigns madness like Menaechmus of Syracuse in Plautus, and mirrors his rival Edmund by deceiving his father at Dover Cliff (although this is to give Gloucester life). Then at the end of *King Lear*, there are a number of comic recognition scenes: Cordelia is rediscovered by Lear – as Palaestra by her father Daemones in Plautus' *Rudens* – but is lost again in death; and the true identity of Edmund and Edgar is established.

These comic elements in what may be Shakespeare's greatest tragedy suggest the truth of Patrick Kavanagh's dictum that 'Tragedy is underdeveloped Comedy'[39].

5 | The Pervasive Presence of Ovid

1

Ovid (43 B.C. – 17 A.D.), was the favourite poet of Shakespeare[1], who appropriated his work, read both in Latin and in translation, in his plays and in his poetry. For the schoolmaster Holofernes in *Love's Labour's Lost*, Ovid 'was the man' 'for the elegancy, facility, and golden cadence of poesy' (4.2.121-2). In 1598, Francis Meres used the theme of reincarnation – that of a Trojan warrior into a Greek philosopher – to suggest the impact of Ovid upon Shakespeare[2]: 'As the soul of Euphorbus was thought to live in Pythagoras: so the sweete wittie soul of Ovid lives in mellifluous and honey-tongued Shakespeare, witness his *Venus and Adonis*, his *Lucrece*, his sugar'd *Sonnets* among his private friends, etc'. But Ovid was not always sweet for Shakespeare: his myth of the rape of Philomela tastes distinctly sour in plays like *Titus Andronicus* and *Cymbeline*.

By far the most important work of Ovid for Shakespeare was his epic poem in fifteen books, the *Metamorphoses*[3], which deals with the innumerable changes into another form undergone by persons from Greek myth. These transformations bring intense states of human emotion to a conclusive end, and can evoke two different reactions: either focus on the new shape that is known to us and so to make the metamorphosis believable; or focus on the human subjects of transformation and so to render it inexplicable[4]. While the epic poems of Homer and of Virgil present a *continuous* narrative that tells one story, Ovid's *Metamorphoses* is an *episodic* epic that tells about 250 stories from Greek mythology, with about 50 of these treated at some length, and so functioning as miniature epics or epyllia. The discrete nature of such stories provided a wonderful fund of material for Shakespeare to appropriate in his poems and in his plays.

Ovid's *Metamorphoses* is full of extreme emotion, of sex and of violence. Which appealed to Shakespeare, and which appeals to the contemporary world. The editors of a recent volume of translations of the *Metamorphoses*, Michael Hofmann and James Lasdun, explain[5]: Ovid deals with modern issues such as 'holocaust, plague, sexual harassment, rape, incest, seduction, pollution, sex-change, suicide, hetero – and homosexual love, torture, war, child-battering, depression and intoxication'.

Other works by Ovid that Shakespeare used also have a sexual content, two of which – *Amores, Love Affairs* and *Ars Amatoria, The Art of Love* – are, in part, parodies. *Amores* is a sequence of poems about Ovid's fictitious mistress Corinna that parodies the serious love elegies of Propertius about Cynthia. In *Ars Amatoria*, Ovid writes a manual of seduction as a teacher of love (*praeceptor amoris*) that parodies Greek and Roman didactic poems on serious topics. The Emperor Augustus, who sought to clean up the sexual mores of the Roman upper classes, was not amused by this poem, and in 8 A.D. exiled Ovid to Tomis on the Black Sea (Ovid never returned to Rome). In *As You Like It* (3.3.5-6), Touchstone relates the characters' exile to that of Ovid: 'I am here with thee and thy goats, as the most capricious poet honest Ovid was among the Goths'. This statement subtly alludes to the erotic content of Ovid's poetry, because the adjective 'capricious' suggests not only the meanings of 'humorous', 'whimsical', but also the meaning 'licentious', since it comes from the Latin for 'goat' *caper*, and since those animals were notorious for lust.

It was not just in Rome that Ovid's poetry about sex was disapproved of: Marlowe's fine translation of the *Amores* was burnt in London by order of the Church authorities in 1599. This act took place in a climate of political censorship that sought to ban plays, satires and epigrams, Marlowe's poems being found with John Davies' *Epigrams*[6].

Then Ovid's *Heroides, Heroines*, is a series of letters by noble women of the past to absent lovers or husbands. Finally, there is the *Fasti*, a long poem about the Roman calendar and events (often religious) associated with it.

2

The great bulk of the myths used by Shakespeare are Greek, and 80% of them come from Ovid[7]. For although there are several systems of mythology in Europe (and many more beyond it), it is Greek myth that has achieved ascendancy in Western culture; as Heidegger says, 'myth itself is Greek'. One reason for this is that the stories of Greek mythology are very entertaining, that they are for Wallace Stevens 'the greatest piece of fiction'. Another reason is that these myths do not exist in a single, canonical form, but appear in many different versions, are always open to new angles; as Calasso says, 'No sooner have you grabbed hold of it than myth opens out into a fan of a thousand segments'[8]. The advantages of that for a creative writer are obvious.

It will be objected that, while Greek myths may have held audiences and readers in Shakespeare's day, they no longer do so, and that to approach these stories in his work is to function like a modern anthropologist investigating a 'primitive' culture. But Greek myth has proved to be remarkably resilient in the modern world, as figures like Oedipus, Medea and Antigone attest. Indeed contemporary European theatre is full of Greek myth: note the astonishing number of appropriations of tragedies by Aeschylus, Sophocles and Euripides that deal with Greek myth in the recent past. In Ireland alone, there have been nearly thirty such plays since 1975[9].

3

Ovid's most telling impact upon Shakespeare lies in his treatment of sexual themes. As Ted Hughes states 'Above all, Ovid was interested in passion', and this is 'what he shared with Shakespeare'. It is as though the bulk of Ovid's poems were a prolonged commentary on Virgil's moralizing aphorism *Omnia vincit Amor*, 'Sexual desire conquers all'. Indeed in the single poem of *Tristia* 2, Ovid held that all Greek and Latin poetry is about love. In appropriating Ovid's use of sexual themes, Shakespeare not only lifts specific topics from the Latin poet, but also makes up fresh material in the *manner* of Ovid: an elaborate, self-conscious style involving wit, paradox, aphorisms (*sententiae*), many forms of word-play[11].

Much in Shakespeare comes from Ovid's *Metamorphoses*, a work that deals with extreme sexual states, not least rape; indeed for Segal, the poem is an 'epic of rape'[12]. The theme of the rape of

Philomela by Tereus in *Metamorphoses* (6.425-674) is found in both *Titus Andronicus* and in *Cymbeline*. That mythical rape anticipates the fate of the daughter of Titus Andronicus, Lavinia, who is raped and mutilated by the sons of Tamora, Queen of the Goths, Demetrius and Chiron, in revenge for the killing of her son Alarbus by Titus. When Tereus rapes Philomela – 'by the barbarous king / So rudely forced'[13] – who is the sister of his wife Procne, he cuts out her tongue to prevent her telling, but she lets Procne know by means of a tapestry she weaves. The two women then take their revenge by killing Tereus' son Itys, and serving his flesh to his father.

Shakespeare multiplies these horrors. Lavinia's mutilation is even more severe, because not just her tongue, but her hands are cut off by the rapists. But Lavinia is still able to indicate that she has been raped by referring to Ovid's tale of Philomela. She tosses a copy of the *Metamorphoses* that is explicitly named in the text by the boy Lucius, grandson of Titus: 'Grandsire, 'tis Ovid's *Metamorphoses*; My mother gave it to me (4.1.42-3). (And Lavinia had read to Lucius 'sweet poetry' and Cicero's work on oratory *Orator* in the manner of the Roman mother Cornelia, who educated in Greek culture her sons, the radical politicians Tiberius and Gaius Gracchus (4.4.11-4))[13a]. Titus sees that Ovid is open at the myth of Philomela (4.1.47-9):

> This is the tragic tale of Philomel,
> And treats of Tereus' treason and his rape;
> And rape, I fear, was the root of thy annoy.

Titus then makes the connection to Lavinia explicit: was she 'Ravished and wronged, as Philomela was?' (4.1.52-3). Lavinia then takes a staff in her mouth, guiding it with her stumps, and writes the Latin word for 'rape', and the names of those who raped her: '*Stuprum* – Chiron – Demetrius'. Earlier in the play (2.4), Titus' brother Marcus links Lavinia's rape to that of Philomela in a speech that is very Ovidian in the way it renders violence the subject of pathos, and that must represent one possible mode of responding to great human suffering (as in the Messenger speeches in Greek tragedy).

When Titus takes his revenge, he does so in spectacular fashion. Just as the mutilation of Lavinia exceeded the myth, so too does Titus' treatment of Demetrius and Chiron: 'For worse than Philomel you used my daughter, / And worse than Procne I will be revenged' (5.2.194-5). Assisted by Lavinia, who receives their blood, Titus cuts the throats of Chiron and Demetrius, and bakes their heads in a paste made of their bones; he then serves this to Tamora, before killing her. Nor is that all: Titus kills Lavinia because of the *shame* she has experienced, citing the example of the Roman Virginius, who killed his daughter Virginia because she had been raped: 'Because she was enforced, stained, and deflowered' (5.3.38). So Lavinia endures a worse fate than Philomela: she is silenced, while Philomela, changed into a nightingale, sings.

Clearly, Rome in *Titus Andronicus* is 'a wilderness of tigers', and Titus quotes Ovid to make the point that the goddess of Justice Astraea has left the earth: *Terras Astraea reliquit* (4.3.4; *Metamorphoses* 1.150). Like many a Renaissance work, *Titus Andronicus* is based on Latin texts, the *Thyestes* of Seneca and the *Metamorphoses* of Ovid. All three texts shock, rebuke the notion that canonical authors do not do horror, sex and violence.

Sexual disaster derived from Ovid's *Metamorphoses* can be found in comedy and romance as well as in tragedy. The rape of Innogen, an English princess, by Giacomo in *Cymbeline* (1610) is potential rather than actual, but still relates to the myth of Philomela. Innogen's commoner husband Posthumus, who is banished to Rome, engages in a wager about her chastity with an Italian man named Giacomo, betting him a diamond ring (which Innogen gave him) and 10,000 ducats that he will be unable to seduce his wife.

Once in England, Giacomo enters Innogen's bedroom by subterfuge, steals her bracelet, and takes note of a mole on her left breast. At the same time, Giacomo directs the audience's attention to the theme of rape by comparing himself (if in a muted way) with Sextus Tarquinius, son of the legendary king of Rome who was notorious for the rape of Lucretia. More: before Innogen went to sleep, she had been reading Ovid's account of the rape of Philomela by Tereus, and finishes at the moment of rape (2.2.44-6): 'She hath been reading late, / The tale of Tereus. Here the leaf's turned down / Where Philomel gave up'. But Giacomo feels that the bracelet and knowledge of the mole is enough: since he has ensured that Innogen appears to be unfaithful, since she has been raped metaphorically, he does not need to rape her in reality. Lavinia's dire fate is not that of Innogen.

Innogen's bedroom contains a representation of Diana, virgin goddess of the wild and the hunt, protector of women. Ovid tells the story of how the hunter Actaeon by accident saw Diana bathing naked, with the result that she changed him into a stag, and he was torn into pieces by his own hounds (*Metamorphoses* 3.158-252). A salutary warning of how the male gaze, directed at a female figure, can lead to radical punishment, this myth of Actaeon is applied in a modified way to the inordinate sexual desire of Falstaff for Mistress Ford and Mistress Page in *The Merry Wives of Windsor*. Indeed Falstaff's follower Pistol explicitly names Actaeon, when he transfers the application of the myth to Ford, potential cuckold (2.1.109-11).

Mistress Ford and Mistress Page are annoyed at Falstaff's advances (they receive identical love letters), and decide to humiliate the amorous knight. He is hidden in a basket of dirty linen, which is thrown into the Thames; disguised as a Mistress Prat, a suspected witch, he is beaten by the jealous Ford; when he is deserted by Mistress Page and Mistress Ford in Windsor Park, he is assaulted by pretended fairies. There Falstaff is disguised as Herne the Hunter of folk culture with the horns of a cuckold (he has no wife), but which suggest the head of a stag, and so the figure of Actaeon. But Falstaff, for all the indignities he suffers, is not killed like Actaeon; this is comedy, not tragedy, and even Ovid notes that some felt the hunter's punishment was too severe (3.253-4).

4

Shakespeare can appropriate Ovid to very positive effect in regard to love (*The Taming of the Shrew*; *The Winter's Tale*), and to power (*The Tempest*).

The subplot of *The Taming of the Shrew* deals with the relationship of Bianca, younger daughter of the rich Baptista Minola of Padua, with Lucentio of Pisa, who loves her at first sight; this is satirized as 'I burn, I pine, I perish' (1.1146). Bianca is to be educated in Greek and Latin, so that the servant Tranio[14] (pretending to be his master Lucentio) brings her 'this small packet of Greek and Latin books' (2.1.96).

In a scene that has no source (3.1), Lucentio, who is disguised as the schoolmaster Cambio, appropriates Ovid's Latin to express his love for Bianca, mistranslating part of a letter of Penelope to Odysseus that deals with the Trojan War (*Heroides* 1.33-4). The Latin translates as 'Here went Simois, here is the Sigeian land, / Here stood the lofty palace of old Priam'. But as he takes the text word for word like a schoolmaster, Lucentio endorses the slogan 'Make love, not war'. And has a go at his rival Gremio ('old pantaloon'):

Hic ibat – as I told you before; *Simois* – I am
Lucentio; *hic est* – son unto Vincentio of Pisa; *Sigeia tellus* –
Disguised thus to get your love. *Hic steterat* – and that
Lucentio comes a-wooing; *Priami* – is my man Tranio; *regia*
– bearing my port; *celsa senis* – that we might beguile the old
panaloon.

But Bianca shows that she is well able for Lucentio by providing an alternative 'translation' ('conster') that makes his prospects very doubtful, and suggests he should be wary of letting Gremio hear him:

Now let me see if I can conster it. *Hic ibat*
Simois – I know you not; *hic est Sigeia tellus* – I trust
you not; *Hic steterat Priami* – take heed he hear us not;
regia – presume not; *celsa senis* – despair not.

The fact that Bianca knows Latin means that she has access to one of the main distinguishing features of the male elite in Elizabethan England, so that she is the equal of Lucentio. Their subsequent marriage will therefore contrast with what many feel happens in the main plot: Petruchio dominates Katherine (the Shrew).

A further Ovidian note occurs when Bianca and Lucentio (as Cambio) discuss their reading (4.2.6-10). Lucentio states that he is reading Ovid's *Ars Amatoria* and that this work about the pursuit of a woman expresses his feelings for Bianca: 'I read that I profess, *The Art to Love*'. Bianca, knowing that Book 3 of this work tells women how to love, retorts 'And may you prove, sir, master of your art'. But not all of Ovid suits the case of Bianca: her relationship with Lucentio has nothing to do with the rape of Io by Zeus, and the attempted rape of Daphne by Apollo that are depicted in Book 1 of the *Metamorphoses* and referred to in the Induction of *The Taming of the Shrew* (2.50-6).

More positive still is the late romance *The Winter's Tale* (about 1609-10). Hermione, wife of Leontes (King of Sicily), is wrongly accused by him of adultery, and is thought to have died. The painter Giulio Romano (1499-1546) sculpts a wonderful lifelike statue of Hermione; as Paulina, wife of Antigonus (Lord of Sicily) says to Leontes, 'As she lived fearless, / So her dead likeness I do well believe / Excels whatever yet you looked upon, / Or hand of man hath done' (5.3.14-7)[15]. At the climax of the play, Paulina brings the statue to life, so that Leontes and Hermione embrace and are united again; as Helena Faucit (who played Hermione) wrote, 'It was the finest burst of passionate speechless emotion I ever saw'[15a].

While his statue scene is Shakespeare's invention (not found in the play's main source Robert Greene's *Pandosto*), it draws on the story of Pygmalion in the *Metamorphoses* of Ovid, who turned it into a major account of wish fulfilment, and who here reverses his usual pattern of turning the animate into the inanimate. Himself in love with statues, Ovid depicts Pygmalion (legendary King of Cyprus) as a timid sculptor who shrinks from real, physical women, and who proceeds to carve an ivory statue of a very beautiful woman. When Pygmalion prayed to Venus, goddess of love, to give him a wife like this statue, she gave the statue life, and he married this woman.

In *The Winter's Tale*, as in Ovid, we see that art outdoes nature, but now does so in the theatre, so that, as Bate says, Shakespeare 'has achieved the seemingly impossible feat of staging an Ovidian metamorphosis'[16]. But one that is more human than Ovid allowed: it is a human being, Paulina, not a goddess, that brings the statue of Hermione to life, and the restored woman is now sixteen years older. With the result that Leontes has to say 'Hermione was not so much wrinkled, nothing / So age'd as this seems' (5.3.28-9).

Ovid provides further material for *The Winter's Tale*, when the flowers of the pastoral landscape are linked, in ways both positive and negative, to Perdita, the last daughter of Leontes and Hermione. Florizel, the son of Bohemia's king, loves Perdita, who has been brought up as a shepherdess, and lauds her as the Roman goddess of flowers, Flora, the dedication day of whose temple was April 28: 'Flora / Peering in April's front' (4.4.2-3). But Flora was raped by the west wind Zephyrus, before he gave her dominion over flowers. Then violets are 'sweeter than the lids of Juno's eyes' (eyelids being a sign of beauty in Shakespeare's day) 'Or Cytherea's breath', i.e. Venus, goddess of love, born near the Greek island of Cythera. But the goddess of corn, Proserpina, lets flowers fall from her lap, when she is abducted from Sicily by the god of the Underworld, Pluto (Dis); this suggests the problematic nature of love, and its proximity to the realm of the dead. Equally well, Phoebus or Apollo as the god of the sun, will not warm primroses, because, as the earliest flowers of spring, they no longer bloom in the summer heat. So all is not well in this pastoral landscape, and yet Proserpina returns each year to the earth and brings with her summer, after the winter of the

Underworld; a cycle enacted in *The Winter's Tale* as success and harmony return to Sicily.

But the central figure of this play's pastoral world is Autolycus, regarded by Homer as 'surpassing all men in stealing and swearing' (*Odyssey* 19.395-6), and by Ovid as making 'white black and black white' (*Metamorphoses* 11.314-5). In Shakespeare, Autolycus is a thief, a con-man, an actor, a pedlar, who seems to be modelled on poor Jacobean vagabonds. His father was Mercury god of thievery and of lying, but also of eloquence: 'I am littered under Mercury' (4.3.24-5). The appearance of this rogue stresses that, even in his late romances, Shakespeare does not shrink from the darker side of things.

A further use of Ovid for positive purposes comes in *The Tempest*, when Prospero employs a speech of Medea (*Metamorphoses* 7.197-209) to renounce his rough magic. When Medea of Colchis (modern Georgia) helped the Greek hero Jason bring the Golden Fleece back to Greece, she fell in love with him and married him. To please Jason, Medea rejuvenates his father Aeson by using magic spells. In order to do this, she seeks the help of elements of nature, as well as the goddess of the Underworld Hecate. Shakespeare read Medea's speech in both Latin and in Golding's translation[17]. Here is Golding and Shakespeare (5.1.33-51):

> Ye airs and winds; ye elves of hills, of brooks, of woods alone,
> Of standing lakes, and of the night, approach ye every one,
> Through help of whom (the crooked banks much wond'ring at the thing)
> I have compelled streams to run clean backward to their spring.
> By charms I make the calm seas rough and make the rough seas plain,
> And cover all the sky with clouds and chase them thence again.
> By charms I raise and lay the winds and burst the viper's jaw,
> And from the bowels of the earth both stones and trees do draw.
> Whole woods and forests I remove; I make the mountains shake,
> And even the earth itself to groan and fearfully to quake.
> I call up dead men from their graves...

> Ye elves of hills, brooks, standing lakes, and groves
> And ye that on the sands with printless foot
> Do chase the ebbing Neptune, and do fly him
> When he comes back, you demi-puppets that
> By moonshine do the green sour ringlets make,

> Whereof the ewe not bites; and you whose pastime
> Is to make midnight mushrooms, that rejoice
> To hear the solemn curfew; by whose aid –
> Weak master though ye be – I have bedimmed
> The noontide sun, called forth the mutinous winds,
> And 'twixt the green sea and the azured vault
> Set roaring war: to the dread rattling thunder
> Have I given fire, and rifled Jove's stout oak
> With his own bolt; the strong-based promontory
> Have I made shake, and by the spurs plucked up
> The pine and cedar. Graves at my command
> Have waked their sleepers, oped, and let 'em forth
> By my so potent art. But this rough magic
> I here abjure...

In his eloquent paraphrase of Medea's speech, Shakespeare radically alters the force of the original. Medea refers to her powers to control and invent nature in the context of *proceeding* to use them; Prospero refers to these powers in the context of *ceasing* to use them. Prospero is changed into something rich and strange; so too is Ovid.

5

Although *A Midsummer Night's Dream* (about 1595) has no single main source, the spirit of Ovid presides over it, as change succeeds change. But while in Ovid metamorphosis brings the action to a close, in Shakespeare it causes action. One obvious type of transformation in *Dream* is that of dreams that may be mysterious and disconnected – the weaver Bottom cannot interpret his dream – or that may be meaningful: Hermia's dreams of a serpent that stands for Lysander's sexual advances, for his penis[18]. In any case, the artist rises above dreams: Shakespeare succeeds in making the disparate elements of the play – aristocrats, artisans, fairies – form a unified whole.

In *Dream*, the classic metamorphosis of comedy is stressed. Men and women who have been lovers, and who have had difficulties in love – 'The course of true love never did run smooth' (1.1.134) – get married in the end: Theseus, Duke of Athens, and Hippolyta, Queen of the Amazons (who frame the play); Hermia and Lysander; Helena and Demetrius. As the King of the Fairies, Oberon, sings, 'So shall all the couples three / Ever true in loving be' (5.1.385-6).

But there are much more unusual transformations in *Dream*. Juice from the pansy makes the recipient fall in love with the first person they see, and so brings about unlikely couples. Since this flower is described by Oberon as 'purple with love's wound' (2.1.166), it is linked to a metamorphosis in Ovid, where the berry of a mulberry tree sheltering the remains of the lovers Pyramus and Thisbe (whose story is told by the artisans) turns purple. Puck (or Robin Goodfellow) squeezes juice into Lysander's eyes, and makes him love Helena instead of his beloved Hermia. Oberon drops the potion into the eyes of Titania, Queen of the Fairies (whose name comes from Ovid), and makes her fall in love with Bottom.

This brings us to a further striking transformation – that of human to animal so prevalent in Ovid – since Bottom is changed by being given the head of an ass; as Quince says, 'Thou art translated' (3.1.98). The closest analogue for this is Ovid's King Midas, who challenged the god Apollo, and was punished by having his ears changed into those of an ass (*Metamorphoses* 11, 174-9). A further analogue is found in Apuleius' picaresque novel *The Golden Ass* (translated into English by William Adlington in 1566), in which the narrator Lucius is transformed into an ass[19]. But the resemblance is only partial: in physical shape, Lucius is fully an ass, Bottom only in part; in mental state, Lucius knows he is an ass, Bottom does not. But both men altered retain human feelings, and Titania's grotesque passion for the ass-like Bottom mirrors that of the woman of Corinth who has sex with Lucius. In due course, the sight of the enchanted lovers is restored by the supernatural agency of Puck.

A more specific debt to Ovid's *Metamorphoses* in *Dream* is found in the myth of the lovers Pyramus and Thisbe that he brought from the East (4.55-166)[20]. While these lovers are transformed into a tree in Ovid, their story in Shakespeare is changed from tragedy in verse into burlesque in prose; a parody of how to translate a Roman text into the present era, as well as a meditation on the illusion of theatre. The myth of the lovers Pyramus and Thisbe is disastrous in nature. Forbidden contact by their parents, they arrange to meet outside the town of Babylon by night. The result is appalling. Pyramus thinks Thisbe killed by a lion, and rams a sword into his body; Thisbe, who is alive, finds him dying, and kills herself. As Pyramus says, 'One night will destroy two lovers' (108).

A group of artisans ('mechanicals') led by Peter Quince the carpenter rehearse and stage a version of Pyramus and Thisbe for the wedding of Theseus and Hippolyta, but are sadly lacking in theatrical skills. As Hippolyta says, 'This is the silliest stuff that ever I heard' (5.1.204). This version involves a crude, outmoded mingling of comedy and tragedy, as its very title shows: 'The most lamentable comedy and most cruel death of Pyramus and Thisbe'. Some detail. Bottom is a most inferior player of Pyramus, who produces malapropisms such as 'odious' for 'odorous'. As does Flute (playing Thisbe), who calls the tomb of Ninus, where the lovers met, 'Ninny's tomb'. Both Bottom and Flute get Greek mythology from Ovid wrong: Cephalus killed his faithful wife Procris by mistake, but the players call him 'Shafulus' and her 'Procrus'. And there is to be a bizarre Prologue in ballad metre stating Pyramus is not killed.

Odder still is the decision that the wall through which Pyramus and Thisbe speak is to be played by an actor. For all that, this myth is akin, in part, to the relationship between Lysander and Hermia, which is forbidden by her father Egeus, so that she steals out from her house to meet Lysander. But Helena in pursuit of Demetrius, who rejects her, notes that another myth of Ovid, in which the god Apollo pursued Daphne, is reversed (2.1.230-1): 'The story shall be changed: / Apollo flies, and Daphne holds the chase'. Gender roles are transformed, Ovid is transformed.

Samuel Pepys held in 1662 that *Dream* was 'the most insipid ridiculous play that ever I saw in my life'[21]. Within the play, Hippolyta thinks otherwise (5.1.23-7):

> But all the story of the night told over,
> And all their minds transfigured so together,
> More witnesseth than fancy's images.
> And grows to something of great constancy;
> But however, strange and admirable.

Then Peter Brook, who directed a famous production of *Dream* in 1970, said 'I think that *A Midsummer Night's Dream* is a perfect Mozartian construction, where you can't cut a note out of the score without harming it'[22]. Crucial to *Dream's* achievement is the theme of transformation, much of which comes from Ovid. The result is, as Rudd nicely says, 'the most magical tribute that Ovid was ever paid'[23].

6

The literary genre known as the 'epyllion' or miniature epic came into being in the Hellenistic period in poems like the *Hecale* of Callimachus (about 310-240 B.C.). The genre flourished in Rome at the time of the Late Republic in the first century B.C.: there is Poem 64 of Catullus (often called 'The Marriage of Peleus and Thetis') that runs to 408 lines, and there are lost poems of that era by Calvus (*Io*) and by Cinna (*Zmyrna*). Central features of these epyllia are the treatment of themes from Greek myth, stress on the psychology of love, the use of digressions. These features are often found in the fifty or so miniature epics narrated in Ovid's *Metamorphoses*, or even in much shorter stories like that of Venus and Adonis.

In Elizabethan England, a vogue for miniature epics developed[24]. Thomas Lodge wrote *Scillaes Metamorphosis* (1589); John Clapham wrote *Narcissus* in Latin (1591), which Shakespeare may have sought to outdo; Marlowe wrote *Hero and Leander* (about 1592); Thomas Heywood wrote *Oenone and Paris* (1594); and Shakespeare wrote *Venus and Adonis* (1593) and *The Rape of Lucrece* (1594), when the theatres were closed for nearly two years because of plague. It is noteworthy that in 1595 Richard Carew linked both *Hero and Leander* and *Venus and Adonis* to Catullus 64[25]. Both Shakespeare's epyllia focus heavily on love and sex in the best Ovidian manner, and proved extremely popular.

Indeed Ovid is linked to *Venus and Adonis*[26] in a variety of ways. The printer of Shakespeare's poem, another Stratford man Richard Field, had worked for Thomas Vautrollier, who published Ovid's *Metamorphoses* in Latin in 1589, and his *Heroides* in Latin in 1594. Then Shakespeare used as epigraph for *Venus and Adonis* lines 35-6 of Ovid, *Amores* 1.15: *Vilia miretur vulgus : mihi flavus Apollo / Pocula Castalia plena ministret aqua*, 'Let the common herd wonder at worthless things: for me let golden Apollo / serve cups full with Castalian water'. These lines come from towards the end of the last poem of Book 1 of Ovid's *Amores* (*Love Affairs*), concluding poems of Augustan poetry books providing a specific personal stamp or 'signature'. Here Ovid follows the poetic doctrine of Callimachus, when he contrasts literary works that are inspired by the god of poetry Apollo, and by the Muses, whose seat is the spring Castalia on Mount Parnassus near Delphi. By using this epigraph, Shakespeare indicates that he is no 'upstart crow' (as held in 1592 by Robert Greene), that he is writing superior verse for a discerning audience, that he can therefore dedicate his poem to Henry Wriothesley, Earl of Southampton, in the first printed book to bear his name.

Just after the lines Shakespeare uses as epigraph for *Venus and Adonis*, Ovid hopes that Apollo will provide him with a wreath of myrtle, which, since it is the plant sacred to Venus, stands for love poetry, and wants his audience to consist of what Shakespeare might call star-crossed lovers. But such lovers would find more than they bargained for in *Venus and Adonis* and *The Rape of Lucrece*.

Written in six-line stanzas of iambic pentameter with a rhyme scheme of a b a b c c, *Venus and Adonis* vastly expands the account of the goddess of love and a boy in Ovid's *Metamorphoses*: 83 lines turn into 1194. This change in length is matched by a change in tone and in characterization. Whereas in Ovid Adonis does not reject the sexual advances of Venus, in Shakespeare he does so, and with passion (compare the rejection in Ovid of the nymph Salmacis' advances by the boy Hermaphroditus). At the same time, *Venus and Adonis* privileges language in such a way that the point of view is always variable; both Venus and Adonis have their say; there is constant use of the red/white colour contrast already found in Catullus 64 (308).

The initial characterization of Adonis as 'a tender boy' (32), who loves the hunt and despises love, links him to Hippolytus, who as a chaste devotee of Artemis / Diana, the goddess of the hunt, rejected the sexual advances of his step-mother Phaedra. Adonis may be the best work of nature, but he refuses to play the role of a lover, stating 'I know not love' (409), and exhibiting 'pure shame and awed resistance' (69). But later he distinguishes between love which is 'all truth' and lust which is 'full of forgèd lies' (804).

Venus appears in a number of guises[27]. She wants to be a huntress like her sister Diana; she is the conqueror of the god of war Mars, who is her 'slave'; she is the goddess of sensual love (*Pandemos*), but not of heavenly love (*Ourania*); and, finally, she is Venus the creator, as in the opening of Lucretius' didactic poem *The Nature of the Universe*. But she also exhibits the characteristics of a human being.

Venus' very elaborate speeches recall the theme of the abandoned heroine in Greek and Latin literature – including Ovid's *Heroides* – such as Medea, Ariadne, Dido. She is frustrated about Adonis: 'She's love, she loves, and yet she is not loved' (610). So in *Venus and Adonis*, as often in Ovid, there is no mutual desire, no love that proceeds smoothly: 'Sorrow on love hereafter shall attend' (1136). The mutual misunderstanding between boy and goddess is therefore tragic for them. But for the reader it is, rather, comic and, at times, farcical; as when the couple find themselves on top of each other, but do not have sex. That mixture is found at the end of the poem: it is tragic that Adonis is killed by a boar, but there is an element of comic resolution when he is removed from the human condition and turned into an anemone. And yet that flower is desired, but not desiring.

Presumably the 'graver labour' promised in the Dedication to *Venus and Adonis*, Shakespeare's second miniature epic *The Rape of Lucrece*[28] was praised by Gabriel Harvey, a contemporary scholar: [28a]

> The younger sort takes much delight in Shakespeare's *Venus and Adonis*: but his *Lucrece* & his tragedy of Hamlet, Prince of Denmark, have it in them, to please the wiser sort.

Written in stanzas of rhyme royal (a b a b b cc) in iambic pentameter, *The Rape of Lucrece* derives mainly from Ovid's *Fasti* 2.685-852 (with some help from Livy 1.57-60). As previously, Shakespeare greatly expands Ovid: 167 lines becomes 1855.

The theme now is not Greek myth, but Roman legend: the rape of Lucretia, wife of Collatinus, by Sextus Tarquinius, son of the king of Rome, Tarquinius Superbus, an event which led to the expulsion of the kings from Rome[29]. That political aspect is stressed by Livy, but Ovid dwells on the pitiful fate of Lucretia, as does Shakespeare. But *The Rape of Lucrece* also strongly emphasizes the evil of Sextus Tarquinius' bestial lust, which contrasts with Lucrece's steadfast chastity, an evil of which he is himself well aware.

After being entertained as a guest by Lucrece, Sextus Tarquinius directs his male gaze upon her with 'lewd unhallowed eye' (392), and get ready to rape her: 'Pawning his honour to obtain his lust' (156)[30]. He offers her an impossible choice: she can be raped, killed and shamed by being placed in a dead slave's bed, or she can agree to be raped by Tarquin. It is noteworthy that the actual rape of Lucrece is not described, but she waxes very eloquent in lamenting her lot. One aspect of this is the way Lucrece cites the rape of Philomela by Tereus that Shakespeare deals with in *Titus Andronicus* and in *Cymbeline*.

More striking is the ecphrasis (description of a work of visual art in literature) about the Trojan War that has a dual source in Book 13 of Ovid's *Metamorphosis*, and in Book 1-2 of Virgil's *Aeneid*. Shakespeare plays down the aspect of Lucrece's rape that relates to Roman politics, but he does introduce a different political theme in his account of Troy. In the Greco-Roman world, the private space of an individual person was affected by the sack of a city like Troy, with women being raped and enslaved. So the use of the Trojan War here adumbrates the rape of Lucrece by Tarquin, who is assimilated to Sinon, the Greek who had the Wooden Horse brought into Troy and so facilitated rape. As Burrow says, 'The way *Lucrece* deliberately brings warriors and images of warfare into a domestic sphere marks it as one of the seminal moments in Shakespeare's career';[31] as in *Macbeth* and *Othello*.

Dishonoured as she is, Lucrece thinks suicide preferable to a life of shame (though she wants her husband Collatinus to take revenge upon Tarquin), and stabs herself. Here she follows the Stoic example of Brutus and Cassius in *Julius Caesar*, and of Cleopatra and Antony in *Antony and Cleopatra*, ignoring Augustine's view that, since she had not committed a crime, she was killing herself in an unjust way[32].

7

Participating in the huge vogue for sonnets, including sequences of them, in Elizabethan and Jacobean England, Shakespeare wrote a very large number: in 1609 a volume of 154 *Sonnets*, together with the poem *A Lover's Complaint* was published[33]. In 1598, Francis Mere posited a connection between Shakespeare's *Sonnets* and Ovid: 'the sweet witty soul of *Ovid* lives in mellifluous and honey-tongued Shakespeare, witness ... his sugred *Sonnets* among his private friends'. But the vast majority of Shakespeare's *Sonnets* were written about a young *man* (1-126), and so against the Ovidian and Petrarchan tradition of dealing with a beloved woman; those *Sonnets* that do deal with a woman (127-52) portray her as unattractive and promiscuous, in a vein of mocking misogyny – unlike the portrait of Ovid's Corinna or Petrarch's Laura[34].

Furthermore, Shakespeare's *Sonnets* need not of necessity be read in sexual terms, as the confessions of an older lover for a beloved boy. What he does in the *Sonnets* to the young men is to express the hope of a lowly player and playwright for social and financial patronage from an aristocratic young man, and to couch this in sexual terms. Sex is therefore a metaphor for the patron / client relationship and not the confessions, however ironic, of a lover like Ovid in the *Amores*[35]. As Kerrigan says, 'The Sonnets are not autobiographical in a psychological mode'[36].

The use of Ovid in the *Sonnets* comes when Shakespeare draws on the *Metamorphoses*, and especially the speech of Pythagoras about change in Book 15; turns epic into lyric; and transforms the theme of metamorphosis *in* Ovid into the metamorphosis *of* the

Roman poet. In these sonnets, images of change and permanence are powerfully stated, and relate in varying ways to the young men. So in *Sonnet 55*, the assertion about the immortality of the young man – 'Nor Mars his sword nor war's quick fire shall burn / The living record of your memory' – comes from Golding's translation of the translation of the *Metamorphoses*: 'Now have I brought a work to end which neither Jove's fierce wrath, / Nor sword, nor fire, nor fretting age with all the force it hath / Are able to abolish quite'[37]. But whereas what is immortal in Ovid is his own verse, what is immortal in Shakespeare is the young man.

Contrasting with this is *Sonnet 64*, where nature constantly changes. Golding is again the source:

> Even so have places oftentimes exchanged their estate,
> For I have seen it sea which was substantial ground alate (formerly).
> Again where sea was, I have seen the same become dry land ...

Shakespeare closely follows Ovid about the changes in nature:[38]

> When I have seen the hungry ocean gain
> Advantage on the kingdom of the shore,
> And the firm soil win of the watiry main,
> Increasing store with loss and loss with store...

But he now applies these changes to his beloved youth whom they may take away from him: 'Time will come and take my love away'.

Most striking of all is *Sonnet 60* that again derives from Golding's Ovid, but radically alters its meaning. Ovid tells of universal change, but suggests that this is in itself a form of permanence. Shakespeare also bows to the passing of time and the inevitability of death, but what he asserts will escape from the ravages of fleeting years is his own verse, his celebration of the young man:[39]

> Things ebb and flow, and every shape is made to pass away.
> The time itself continually is fleeting like a brook.
> For neither brook nor lightsome time can tarry still. But look
> As every wave divers other forth, and that that comes behind
> Both thrusteth and is thrust itself: Even so the time by kind
> Do fly and follow both at once, and evermore renew.
> For that that was before is left, and straight there doth ensue
> Another that was never erst.

> Like as the waves make towards the pebbled shore,
> So do our minutes hasten to their end;

> Each changing place with that which goes before,
> In sequent toil all forwards do contend.
> Nativity, once in the main of light,
> Crawls to maturity, wherewith being crowned,
> Crookèd eclipses 'gainst his glory fight,
> And Time that gave doth now his gift confound.
> Time doth transfix the flourish set on youth,
> And delves the parallels in beauty's brow,
> Feeds on the rarities of nature's truth,
> And nothing stands but for his scythe to mow.
> And yet to times in hope my verse shall stand
> Praising thy worth, despite his cruel hand.

And so it has: Ovid's confident assertion that 'I will be read on the lips of the people' (*ore legar populi*)[40] has proved equally right in the case of William Shakespeare, Gentleman.

6 | The Matter of Virgil

1

Eliot asserted of Virgil that he 'acquires the centrality of the unique classic; he is at the centre of European civilization, in a position which no other poet can share or usurp'[1]. Despite the fact that, in the early modern period, Virgil was variously a moralist, a magician, an exemplary user of language[2], this is hyperbole that was not endorsed by Shakespeare (who now holds that position himself). The significant appropriation of Seneca, Plautus and Ovid by Shakespeare can be defined in a clear way: Seneca's tragedies provided the revenge play, and the theme of evil in the ruler; Plautus provided the play of sexual resolution, and stock characters like those who help make up Falstaff; Ovid provided the vast bulk of Shakespeare's Greek mythology, and a sweet witty style. But it is far less easy to define what Virgil offered to Shakespeare, for it seems that this Latin author appears in him as part of the general cultural capital of the age, as a diffuse element without a single clear-cut function[3]. As Pitcher says, 'The Virgilian presence in *the Tempest* is often of this spectral kind, a half-seen image of death, or damnation, or despair at the back of an episode, a line, or even a single word'[4]. So the statement at the base of the monument to Shakespeare at Stratford that he was in his art a Vergilius Maro (*arte Maronem*) is false.

Genre may be the key to Shakespeare's tangential encounter with Virgil: the *Aeneid* is a *continuous* epic poem about the foundation of Rome, but Shakespeare, dramatist and poet, does epic only in miniature form, the epyllion. Hence he looted Ovid's *Metamorphoses* on a grand scale, because this is an *episodic*, not a continuous epic, dealing with some 250 stories – about 50 of them miniature epics – that readily lend themselves to detached treatment. So it is significant that the three parts of the *Aeneid* most prominent in Shakespeare – the stories of Dido and Aeneas, of the fall of Troy, and of Aeneas' descent to the Underworld – can all be regarded as miniature epics, and so equally available to him.

2

One of the great love stories in Latin literature, the tale of Dido[5] and Aeneas told by Virgil in the *Aeneid* portrays, in stark terms, the clash in Roman life and letters between public and private values: the Trojan hero Aeneas must found the Roman state and so abandon Dido; Dido privileges sexual love and marriage and, when abandoned, commits suicide. The matter, however, is not so simple. Dido has previously been married in Tyre to her uncle Sychaeus, who was murdered by her brother Pygmalion, after which she came to Carthage; in *Aeneid* 6 she is reunited with Sychaeus and spurns Aeneas ('one of the most civilized passages in literature', said Eliot)[6]. Aeneas was also married previously to Creusa, who dies after Troy is captured by the Greeks. Furthermore, there is an alternative version of Dido's time in Carthage: after obtaining land by deception to found the city, she became an exemplary ruler, who was famous for chastity and devotion to the dead Sychaeus, and who committed suicide rather than marry a local prince named Iarbas. Aeneas, brought into the story by Virgil, does not appear in this version, and Dido is often viewed in later eras as a paradigm of the chaste ruler. Since an alternative name for her is Elissa, she was easily assimilated to Elizabeth, the Virgin Queen.

The intricacies involved in the Dido story are most clearly set out in Act 2, Scene 1 of *The Tempest*[7]. The context is that Claribel, daughter of the king of Naples Alonso, has married the king of Tunis, and that the councillor Gonzalo wishes to identify modern Tunis with ancient Carthage, the city of Dido. The lord Adrian sees Claribel as a 'paragon' that has not existed (says Gonzalo) 'since widow Dido's time'. This is the chaste Dido without Aeneas, but Antonio, the usurping Duke of Milan, insists on the liaison between the two: 'widow? A pox o' that! How come that widow in? Widow Dido!' There is a further complication when Sebastian (brother of Alonso) draws attention to that fact that the widower Aeneas is also far from innocent: 'What if he had said "widower Aeneas" too?' It is as though Shakespeare's natural tendency towards strategic opacity has been mapped on to Virgil's epic poem, as though he accepts the contemporary view that both Dido and Aeneas are partly to blame for what happened.

The appearance of Dido and Aeneas in *Antony and Cleopatra* is also problematic[8]. When Antony thinks that Cleopatra is dead, and plans to join her, he places the two of them in the Elysian fields with other pairs of lovers such as Dido and Aeneas, while calling to her servant Eros, whose name in Greek means 'sexual love' (4.15.50-54):

> Eros! – I come, my queen. – Eros! – Stay for me.
> Where souls do couch on flowers we'll hand in hand,
> And with our sprightly port make the ghost's gaze.
> Dido and her Aeneas shall want troops,
> And all the haunt be ours. Come, Eros, Eros!

The problem is, of course, that in the Underworld Dido is reunited with her husband Sychaeus, and spurns Aeneas (as well she might). What then does this passage suggest? Is Shakespeare confused or is Antony? Did the author remember that the historical Antony died before the *Aeneid* was written? Does Antony think that his own doomed, but continuing love for Cleopatra can somehow rewrite Virgil, so that a central pair of lovers in Latin literature mirror contemporary lovers in Roman history? After all, Cleopatra sees herself as Dido, when she echoes Ovid, *Heroides* 7.139: Dido says to Aeneas, 'But the god orders you to go. I would he had forbidden you to come'; Cleopatra says to Antony about his wife Fulvia 'What, says the married woman you may go? / Would she had never given you leave to come' (1.3.20-21).

A reference to Dido may hardly involve Virgil at all. In one of the statements that Lorenzo makes in the love duet in *The Merchant of Venice*, he invokes Dido (5.1.9-12):

> In such a night
> Stood Dido with a willow in her hand
> Upon the wild sea banks and waft her love
> To come again to Carthage.

The tone in this portrait of the abandoned Dido derives in general from Ovid, *Heroides* 7; the specific detail of the sea shore comes from Ariadne deserted on the island of Naxos by Theseus, as told in Chaucer's *Legend of Good Women*; the willow is a general symbol of betrayed love, as in Desdemona's 'willow song' in *Othello* (4.3.38-55).

3

In the Renaissance, the fall of Troy was viewed as one of the major events in history, a main source for which was the account given by Aeneas in Book 2 of the *Aeneid*[9]. In *Julius Caesar* (1.2.112-15)[10], Shakespeare invents a situation in which the conspirator Cassius rescues the helpless Caesar from the Tiber, and compares this with Aeneas rescuing his father Anchises from the burning city of Troy, this being for Seneca and for Renaissance writers an archetypal act of piety (*pietas*):

> I, as Aeneas, our great ancestor,
> Did from the flames of Troy upon his shoulder
> The old Anchises bear, so from the waves of Tiber
> Did I the tired Caesar.

But this is ironic: Cassius goes on to *kill* Caesar in Rome; Anchises, old and weak, dies of natural causes in Sicily.

When at the end of *Titus Andronicus* (5.3.79-86), Marcus Andronicus (brother of Titus) asks his son Lucius to explain the situation in Rome, he draws a parallel with the way Aeneas 'our ancestor' told Dido the story of the fall of Troy, termed 'our Rome'. Marcus refers, in particular, to the deceitful Simon who persuaded the Trojan to admit into their city the Wooden Horse ('fatal engine') that contained Greek soldiers. This story mirrors five separate acts in *Titus Andronicus*, four of which are perpetrated or engineered by Demetrius and Chiron, sons of Tamora, Queen of the Goths and later Empress of Rome: the rape of Lavinia, daughter of Titus Andronicus; the killing of Bassianus, brother of the Emperor Saturninus; the banishment of Lucius; the deaths of Lucius' brothers Quintus and Martius; the remaining act is the killing of Titus by Saturninus. As always, *Titus Andronicus* runs to excess, here the excess of violent treachery.

When Hamlet in Act 2, scene 2 of his name play wishes to think of a speech for the Player, it is again 'Aeneas' tale to Dido' that is in question, and specifically the murder of Priam, King of Troy. The speeches made by Hamlet and by the First Player seem to derive from Marlowe's version of the story that was written about 1586, and that now in 1600 could seem old-fashioned, even archaic, when compared to the modern, flexible style of *Hamlet*[11]. But the old style still has the energy of the type that the Player puts into his speeches about figures from Greek mythology such as Hecuba, wife of Priam, and that seems excessive to Hamlet: 'What's Hecuba to him, or he to

Hecuba, / That he should weep for her?' (2.2.547-48). But Hamlet comes to find his own answer to that rhetorical question that appears to expect the answer 'nothing': a different play, *The Murder of Gonzago*, will trap Claudius into tacitly admitting he has murdered Hamlet's father: 'The play's the thing / Wherein I'll catch the conscience of the king (2.2.593-94).

4

It is accepted by all that *The Tempest* has no single main source; among the lesser sources that have been suggested for this short late play is the *Aeneid* of Virgil[12]. But the precise way that the *Aeneid* is used is problematical. While *The Tempest* clearly appropriates a number of passages from the *Aeneid*, the overall significance of this process is opaque: the Latin epic is no skeleton key to this play. Indeed Virgilian passages that are purloined may be part of the general cultural capital of the Jacobean era. For example, it is often stated that the storm at the beginning of *The Tempest* derives from the storm at the beginning of the *Aeneid*, but storms occur regularly in various Greco-Roman literary genres, in other epics such as the *Odyssey* and Lucan, in New Comedy, in the Greek novel, in Roman tragedy; and, of course, in life, as with the storm in the Bermudas in 1609 that is an accepted source for *The Tempest*.

Then a parallel, even if established, may only partly fit the situation. When Ferdinand first exclaims on seeing Miranda 'Most sure the goddess / On whom those airs attend' (1.2.421-22), he echoes *O dea certe*, 'O certainly a goddess', used by Aeneas of his mother the goddess Venus (*Aeneid* 1.338), but Miranda can never be a goddess. More telling is the way that Ariel 'like a harpy', a violent, predatory bird, ensures that the banquet to be enjoyed by Alonso, Sebastian and Antonio 'vanishes', in the way harpies prevent Aeneas and his men eating in *Aeneid* 3. But even here the parallel, though close, is localized, and does not involve an extended comparison between Aeneas and the three men of *The Tempest*.

Much more obviously Roman is the masque[13] in *The Tempest* that relates to those written by Ben Jonson and performed at the court of James I; these highly elaborate works involved music, song, dance, gorgeous costumes and complicated stage machinery, and were designed to bolster the status quo. Shakespeare's masque is performed for the betrothal of Ferdinand and Miranda by a number of goddesses from Roman mythology, who are summoned up by Prospero: Iris, goddess of rainbow, and messenger of the gods;

Juno, wife of Jupiter and so queen of the gods; and Ceres, goddess of the earth and of crops. Juno and Ceres function, in part, like a *deus ex machina* in Greek tragedy, who ascends or descends on the stage by means of a machine, and who brings about some resolution in the play; here the stage direction at the end of the masque (4.1.143) reads '*Juno and Ceres ascend in their chariot*'.

We expect therefore that this masque will involve resolution and so it proves: Iris brings together Ceres and Juno in a way that 'reconstitutes the fragmented world of the play'[14]. Played by the spirit Ariel (whose 'saffron wings' comes from the *Aeneid* (4.1.78; 4.700), Ceres presides over the civilizing invention of agriculture, which provides human beings with crops, notably wheat, in summer (winter is abolished in this brave new world). Juno brings power, being for Ferdinand 'a most majestic vision' (4.1.118), and, because she presides over the bonds of marriage (*Aeneid* 4.60-61), she endorses the impending marriage of Miranda and Ferdinand. At the same time, Miranda's virginity, which is vital to Prospero's political future, routs the attempt by the divine powers of sexuality, Venus and her son Cupid, to rape Ceres' daughter Proserpina. All might seem well, but the masque ends on a discordant note: Prospero refers to Caliban's plot against his life in a kind of anti-masque, a form that stresses the negative.

5

Since much recent work on *The Tempest* has focused on the themes of imperialism and colonialism[15], it is desirable to examine briefly these themes in relation to the *Aeneid*, in order to see if we can posit a more clear-cut interaction between the two texts. In *The Tempest*, Prospero is a displaced imperialist who colonizes the island, and enslaves the spirit Ariel and the ambiguous, but human figure Caliban, who exhibits the typical dependence of the colonized. This scenario might suggest the way the England of Shakespeare controlled the land, resources and inhabitants of Ireland and of Virginia. It has also suggested to recent interpreters of *The Tempest* the impact of colonial powers on Africa, Asia and Latin America; as Octave Mannoni says, 'Colonial countries are still the nearest approach possible to the archetype of the desert island'[16].

Can any of this be connected to the *Aeneid*? The island of *The Tempest* has a setting in the south Mediterranean, as do the wanderings of Aeneas. In the manner of Prospero, Aeneas is clearly engaged in the imperial conquest of Italy (this mirrors the later acquisition of Empire by Rome). Both men have a ruthless streak: Prospero is a slave owner, Aeneas sacrifices eight men in cold blood to avenge the death of his ally Pallas. Indeed the *Aeneid* ends with the merciless killing by Aeneas of the Italian hero Turnus (who wears the sword-belt of Pallas). But here the comparison breaks down, for in the Epilogue to *The Tempest* Prospero prays for forgiveness, as Aeneas does not. *Pace* Eliot, Virgil is no proto-Christian, but Prospero appears to be one. Once more attempts to find a skeleton key to *The Tempest* in the *Aeneid* succeed only to a limited extent.

7 | The Uses of Latin

1

Far more than Greek, Latin is the central language of Europe[1]. An Indo-European language that comes from west central Italy, Latin has existed for over 2,500 years, and came to be the main language first of Italy and then of the Roman Empire. In various parts of the Empire, colloquial or Vulgar Latin developed into the Romance languages, including French, Italian, Spanish and Portuguese. Meanwhile, more elevated Latin came to fulfil vital roles in the Church, in education, in scholarship and in culture. Latin was used in the liturgy of the Roman Catholic Church until the 1960s, and remains the official language of that Church to this day.

Latin was gradually ceasing in the sixteenth century to be the major language in which books were published, so that Shakespeare's plays were presented to readers in English[2]. But Latin continued to play a number of important roles: as the language of international affairs; as a means of communication among the educated; as the essential subject in grammar schools, like the one Shakespeare attended in Stratford (see Chapter One, section 2); as the medium of instruction in the universities, Oxford and Cambridge. Knowledge of Latin was therefore a mark of privilege, available only to an educated elite who had access to various forms of power and distinction within society.

Accordingly, Latin comes under attack from the leader of the rebellion by the lower classes in *2 Henry VI*, Jack Cade (this recalls the Peasant's Revolt of 1381)[3]. Capable of a savagery that both contrasts with and mirrors the intrigues of the aristocratic York, Cade condemns Lord Saye, Lord Chamberlain and Treasurer of England, to death for corrupting 'the youth of the realm in erecting a grammar school', one in which Latin is taught. Cade also censures Saye for having men about him who 'usually talk of a noun and verb', which are 'The two most important classes'[4] of words in the English language (4.7.31-32, 36). When Saye uses Latin to describe the men of Kent – 'tis *bona terra, mala gens*, 'a good land, bad people' – Cade says 'Away with him, away with him! he speaks Latin' (4.7.53-54). Latin therefore symbolizes the established order, the privilege of class. But it also, of course, is part of Renaissance humanism, of civilization. Cade's Utopia is anti-intellectual.

2

Shakespeare makes use of Latin in his plays in a number of ways: direct quotation from Latin authors; Latin proverbs; Latin-based names; Latin-based words.

In *2 Henry VI*, quotations from Cicero, Virgil and Lucan serve to link ancient and modern. When the Duke of York reads an ambiguous statement about himself and King Henry (1.4.61), he cites an analogue from Cicero (*De Divinatione* 2.56), the response of the Delphic Oracle to Pyrrhus, king of Epirus, when asked if he would conquer Rome: *Aio Aeacidam Romanos vincere posse*, 'I say the son of Aeacus the Romans can conquer'. Then Duke Humphrey, Lord Protector of England, replies (2.1.4) to an attack on him by his uncle, Cardinal Beaufort, by citing a famous line from the beginning of Virgil's *Aeneid* (1.11) about the goddess Juno's enmity towards Troy and the Trojan hero Aeneas: *Tantaene animis caelestibus irae?* 'Can there be such anger in heavenly minds?' When Suffolk faces death (4.1.117), he says *Paene gelidus timor occupat artus*, 'Cold fear almost seizes my limbs'; this conflates the statement about the Italian hero Turnus brought about by the Fury Allecto in Virgil's *Aeneid* – *subitus tremor occupat artus*, 'sudden fear seizes his limbs' and the statement about those facing Julius Caesar in Lucan: *gelidus pavor occupat artus*, 'cold fear seizes his limbs' (*Aeneid* 7.446; Lucan 1.246).

Much given to the use of proverbs, Shakespeare employs a number of Latin examples. When Gower at the beginning of *Pericles* wants to praise the story he is introducing, he invokes the Latin proverb '*Et bonum quo antiquius eo melius*', 'The older a good thing is, the better it is'. Then the statement by the pedant Holofernes in *Love's Labour's Lost* (4.2.79) '*vir sapit qui pauca loquiter*', 'the man is wise who says little' seems to mock his own prolixity. When Lucio in *Measure for Measure* uses, of the Duke Vincentio, the proverb

'*Cucullus non facit monachum*', 'A hood does not make a monk', he disputes the fact that the hood worn by the disguised Duke makes him a proper friar (but there is irony in the fact that he believes the Duke to be a friar). Related to these Latin proverbs is the maxim from Lyly's *Grammar, diluculo surgere saluberrimum est*, 'It is very healthy to rise at daybreak', that Sir Toby Belch quotes at his friend Sir Andrew Aguecheek in *Twelfth Night* (2.3.1-2).

A further use of Latin by Shakespeare occurs when the name of a person derives from that language. This process is specially marked in the case of young women in the late romances. There a Latin-based name may replicate the practice in Greek tragedy of regarding a name as something unpleasant, as the name Helen in Aeschylus' *Agamemnon* is seen to begin with the syllable 'hel' meaning 'to destroy': in *The Winter's Tale*, the daughter of King Leontes and Hermione of Sicily is missing for many years in Bohemia; and so properly called Perdita, Latin for 'last woman'. On the other hand, a Latin-based name can be positive: in *Cymbeline*, the daughter of Cymbeline, King of Britain, is named Innogen, which suggests English 'innocence' from Latin *innocens*, and, when she is disguised as a page, she has the name Fidele, which suggests Latin *fidelis* meaning 'faithful', and so draws attention to her fidelity to her husband Posthumus Leonatus. Equally well, the name of Prospero's daughter in *The Tempest*, Miranda, which is Latin for 'woman to be admired', stresses her fine qualities.

On occasion, Shakespeare's text alerts us to this process: in *Pericles*, Marina, whose name means 'woman of the sea', states that I am 'Call'd Marina / For I was born at sea' (5.1.155). Again, in *The Winter's Tale*, Hermione says to Antigonus in a dream 'for the babe / Is counted lost for ever, Perdita / I prithee call't' (3.3.31-3). Similarly, when in *Love's Labour's Lost*, the pedant Holofernes regards Ovid as the exemplar of what is best in poetry, he draws attention to the fact that his cognomen or family name 'Naso' means 'nose' in Latin: 'Ovidius Naso was the man; and why indeed 'Naso' but for smelling out the odoriferous flowers of fancy, the jerks of invention?' (4.2.123-25).

3

More than most languages, English borrows foreign words with promiscuous zest. By far the largest number of these loanwords come from Latin, either directly or mediated through French: a realistic estimate of the percentage of Latin-based words in English is 50%[5]. In Old English, there is a trickle of these words; in Middle English, a much greater amount. But a very large number of loanwords from Latin flowed into English between 1580 and 1660 in order to meet the needs of a more complex society; some 10,000 new words were introduced, nearly all from Latin, and about half of these lasted in the language. This period included all of Shakespeare's mature life, and he followed the practice of other writers is using new words based on Latin, and in coining not a few himself[6]. All of which shows that English has a special lexical relationship to Latin: it taps the vocabulary of Latin – especially verbs, nouns and adjectives – to create new words by treating these resources as if they belonged to English (as some Indian languages do with Sanskrit). As Defoe said, 'an Englishman has his mouth full of borrow'd phrases... he is always borrowing other men's language'[7].

It is a mistake to believe that Latin-based words that are often long and abstract are of necessity less strong, less effective than short, concrete Anglo-Saxon words. They are often powerful and imperious, suggesting the fact that, although Rome relinquished control of England early in the fifth century, the language of the Romans has now, in the Renaissance, re-entered England as a vital part of the English language. Shakespeare uses these Latin-based words to excellent effect (section 4), but they can of course, be employed in a highly pedantic way – as we see in the case of the schoolmaster Holofernes in *Love's Labour's Lost*, who speaks both words in Latin and exotic Latin-based words.

Love's Labour's Lost is a comedy that is centrally concerned with language, and contains more new words than any play of Shakespeare's except *Hamlet*: it passes, as Pater says, 'from the grotesque and vulgar pedantry of Holofernes, through the extravagant but polished caricature of Armado, to become the peculiar characteristic of a real though still quaint poetry in Biron himself, who is still chargeable even at his best with just a little affectation'[8]. Holofernes is given to quoting sentences, phrases and words in Latin in a pedantic way, and may be viewed as a fraud, because the Latin he knows is that which any Elizabethan schoolboy would have learned in a grammar school. So when Holofernes says to the curate Nathaniel about Armado '*Novi hominem tamquam te*', 'I know the man as I know you', this comes from that basic text-book Lyly's *Grammar* (5.1.9). So when he recognizes Latin lines by the pastoral poet Mantuan (1447-1516)[9], this is because it was standard reading in the schools. But when Holofernes is going to quote Horace, he can't recall the passage.

No wonder, then, that Holofernes produces bad Latin. When Sir Nathaniel correctly says *bene intelligo*, 'I understand well', he wrongly thinks that the correct form of the adverb should be *bone*: '*Bene? Bene* for *bone?*' The Irony of Holofernes' bad Latin is stressed , when he cites Priscian, who wrote a voluminous treatise on Latin grammar in the sixth century A.D., and alludes to the proverb 'to break Priscian's head' that means to use bad Latin, in order to justify the wrong form *bone*: 'Priscian's a little scratched'.

In Elizabethan England, there was a campaign waged against what were called 'inkhorn' words, those perceived to be derived from Latin or Greek in a pedantic way. Holofernes' account of Adriano, which shows his liking for synonyms, indicates the merit of this campaign (5.1.9-14): 'His humour is loftie, his discourse peremptory, his tongue filed, his eye ambitious, his gait majestical, and his general behaviour vain, ridiculous, and thrasonical. He is too picked, too spruce, too affected, too odd, as it were, too peregrinate, as I may call it'.

Some of those Latin-based words such as 'ambitious', 'ridiculous', and 'affected' seem, though recently coined, to be acceptable. But the adjective 'thrasonical' meaning 'boastful' that comes from the braggart solider in Terence's comedy *Eunuchus*, and the adjective 'peregrinate' meaning 'foreign' that comes from Latin *peregrinus* are recent and exotic coinages that are abnormal in English, and have not lasted. As Holofernes' disclaimer 'as I may call it' seems to recognize.

Explicit contempt for English compared with Latin is provided by Armado. Liking to replicate phrases, he quotes Caesar's boast after the battle of Zela in 45 B.C. *veni, vidi, vici*, translates it 'in the vulgar' as 'he came, see, and overcame', but then exclaims 'O base and obscure vulgar' (4.1.67). Armado later prefers an affected and comic Latin-based word to what he regards as an English vulgarism: 'the posteriors of this day, which the rude multitude call the afternoon' (5.1.79-80).

Finally, *Love's Labour's Lost* boasts the largest word in Shakespeare, the dative/ ablative plural of a mediaeval Latin noun meaning 'the state of being greatly honoured': '*honorificabilitudinitatibus*' (5.1.40). As Hamlet says, 'Words, words, words' (2.2.189).

4

Shakespeare often employs Latin-based words to powerful effect, both those already in the language and those he himself coined; he appears to have introduced more than 600 Latinate neologisms[10] into English, many of which have lasted, and now seem just normal English. Examples include 'addiction', 'compulsive', 'fixture', 'laughable', 'pious', 'radiance', 'sympathize', 'uneducated'. Horace says that new and invented words will have authority if they are used sparingly, but such restraint is foreign to the limitless linguistic exuberance of Shakespeare (*Ars Poetica* 52-53).

Sometimes Shakespeare uses several Latin-based words in the same sentence to great effect. The famous lines in *Hamlet* (1.1.165-6) about the dawn draw on the very rare Latin adjective *russus* meaning 'red' and the mediaeval Latin noun *mantum* meaning 'cloak': 'But look, the morn in russet mantle clad / Walks o'er the dew on yon high eastern hill'. When Coriolanus wishes to express his jaundiced view of the common people, he employs two Latin-based words: 'dissentious' from *dissentire* meaning 'to disagree', and 'opinion', which here means the opposite truth, from *opinio*: 'What's the matter, you dissentious rogues / That, rubbing the poor itch of your opinion, / Make yourselves scabs?'(1.1.161-3).

But very often it is a single word derived from Latin that becomes effective in Shakespeare. When Touchstone dilates on sex among animals in *As You Like It* (3.2.76), he refers to 'the copulatio of cattle', the first noun coming from Latin *copulation* and dating from 1483; later, he speaks of 'country copulatives' meaning couples who are united in marriage and in copulation. Modern poets know the force of the noun and verb here: in Eliot's 'Sweeney Agonistes', Sweeney sees life as 'Birth, and copulation and death'; in Yeats's striking version of heaven, 'Nymphs and satyrs / Copulate in the foam'[11].

Words derived from Latin may have a religious aspect. When the Porter in *Macbeth* uses the word 'equivocator' that comes from late Latin *aequivocare* meaning 'to use words of more than one sense, he is talking about how drink may or may not lead to sex, but suggests the practice of mental reservation employed by persecuted Jesuits in England. In Shakespeare's remarkable poem 'The Phoenix and the Turtle', terms from scholastic philosophy that relate to the Trinity and come from Latin – *essentia, distinguere, divisio* – are used to describe a union between the phoenix and the turtle that involves distinction without difference (25-8):

> So they loved as love in twain
> Had the essence but in one,
> Two distincts, division none.

Shakespeare's use of Latin-based words can be found in stylistic tricks such as the employment of compound adjectives and of hendiadys, 'a figure of speech in which a single idea is expressed by two words connected by a conjunction' (OED). Like Hopkins,[12] Shakespeare makes frequent use of compound adjectives that achieve compression by avoiding a relative clause: 'green-eyed jealousy is jealousy which possesses green eyes' (*The Merchant of Venice* 3.2.110). In *Measure for Measure* (5.1.43), Isabella calls Angelo in relation to herself 'a virgin-violator', using the Latin words *virgo* and *violare*. The figure of hendiadys permeates *Hamlet* and can occur in words based on Latin[13]. When the Ghost appears, Hamlet uses two very similar words that come from church Latin *angelus* and classical Latin *minister* (1.4.39): 'Angels and ministers of grace defend us!' Equally well, in Hamlet's famous statement about life, his two references to the sky as 'this most excellent canopy' and this 'brave o'erhanging firmament' both derive from Latin words: mediaeval Latin *canopeum* ('a net over a bed') and classical Latin *firmamentum* meaning a 'support' or 'prop' (2.2.265-6).

An even more potent use of Latin-based words occurs when they are juxtaposed with Old English ones. There is a classic example near the end of *Hamlet*, when Hamlet speaks to Horatio (who has thought of suicide) (5.2.330-3):

> If thou didst ever hold me in thy heart
> Absent thee from felicity awhile
> And in this harsh world draw thy breath in pain
> To tell my story.

Hamlet mixes Old English words such as 'heart', 'world', 'draw', 'breath' with Latin-based words such as 'Absent' from late Latin *absentare*, 'felicity' from Latin *felicitas*, 'pain' from Latin *poena*, story from Latin *historia*, so as to produce a very satisfying register of language.

Another striking example of this linguistic process occurs in *Macbeth*, when Macbeth contemplates the murder of Duncan (1.7.1-7):

> If it were done when 'tis done, then 'twere well
> It were done quickly. If th'assassination
> Could trammel up the consequence and catch

> With his surcease, success, that but this blow
> Might be the be-all and the end-all-here,
> But here, upon this bank and shoal of time,
> We'd jump the life to come.

The words 'assassination' and 'trammel' come respectively from late Latin *assassinus* and *tramaculum*, the words 'consequence' and 'success' from Latin *consequential* and *successus*. But these Latinisms are balanced by words or phrases from Old or Middle English: the thrice repeated 'done'; the nouns 'bank' and 'life'; the invented phrase 'the be-all and the end-all'. Here again new Latin and old English become powerful. As Richard Carew said, 'the long words that we borrow, being intermingled with the short of our own store, make up a perfect harmony'[14].

Such a conjunction of Latin-based and Old English words can be just an example of hendiadys that aims to stress an emotion: 'Dear amity and everlasting love' (from Latin *amicitia*, 'friendship'; *King John* 5.4.20). But the use of synonyms[15] becomes more subtle, when the Latin-based word of one speaker is humorously glossed by an Old English word of another speaker: Armado: 'Boy, what sign is it when a man of great spirit / grows melancholy?' Moth: 'A great sign, sir, that he will look sad?' (from Late Latin *melancholia*; *Love's Labour's Lost* 1.2.1-3). But Armado expected the answer that he is in love.

Shakespeare not only uses Latin-based words, but also shows himself conscious of the process. A character may indicate how an English word comes from Latin, as Justice Shallow in *2HenryIV* (3.2.67-70): '"Better accommodated" – it is good; yea, indeed, it is. Good phrases are surely, and ever were, very commendable. "Accommodated – it comes of '*accomodo*'. Very good, a good phrase"'. Equally, the Latin-based word may be glossed by an English equivalent. In *Love's Labour's Lost* 3.1.133-36), Costard refers to Armado's giving him money for bringing a letter to the country maid Jaquenetta: 'Now I will look to his remuneration. "Remuneration"! O, that's the Latin word for three farthings. Three farthings – remuneration'. Sir Toby Belch in *Twelfth Night* (2.3.67-68) is very clear when speaking of his kinswoman Olivia: 'Am I not consanguineous? Am I not of her blood?'

Shakespeare also knows that an English word that is derived from Latin can alter its meaning: as the verb 'occupy' from *occupare*. Railing in *2 Henry IV* (2.3.67-68) against the title 'captain' being applied to Pistol, the whore Doll Tearsheet says

'God's light, these villains will make the word as odious as the word 'occupy'; which was an excellent good word before it was ill sorted'. In the past, the verb 'occupy' meant 'take possession of', but now it means 'to have sexual intercourse with'. It is a nice irony that a worker in the sex industry should object to a once innocent noun now having a sexual connotation; nice too that Doll's verb – 'sorted' comes from the Latin *sortiri* meaning to 'fix' or 'assign'. Ben Jonson knew what was happening here: 'Many, out of their owne obscene Apprehensions refuse proper and fit words; as *occupie, nature,* and the like'[16].

Not all Latin-based words invented by Shakespeare were successful. Two examples from *Measure for Measure* (4.1.28; 5.1.101) will make the point. Isabella says of Angelo that he 'hath a garden circummur'd with brick', where the verb comes from the rare Latin adjective *circummuranus*, 'walling round', and has remained exotic. Whether a Latinate word will survive or not is arbitrary, as this example shows: in Isabella's reference to Angelo's sexual desire as 'his concupiscible intemperate lust', the first adjective from late Latin *concupiscibilis* meaning 'violently desirous' is clearly an 'inkhorn' term that had no future in English, while the second adjective from Latin *intemperans* is now part of normal English. Again, Latinate diction in Shakespeare can be bombastic, but may be deliberately so, as with speeches in *Troilus and Cressida* by politicians, a breed given to empty rhetoric. Consider, for example, part of Hector's speech to Diomedes that ends the duel between Hector and Ajax (4.5.122-30): 'The obligation of our blood forbids / A gory emulation 'twixt us twain ... my mother's blood / Runs on the dexter cheek, and this sinister / Bounds in my father's, by Jove multiptent'. Here the Latin-based words 'obligation', 'emulation', 'dexter' (right), and 'sinister' (left), together with the first occurrence of 'multipotent' (powerful in many ways), combine to produce an effect of insincerity[17].

5

Tennyson's claim that Virgil is 'lord of language' can surely be applied to Shakespeare: the sheer volume of his phrases that have entered everyday English attests to that. Consider the following, from *Hamlet* alone:[18]

Frailty, thy name is woman.

Something is rotten in the state of Denmark.

Brevity is the soul of wit ...

Use every man after his desert, and who would 'scape whipping?

Though this be madness, yet there's method in't.

Assume a virtue if you have it not.

There are more things in heaven and earth, Horatio, than are dreamt of in your philosophy.

The play, I remember, pleased not the million; 'twas caviare to the general.

Tennyson goes on to praise the phrases and words of Virgil: 'All the chosen coin of fancy / flashing out from many a golden / phrase'; 'All the charm of all the Muses / often flowering in a lonely word'[19]. Latin-based words in Shakespeare can exemplify these statements: from *Hamlet*, the phrase 'But look, the dawn in russet mantle clad...'; from *Love's Labour's Lost*, the adjective 'odoriferous' applied to the poet Ovid. As Steven Pinker says, 'A word, in a word, is complicated'[20].

8 | Greek Themes in Shakespeare

1

Shakespeare had direct access to the Roman world, but his access to Greek material was nearly always indirect; like Polonius, he 'finds directions out' by roundabout means (*Hamlet* 2.1.63).

Shakespeare gets his Greek mythology, so prevalent in his work, from the Latin poet Ovid, although Ovid's *Metamorphoses* is 'Greek in matter, in manner, and even in versification'[1]. He reads the Greek historian Plutarch in English translation in order to deal with Roman history. He does not know Greek tragedy, and his knowledge of the Greek philosophy of Plato and Aristotle comes either from Latin translation or from Castiglione's *The Book of the Courtier*. This stress on translation continues in the case of the Greek epigram used at the end of the *Sonnets* read by Shakespeare in Latin or a modern language, and in the case of Greek novels such as that of Heliodorus. Two plays with Greek themes – *Pericles* and *Timon of Athens* – are written in collaboration; a third such play, *Troilus and Cressida*, is partly mediaeval in character.

But, in a way, none of this matters: Shakespeare possesses the inestimable gift of transforming his sources, direct or indirect, into something special, something rich and strange.

One obvious reason that Greek themes do not loom nearly so large in Shakespeare is his lack of direct knowledge about the Greek world. But it is also true that Renaissance England was ambivalent about the Greeks. At one level, Greek culture was prized (though available only to the few); at another level, there is contempt for the Greeks[2]. As is made clear by the phrase 'merry Greeks' that connotes debauchees and cheats (especially at cards), and is applied by Cressida to Helen: 'a merry Greek indeed' (*Troilus and Cressida*

1.2.110). This ambivalence about the Greeks was nothing new, being very prevalent in Rome. Having conquered Greece, Rome was, in cultural terms, conquered in its turn; as Horace famously said, 'Captured Greece took her rough victor captive and brought the arts to rustic Latium'. But the Romans tended to despise contemporary Greeks: in Plautus, the verb *pergraeceri* meaning 'to play the Greek' connoted 'to be debauched'; later, Juvenal writes that 'I cannot stand a city of Greeks', people who are Jacks of All Trades. But then Robert Greene brought the same charge against Shakespeare, calling him 'an absolute Johannes Fac-totum'[3].

2

The impact of Greek tragedy on dramatists in the modern period of European history has been immense, but it had little currency in Shakespeare's England[4]. Few could read the difficult Greek of Aeschylus, Sophocles and Euripides, and Shakespeare certainly could not. Since translations of these authors into English were very few in number, the only way Shakespeare could have serious access to Greek tragedy was Latin translations (by Erasmus, Buchanan and others). His Latin was well up to this, but the case that he read these Latin translations is far from convincing[5]. A certain feel for Greek tragedy might have come to Shakespeare from reading Seneca's plays that deal with Greek mythology; as C. and M. Martindale say, 'the most plausible view remains that Seneca was the closest Shakespeare ever got to Greek tragedy'[6]. More obviously, Seneca, together with Plutarch, provided Shakespeare with a precedent for making characters – Hamlet, Othello, Antony – more human and more introspective than is the case in Greek tragedy.

For all that, some affinities between Shakespeare and the Greek tragedians can be posited; Silk adverts to three shared elements: a necessity to act (*must*), an element of excess (*too*), and the identity of the character (*name*)[7]. So Creon in Sophocles' *Antigone* (1106) says 'we must fight necessity'; Othello says of Desdemona 'Yet she must die' (5.2.5). So Cadmus in Euripides' *Bacchae* (1249-50) states of Dionysus that 'the god ruined us justly, but too much'; Macbeth speaks of his 'vaulting ambition which o'erleaps itself'. So Sophocles' Oedipus (397) refers to himself, with multiple irony, as 'The knowing nothing Oedipus'; Cleopatra asserts that 'I will be Cleopatra' (3.13.187).

3

The relationship of Shakespeare to Greek philosophy is less tenuous then to Greek tragedy[8]. While he did not read classical Greek, he could have read translations of Plato into Latin and the mediation of Platonic doctrine in Castiglione's very influential *The Book of the Courtier*, translated into English by Thomas Hoby in 1561. So to analyse Platonism in Shakespeare, we must turn to its modification in the Italian Renaissance, which fused Plato's thought with that of later Neoplatonic system. Marsilio Ficino maintained Plato's preference for a chaste homosexual relationship between men. But in Pietro Bembo, love becomes heterosexual, being directed by men towards women, sexual in youth, spiritual in old age. That doctrine of Bembo is found in turn in Castiglione, where he is one of the main characters; he further posits the notion there that the man is the educator of the woman.

Ficino maintained that response to Beauty in the person comes through the senses of eye and ear, not through smell or touch; certainly, the Greeks and Romans saw sexual attraction in visual terms: as Propertius said, *oculi sunt in amore duces*, 'eyes are leaders in love' (2.15.12). But Shakespeare adapts Platonism for his own ends, critiquing it in an intermittent but potent way in his epyllion *Venus and Adonis*. When Venus dilates on the attractiveness of Adonis' voice, she enlists not just the senses ratified by Ficino, ear and eye, but also the senses of touch and smell, together with the notion of sensory deprivation (433-48). Indeed Venus rebukes Plato's *Symposium* by elevating taste to the highest level in her response to Beauty. Once Adonis has died, Venus identifies him with absolute Beauty in a way Platonism could not endorse:

> The flowers are sweet, their colors fresh and trim,
> But true sweet beauty lived and dies with him[9].

Equally well, in the Threnos (Lament) of the difficult poem *The Phoenix and the Turtle*, Shakespeare overturns Plato's conviction that the material world is unreal by asserting that the death of the two earthly birds ensures that 'Truth and beauty buried be', and that now only a semblance of truth remains: 'Truth may seem, but cannot be' (62, 64)[10].

Platonic links exist between *Venus and Adonis* and the *Sonnets*. The beloved young man of *Sonnet 53* is not merely a paradigm for male beauty like that of Helen of Troy, and for nature in the seasons of spring and autumn; this man is further a person who, by transcending the 'shadows', the particulars of the material world, functions like a Platonic Form, a universal. Then the theme of procreation advocated by Venus Pandemos, the earthly goddess of Italian Platonism, is found in Shakespeare when she tells Adonis to procreate, and when he so advises the young men in *Sonnets* 1-17.

This use of Platonism, however much adjusted to the body, was not to everyone's taste. In Jonson's play *The New Inne* (1629), Lord Beaufort wants treatment of love to be plain and simple as in Ovid's amatory works:

> I relish not these *philosophical* feasts;
> Give me a banquet o'sense, like that of Ovid.

4

Shakespeare's last two *Sonnets* – 153 and 154 – derive from a six-line epigram in the *Greek Anthology* (9.627) by a Byzantine poet of the fifth century Marianus Scholasticus that he came across in a translation or version into Latin or a modern language[11]. Already in the Hellenistic period, the Greek epigram made love a central theme, treating it in an urbane, knowing, cynical way; this tradition was continued in Greek verse in the Roman and Byzantine periods.

These last two sonnets should be read in the light of a poetic pattern found in literary works in Elizabethan England, in which a sequence of sonnets is followed by a lyric or epigrammatic coda, and then by a long poem[12]. So Daniel's *Delia* of 1592 contains 50 sonnets about the poet's harsh mistress, a short poem in trochaic tetrameters, and a long poem called *The Complaint of Rosamund* that deals with the woman's seduction and suicide. Similarly, Shakespeare's publication of 1609 contains 152 sonnets, a further two sonnets that relate to Greek epigram, and a long poem called *The Lover's Complaint* that deals with the seduction of a young woman.

Here are the epigram by Marianus Scholasticus and Shakespeare's two sonnets relating to it:

> Beneath those plane trees overcome by gentle sleep,
> Love slept, having handed over his torch to the Nymphs. But the Nymphs said to each other 'Why are we waiting?' Would that with this, they said, we could quench the fire in the hearts of humans. When the torch set fire even to the water, the Love Nymphs from then on fill the bath with hot water.

Cupid laid by his brand and fell asleep.
A maid of Dian's this advantage found,
And his love-kindling fire did quickly steep
In a cold valley-fountain of that ground;
Which borrowed from this holy fire of Love
A dateless lively heat, still to endure,
And grow a seething bath, which yet men prove
Against strange melodies a sovereign cure.
But at my mistress' eye Love's brand new-fired,
The boy for trial needs would touch my breast;
I, sick withal, the help of bath desired,
And thither hied, a sad distempered guest,
But found no cure; the bath for my help lies
Where Cupid got new fire – my mistress' eyes.

The little Love-god lying once asleep
Laid by his side his heart-inflaming brand,
Whilst many nymphs that vowed chaste life to keep
Came tripping by; but in her maiden hand
The fairest votary took up that fire,
Where many legions of true hearts had warmed,
And so the general of that desire
Was, sleeping, by a virgin hand disarmed.
This brand she quenche'd in a cool well by,
Which from Love's fire took heat perpetual,
Growing a bath and heathful remedy
For men diseased; but I, my mistress' thrall,
Came there for cure, and this by that I prove:
Love's fire heats water, water cools not love.

Sonnets 153 and 154 reflect the fact that the Dark Lady of *Sonnets* 127 to 152 has been associated with Cupid, the god of Love (as in 137 and 145), and render visible the concepts of work in that sequence. In the two sonnets that function as coda, Cupid turns into 'Love' and becomes 'the general of hot desire', as his torch ('brand') symbolizes passion in a phallic way. He is contrasted with the chaste nymphs who attend Diana, goddess of chastity, and who seek to quench Cupid's fire in cold water. But this fire is revived in a hot bath that shows how male sexual desire is perennial, suggesting the sweating tubs used to cure venereal disease in Jacobean England. Shakespeare himself is at this level, since he cannot be cured by the bath, and so is set on fire once more by his mistress' eyes. The last line of *Sonnet* 154 sums up the situation in a suitable epigrammatic vein: 'Love's fire heats water, water cools not love'.

5

Although it was omitted from the First Folio of 1623, *Pericles*[13] was very popular with both gentry and groundlings in the early decades of the seventeenth century; a fact that caused Ben Jonson to regret that people were keen to see 'some mouldy tale, like *Pericles*' instead of his own work (*The New Inn*)[14]. Just as up to half the plays of Renaissance England were written in collaboration, so Shakespeare wrote *Pericles* with George Wilkins, who belonged to the seedy side of London life. He was a pimp who ran a tavern that doubled as a brothel, and often faced criminal charges of violence against women who were (or were said to be) prostitutes. Wilkins was successful with his play *The Miseries of Enforced Marriage*, put on by Shakespeare's company, the King's Men, about 1606[14a].Wilkins was responsible for the opening nine scenes of *Pericles*, Shakespeare for Scenes 10 and 22, which are generally held to be superior. As Muir says, 'It is a thrilling moment in the theatre when at the beginning of Act III (Scene 10), the voice of Shakespeare is heard indubitable and potent, with a tempest at sea to match the storm in *King Lear*'[15].

The sources for Shakespeare's late romances such as *Pericles* (1607/8) are complex, a confluence of late plays by Euripides such as *Ion*, Greek New Comedy by Menander (342 – about 292 B. C.) and others that was mediated to the Renaissance by the Roman comic dramatists Plautus and Terence, and the Greek and Roman novel. For the Greeks and Romans did write novels, and a number of these were available in English translation in Shakespeare's day: *Aethiopica* of Heliodorus by Thomas Underdowne (1569); *Daphnis and Chloe* of Longus by Angel Day (1587); *Clitiphon and Leucippe* of Achilles Tatius by William Burton (1597). Indeed Shakespeare refers to Heliodorus' character the Egyptian thief in *Twelfth Night*, and *Pericles* employs a major array of the narrative devices of fiction[16].

The main source for *Pericles* is the Latin story of *Apollonius of Tyre* (about sixth century AD), which seems to be based on an original Greek novel. The immediate versions of *Apollonius* used by Shakespeare are Book 8 of John Gower's *Confessio Amantis* (1393), and Lawrence Twine's novel *The Pattern of Painful Adventures* (1576), which was used for the brothel scenes.

The plot of these genres of Comedy and the Novel often involves the following features:

The action takes place throughout the Mediterranean.
A shipwreck separates family members or lovers.
A person thought to be dead comes alive.

A recognition scene (*anagnorisis*) brings about the restoration of a lost order, whether in the family or between lovers.

Religion is vital, and may involve the appearance of a god.

These features are all present in *Pericles*. The action takes place throughout the Mediterranean and Middle East: Mytilene on the island of Lesbos; Ephesus in Asia Minor; Antioch in Syria; Tyre in Phoenicia; Pentapolis in North Africa. A shipwreck separates Pericles from his daughter Marina, and from his wife Thaisa, who dies, but later comes to life; in two separate recognition scenes, Pericles is reunited with Marina, and with Thaisa. The goddess Diana appears to Pericles, and tells him to go to Ephesus, where he finds Thaisa.

The intensive travel of Pericles between actual places suggests a metaphorical journey of self-discovery: he undergoes and transcends suffering, since he loses and regains his wife and daughter. Indeed the father-daughter relationship may have a personal meaning for Shakespeare, because, about the time of *Pericles*, his favourite daughter Susanna gave birth to a daughter (in February 1608). In any case, Frye notes that 'Of all fictions, the marvellous journey is the one formula that is never exhausted'[17].

In his poem 'Autolycus', Louis MacNeice nicely indicates what is happening in *Pericles* and the other late romances[17a]:

> In his last phase when hardy bothering
> To be a dramatist, the Master turned away
> From his taut plots and complex characters
> To tapestried romances, conjuring
> With rainbow names and handfuls of sea-spray
> And from them turned out happy Ever-afters.

The presiding deity in *Pericles* is malevolent Fortune, who came to prominence in the Hellenistic period as *Tukhé*, and is a key player in Apuleius' novel *The Golden Ass* as *Fortuna*. Pericles is a good man who provides food for the starving in Tarsus, a soldier-musician of authority, a man who can (like Oedipus) solve riddles. But Pericles is the plaything of Fortune, who is shipwrecked not once but twice, losing his wife Thaisa. Neptune, god of the sea, is here hostile to Pericles, but his reunion with Marina, in the quiet harbour of Mytilene, occurs during the annual festival of Neptune on July 23. Pericles' suffering brings him to say he is 'A man, whom both the waters and the wind / In that vast tennis-court hath made the ball for them to play upon'(Scenes 5.99-101)[18]. Marina also suffers greatly. She is about to be murdered on the order of Dionyza, wife of the Governor of Tarsus Cleon, who is jealous of her when she is abducted by pirates and taken to a brothel in Mytilene. But there her remarkable virtue enables her to preserve her virginity, to freeze the god Priapus (Scene19, 12), the god of fertility and rampant phallic sexuality, who was a symbol for the Elizabethans of lechery. Indeed in her gait Marina is compared to Juno, queen of the gods.

The climax of *Pericles* comes in scenes 20-22 with the recognition by Pericles of his daughter Marina and his wife Thaisa. Such happy events are common in Comedy, as when Daemones in Plautus' play *Rudens* has his daughter Palaestra restored to him. But the reuniting of Pericles with Marina (which is non-sexual, unlike the incest between Lysimachus and his daughter) moves well beyond that kind of stock happy ending, and suggests a greater form of restoration, one that is religious in character. Hence Eliot writes of 'the speech of creatures who are more than human, or rather, seen in a light more than that of day'[19]. A point highlighted by the fact that Pericles says that he hears 'the music of the spheres', music thought to be made by the heavenly bodies in their circular revolution round the earth, and normally not heard by humans.

This religious aspect of *Pericles* is confirmed by the multiple involvement in the play of Diana, the virgin goddess of the wild, of childbirth and of chastity. Pericles invokes Diana, when his wife Thaisa is giving birth to Marina, while Marina, epitome of chastity, prays to the virgin goddess. In a spectacular epiphany, Diana appears to Pericles in a dream, and directs him to the city of Ephesus, where Thaisa is her priestess in the famous temple. So the play *Pericles* concludes with Pericles reunited with his wife and daughter in one of the most celebrated religious sites of the Greco-Roman world: 'Great is Diana of the Ephesians'[20]. Furthermore, the comic and romance requirement of a marriage is met as Marina is to wed Lysimachus, governor of Mytilene. But in *Pericles* we do not have just what Henry James called 'The time honoured bread-sauce of the happy ending';[20a] rather, Shakespeare is pointing out that the tragic ending of *Hamlet* and other plays is only half the human story, that an ending with the restoration of old order and getting ready for new order, an ending of wonderful harmony, is the other half. We are not required to adjudicate between the two.

There is also a Greek religious aspect in *The Winter's Tale*. When Leontes, king of Sicily, is suspicious that his wife Hermione has committed adultery with his friend Polixenes, king of Bohemia, he seeks advice from the oracle of the god Apollo on the island of Delos in the centre of the Aegean, where the god was born: 'The god suddenly will here / The truth of this appear' (2.3.199-220). Apollo's reply is crystal clear, unlike many ambiguous oracles in the Greek world (3.2.130-4): '"Hermione is chaste, Polixenes blameless, Camillo a true subject, Leontes a jealous tyrant, his innocent babe truly begotten, and the King shall live without an heir if that which is lost be not found'". At the end of the play, all this is proved to be true, including the finding of Leontes' lost daughter, Perdita.

6

Probably written in early 1606, *Timon of Athens* belongs to a period when Shakespeare was writing some of his greatest tragedies: *Othello, King Lear, Macbeth, Antony and Cleopatra*. But *Timon of Athens* was written in collaboration with the experienced dramatist Thomas Middleton[21]. Shakespeare concentrated on the opening of the play, the scenes dealing with Timon, and the conclusion; Middleton dealt with the scenes involving secondary characters like Alcibiades and the Steward, and with the banquet scene (2). What Middleton brought in particular to *Timon of Athens* was his expertise in satirical portrayal of city life.

Timon of Athens was a semi-legendary figure, who was renowned in the Greco-Roman world and in the Renaissance as a person who hated humanity, as a misanthrope. Shakespeare knew of Timon from a digression in Plutarch's *Life of Antony* (also available to him in William Painter's *The Palace of Pleasure*, 1566). He also knew of Timon from the dialogue 'Timon, or the Misanthrope' by the Greek satirical writer Lucian (born about 120 A.D.), which he could have read either in Erasmus' translation into Latin (1528), or in French. But while Shakespeare's Roman plays take much of their plot from Plutarch, the two dramatists of *Timon of Athens* forged an original plot from the two Greek writers. Central here is the elaborate portrayal of Timon (probably played by Richard Burbage), and the viewing of his life as a tragedy. Indeed George Steiner, who drastically limits the number of plays to which he allows the title 'tragedy', affirms that *'Timon of Athens* is pure tragedy' on the grounds that it abolishes textuality, abolishes words, when Timon bids 'language, cease' (14.755)[22]. We hear no cry of 'I will be Timon'.

In this play of minimal plot and a sense of futility that anticipates Beckett, Timon is a man who is defined entirely by his wealth, so that the appropriate text is 'the root of all evils is the love of money' from Paul[23]. It is because of 'gold' (the word occurs 36 times) that

Timon is popular, because he is bereft of gold that he becomes unpopular. Initially, Timon's ostentatious display of wealth is paraded, his 'bounty' heavily stressed: he pays five talents – 56 pounds of silver – to secure the freedom of one man. But when everything is measured by money, it becomes both a symbol of man's greed, and the economic basis of society (as in Jacobean England and the contemporary West). Granted at last this insight, Timon rails against gold (14. 382-90):

> O, thou sweet king-killer, and dear divorce
> 'Twixt natural son and sire; thou bright defiler
> Of Hymen's purest bed; thou valiant Mars;
> Thou ever young, fresh-loved, and delicate wooer,
> Whose blush doth thaw the consecrated snow
> That lies on Dian's lap; thou visible god
> That sold'erest close impossibilities
> And mak'st them kiss, that speak'st with every tongue
> To every purpose...

Marx used tirades like this to support his view that money is a means of converting human values to market values, and so as a way in which people are alienated from their personal lives. In the Athens of Timon, this scenario is all too obvious, and extends to love, as the prostitutes indicate[24].

When Timon possesses wealth, he lives in Athens; when he loses his wealth and is abandoned by his so called friends, he goes to live in the woods; his language changes too from delicate to vulgar. Now Aristotle held that 'a human being is a political animal', that is a person who lives in a *polis*, a city-state like Athens, and that a person who does not do so is either a beast or a god (*Politics* 1.2). Timon is not a god, but he does indeed classify himself to Alcibiades as 'a beast' (14.49). Aristotle's doctrine that virtue is the *mean* between two extremes also applies to Timon, because he is at first an excessive lover, then an excessive hater of mankind, failing to find a middle way[25]; as Apermantus says to him, 'The middle of humanity thou never knowest, but the extremity of both ends' (14.302-3). For Timon becomes one with Yeats's character Ribh, who says 'I study hatred with great diligence / For that's a passion in my own control'[26]. Timon is very clear about this: 'I am Misanthropos, and hate mankind'; 'Henceforth hated be / Of Timon man and all humanity' (14.53; 11.103-4). A sarcastic Plutarchan example of which occurs when Timon, before he cuts down his fig tree, offers it to any Athenian citizen who wants to hang himself (14.740-7).

Timon's hatred for people and for life derives from his resentment at the way in which he has been treated by those he thought friends. His *specific* form of resentment is pointed up by the *general* contempt for society felt by the Cynic philosopher Apemantus (possibly played by the comic actor Robert Armin). Cynics believed in rejecting the conventions and multiple follies of mankind, in espousing simple living, in castigating luxury. Their founder was Diogenes (about 400-325 B. C.), and Hazlitt noted that 'The soul of Diogenes appears to have been seated on the lips of Apemantus'[27]. That Cynics were considered scarcely human was shown by the fact that their name was supposed to come from the Greek work *kuón*, meaning 'dog'. Accordingly, the Painter says to Apemantus 'You're a dog' (1.204). Which leads Timon to qualify Horace's maxim (*Epistles* 1.2.62) *Ira furor brevis est*, 'anger is a brief madness', by adding that 'yon man is ever angry' (2.28-9; by Middleton).

But even very bitter people like Timon need someone to express their resentment to; as Cicero says (*On Friendship* 87), a misanthrope like Timon 'cannot refrain from seeking out someone to whom he can spew out the poison of his bitterness'. So when Timon is living in the woods, he vents his anger on the prostitutes Phrynia and Timandra; on Apemantus; on the Poet and the Painter, whom he drives away; on two senators opposed to Alcibiades. Towards the end of *Timon of Athens*, there are no fewer than three two-line epitaphs for Timon, which appear to contradict each other, but could be seen to indicate different aspects of his character. The first of these epitaphs asserts that Timon has lived beyond his time, that he is not a man and so a beast, that it is therefore fitting that a beast read the lines (an adynaton, an impossibility, 16.3-4):

> Timon is dead, who hath outstretched his span.
> Some beast read this; there does not live a man.

Near the very end of the play, Alcibiades provides two epitaphs for Timon that are taken almost verbatim from North's Plutarch, who attributes the first to Timon and the second to the Hellenistic poet Callimachus (in fact by a professional writer of epigrams, Hegisippus, about 300 B.C.)[28]. The first of these denigrates both Timon himself and those who remain alive, in which he wishes to remain anonymous; the second gives the name Timon, stresses his hatred rather than his love, and tells the readers to go on their way after cursing him (17. 71-4):

'Here lies a wretched corpse, of wretched soul bereft.
Seek not my name. A player consume you wicked caitiffs left'.

'Here lies I, Timon, who alive all living men did hate.
Pass by and curse thy fill – but pass, and stay not here thy gait'.

So these three epitaphs establish that Timon is a superannuated, bestial hater of mankind and of himself; that he wishes and does not wish to be named in death; that he curses people, and wants them to curse him; that these people should pass by regardless.

The portrait of the Athenian leader Alcibiades in *Timon of Athens* (which is mostly by Middleton) is wholly inadequate, because it does not use Plutarch's *Life*, and compares very unfavourably with that of Brutus, Antony and others in the Roman plays[29]. Alcibiades was a ambitious politician and general during the Peloponnesian War between Athens and Sparta (431-04 B.C.), supporting the radical democratic faction, and pursuing a policy of imperialism in the Western Mediterranean. He was one of the main proponents of the failed Athenian expedition to Sicily (415-3 B.C.), from which Athens never fully recovered. But since Alcibiades was recalled to Athens from Sicily to answer charges of profaning sacred statues and rites, it could be argued that he was not given a proper chance in Sicily. In any event, Alcibiades defected to Sparta, advising on tactics against Athens. But he then changed again and after several impressive naval victories over Sparta in the Aegean, he was ultimately recalled to Athens as general. Alcibiades remains a controversial figure to this day. Aristophanes may have got to the core of the matter, when he had Aeschylus say in *The Frogs* that it is unwise for the city-state to raise a lion cub inside, but, if it does, it should tolerate its ways[30].

What Alcibiades does in *Timon of Athens* is to function as a foil to Timon (this comes, in part, from Plutarch). Middleton's portrait in Scene 2 turns Alcibiades from being a rich aristocrat into a poor soldier, the opposite of Timon who gives him a present. When Alcibiades pleads to the Senate on behalf of his soldier who is accused of manslaughter (Scene 10 by Middleton, for which there is no Greek authority), the stress on the man's past merits in defence of Athens mirrors the situation of Timon, who feels his past generosity should be returned. But the Senate's decision to banish Alcibiades could be taken to reflect the labelling by Athens of the historical figure as a traitor. At the end of *Timon of Athens*, Shakespeare has Alcibiades lead an army against Athens against the evidence of history, but calculated to appeal to Timon[31].

Further plays of Shakespeare set in Athens are *A Midsummer Night's Dream* and *The Two Noble Kinsmen* (written in collaboration with John Fletcher). But the Athens here is mediaeval in character, largely derived from Chaucer's *Knight's Tale*. Theseus, Duke of Athens, is to be married to the Amazon Queen Hippolyta, and there is a marriage Song (epithalamion) for them at the beginning of *Kinsmen*. Theseus has conquered Hippolyta in war, which suggests male control over a subversive female warrior, and exerts in *Dream* patriarchal power over Egeus' daughter Hermia by enforcing his demand that she marry Demetrius (which she does not want to do). In *Kinsmen* Theseus defeats the evil ruler of Thebes, Creon, who denies burial to men who fought against him (the Seven against Thebes). But *Kinsmen* is at a very oblique angle to ancient Greece: 'an imaginary Greece is endowed with chivalric ideals in a medieval tale which is held up for admiration in a seventeenth-century play'[31a].

7

Probably written in 1602, *Troilus and Cressida* was rarely staged until the twentieth century[32]. Set at the time of the Trojan war between the forces of Greece and those of Troy, the play combines a plot about the war with a plot about the love between Troilus, son of king Priam of Troy, and Cressida, a young Trojan woman, whose father Calchas defected to the Greeks. This love plot is not Homeric, but mediaeval, derived from Chaucer's poem, *Troilus and Chrisyde*[33]. But Shakespeare probably read and used George Chapman's translation *Seven Books of the Iliad of Homer* (1-2, 7-11). This fine work of 1598 brings great energy to Homer (of whom he claimed to have had a vision) by employing the vigorous rushing language of Elizabethan drama, and capturing what Chapman himself calls 'the divine fury' of the Greek poet[34]. As Keats said of Homer's demesne, 'Yet did I never breathe its pure serene / Til I heard Chapman speak out loud and bold'[35].

The genre of *Troilus and Cressida* is notoriously hard to pin down. Those who feel it is a comedy can point to the witty discussion between Cressida and her uncle Pandarus about Troilus, to the failure of the Trojan warrior Aeneas to recognize Agamemnon, to the fact that the Prefatory letter of the Quarto links the play to the comic dramatists Plautus and Terence. Those who feel *Troilus and Cressida* is a tragedy can point to the broken love affair of Troilus and Cressida, and to the killing of Hector by Greek troops. But the overall, prevailing tone of this play is *satiric*, in the mode of Juvenal and Swift; as its ending, in which Troilus and Cressida are not married and do not die, indicates.

The generic instability of *Troilus and Cressida* is stressed by the fact that the viewpoint changes from scene to scene in a way that is unique even for Shakespeare; for example, the first five scenes present, in succession, the views of Troilus, Cressida, Ulysses, Thersites and Hector[37].

The sceptical satire of *Troilus and Cressida* (which made it suddenly popular in the twentieth century) relates to a number of core issues: war, love, identity, language. Sombre accounts of these issues point to the fact that this is not the heroic world of Homer's *Iliad*, but a debased and morally dubious universe, in which the characters are highly self-conscious, knowing less about each other than the audience does.

A good example of how *Troilus and Cressida* critiques the heroic world comes in Ulysses' famous speech on 'degree' (1.3.75-137), on the order he thinks necessary in Greek society to prevent chaos; this is the sort of self-serving stuff for which politicians are notorious, and which is typical of the crafty Ulysses of post-Homeric tradition. Further examples of how the two sides are less than splendid are found in the debates among the Greeks about their lack of success in the war and among the Trojans about whether Helen should be returned to Greece (the latter a usual topic in Elizabethan schools).

For the Greek camp is divided against itself. Ulysses attacks Patroclus who, egged on by Achilles, is seen to be idle and to be 'mocking our designs; (1.3.146). The aged and tedious Nestor holds that Ajax, who is illiterate, is 'grown self-willed' (1.3.188). But Ulysses rigs a lottery, so that Ajax, not Achilles, fights Hector. And Achilles himself is surly, petulant and arrogant. Equally, the Trojans do not come out of this well: they squabble among themselves about whether Helen should be returned to Greece, and Helen herself is portrayed as being little better than a bimbo.

In *Troilus and Cressida*, romantic love is also undercut by the lovers. Troilus can say to Pandarus 'I tell thee I am made / In Cressida's love' (1.50-1), but he is also realistic in speaking to Cressida about love and sex: 'This is the monstruosity in love, lady, that the will is infinite, and the execution confined; that the desire is boundless, and the act a slave to limit'(3.2.79-81). Shakespeare here anticipates a crucial insight of Freud into the human sexual condition: we have to reckon with the 'strange possibility that something in the nature of the sexual instinct is unfavourable to the achievement of absolute gratification'[36].

When Cressida is handed over to the Greeks in exchange for a Trojan prisoner Antenor, she succumbs to the advances of Diomedes, no longer the chivalrous warrior of the *Iliad*. Since she is seen to be false by Troilus, he feels she has no core values, no fixed identity: 'This is, and is not, Cressid' (5.2.149).

But the person who is supreme at debunking everything is Thersites, the only low-born character among the Greeks at Troy. Chapman describes his approach like this (2.181-4):

> A most disorder'd store
> Of words he foolishly pour'd out: of which his mind held more
> Than it could manage: any thing with which he could procure
> Laughter, he never could contain.

Thersites is not only a Fool, a licensed jester, but also something of a Cynic like Apemantus in *Timon of Athens* (Ajax calls him 'Dog!' 2.1.6). Thersites' most striking critique of essentialist views, and implied support for theories of social construction comes in his rhetorical question 'What's aught, but as 'tis valued?' (2.2.53). As with so many rhetorical questions, the answer is negative, 'Nothing'. So Thersites sees the things specially valued in his society as fighting – a disease that promotes butchery – and sex, appetites like that for food which are all that exist: 'Lechery, lechery, still wars and lechery; nothing else holds fashion! A burning devil take them!' (5.2.197-9). Accordingly, Thersites tells Patroclus, the special friend of Achilles, that he is Achilles' 'masculine whore' (5.1.17); this draws not on the *Iliad*, where there is no homosexual relationship between Achilles and Paroclus, but on later Greek tradition[37].

In the *Iliad*, Thersites rails against Greek leaders; in *Troilus and Cressida*, believing everyone to have feet of clay, he is totally vicious (5.4.2-14):

> That dissembling abominable varlet, Diomed, has got the same scurvy doting foolish young knave's sleeve of Troy there in his helm. I would fain see them meet: that some young Trojan ass, that loves the whore there, might send that Greekish whoremasterly villain with the sleeve back to the dissembling luxurious drab of a sleeveless errand. O'th'other side, the policy of those crafty-swearing rascals, that stale old mouse-eaten dry cheese, Nestor, and that same dog-fox, Ulysses, is proved not worth a

blackberry. They set me up in policy that mongrel cur,
Ajax, against that dog of as bad a kind, Achilles...

Language and imagery in *Troilus and Cressida* assist in the debunking of the heroic and of romantic love. While Latin-based words are often powerful in Shakespeare, here they draw attention to the emptiness of political rhetoric, the contrast between words and deeds. For example, Agamemnon's speech that opens Act 1, scene 3 contains curious words such as 'conflux', 'tortive', 'protractive', 'persistive'[38]. Then the dominant image in the play is that of cooking and eating[39], which is used to make the point that sex is an appetite, and so something that is wholly of the body. As Troilus says of Cressida: 'Th'imaginery relish is so sweet / That it enchants my sense. What will it be / When that the wat'ry palate tastes indeed / Love's thrice-repurèd nectar? ' (3.2.17-20).

Despite this stress on the body, *Troilus and Cressida* is more intellectual than any other play of Shakespeare, and may have been played before a learned audience at one of the Inns of Court. Indeed philosophers make several startling appearances in the play in order to provide authority for particular points of view. The Trojan hero Hector tells Paris and Troilus that they have spoken well, but superficially in the debate about Helen's fate 'not much / Unlike young men whom Aristotle thought unfit to hear moral philosophy' (2.2.166-8; *Nicomachean Ethics* 1. 3)[40]. The Greek hero Ulysses is found reading 'A strange fellow' that holds to an Elizabethan view that a person cannot know their own deeds, but must rely on others to recognize them. This book has seemed to some to be Plato or Cicero, but it is more likely 'to be being read, even perhaps written, between the two characters'[41]. In any case, the fellow, like Aristotle, brings outside intellectual authority to bear on issues.

8

George Steiner states that 'It is a great and mysterious stroke of fortune that Shakespeare escaped the fascination of the Hellenic'[42]. The preceding pages have shown that he did not *fully* get away from Greek themes, although they count for much less in his work than Roman ones. That he could not have total access to Greek material is not at all mysterious, since his schooling did not provide it, and since very few men at the time enjoyed such access. Was this a great stroke of fortune, implying that Shakespeare would have been swamped by Greek material? His relationship to the form of ancient drama he was fascinated with, to the Latin tragedies of Seneca, to the Latin comedies of Plautus, suggests otherwise: he stole from these authors, but produced something radically new, as the cases of *Macbeth* and *As You Like It* respectively establish.

For Shakespeare was committed to a form of *open* drama, as Greek and Roman writers were not. This type of drama involves an ability to write *both* tragedies *and* comedies, together with the mingling, in the one play, of comic and tragic elements; a mixture of verse and prose in the one play; a combination of elevated and low language; a focus on the writing of *history* plays, both English and Roman. No Greek or Roman dramatist wrote like that.

Conclusion

Towards the end of his massive poem *The Cantos*, Ezra Pound asserts 'And I am not a demigod, / I cannot make it cohere'[1]. To which William Shakespeare could reply 'I have no wish to make it cohere'. For Shakespeare is not in the business of providing some kind of didactic, totalizing view of the world: he is content to portray it, in magnificent fashion, in all its variety, its glory and its perversity, and to leave it at that. Shakespeare therefore exemplifies Bakhtin's belief that nothing final can be said about the world, that it remains forever in a radically unfinished state, that literature can interpret that state[2].

This opacity leaves unsettled the question of Shakespeare's originality. Extreme positions can be taken about originality in literature: Racine in his Preface to *Bérénice* asserts that 'All creativity consists in making something out of nothing'; Emerson in his essay on Shakespeare takes the polar opposite view: 'The greatest genius is the most indebted man'[3]. Whatever the truth of Emerson's maxim in general, Shakespeare certainly exemplifies it. Since inventing plots was not a gift he possessed, only a handful of plays, out of some forty, lack a main source: *Love's Labour's Lost, A Midsummer Night's Dream, The Merry Wives of Windsor, The Tempest*, possibly *Titus Andronicus*.

But as Shakespeare practices a form of Renaissance imitation (*imitatio*), he moves far beyond mere copying to a type of originality that Roman critics called 'invention' (*inventio*), to what Shakespeare himself termed 'the brightest heaven of invention'[4]. Identifying a source is a necessary first step, but then we need to analyse what the writer does with it. As Quintilian points out, imitation by itself is not sufficient, since invention comes first, is pre-eminent.[5]

Shakespeare is, in drama and in poetry, one of the greatest inventors. As such, he frequently transforms material from the Greek and Roman world; as Yeats said, 'Ancient salt is best packing'[6]. So Plutarch's *Lives* gave Shakespeare the plot for the three major Roman plays of *Coriolanus*, *Julius Caesar*, and *Antony and Cleopatra*. Plautus in his plays *Menaechmi* and *Amphitruo* provided the plot for *The Comedy of Errors*, and, in terms of comic action, lies partly behind other Shakespearean comedies such as *As You Like It* and *Twelfth Night*.

Vital material was provided to Shakespeare by two other Roman writers. Seneca's tragedies not only helped to develop the revenge play as in *Titus Andronicus* and *Hamlet*, but also offered a paradigm for the theme of evil in the ruler in *Richard III*, and especially in *Macbeth*. Ovid's epic poem *Metamorphoses* provided nearly all the Greek mythology that is so prevalent in the plays, as well as the story for the miniature epic *Venus and Adonis*.

Shakespeare also made limited use of some other Greek material. The Greek novel lies behind *Pericles*, Plutarch behind *Timon of Athens*, Homer, to an extent, behind *Troilus and Cressida*.

Shakespeare may not have been a learned man (as Jonson thought himself to be), but he was very well educated, and used his knowledge of the Greek and especially of the Roman world to exquisite effect. Auerbach's summary of Rabelais' use of Greek and Roman models nicely encapsulates what is at stake: 'Yet his endebtedness to antiquity does not imprison him within the confines of antique concepts; to him antiquity means liberation not servitude'[7]. This is certainly the freedom of influence.

Notes

Notes To Preliminaries

1 Coleridge

2 Dryden in *William Shakespeare: The Critical Heritage*, ed. B. Vickers, Volume I, 1623-1692 (London/New York 1974), 138.

3 James Agate in *Oxford Dictionary of Literary Quotations*, ed. P. Kemp (Oxford 1999), 327.

4 Shaw, quoted by C. A. Berst in *The Cambridge Companion to George Bernard Shaw*, ed. C. Innes (Cambridge 2004), 61.

5 C. Leech, *Tragedy* (London 1969), 50.

6 For Shakespeare's scepticism see G. Bradshaw, *Shakespeare's Scepticism* (Ithaca 1990); M. Bell, *Shakespeare's Tragic Skepticism* (New Haven / London 2002).

7 Montaigne, quoted in Bell (note 5), 14-15; John Donne, 'The First Anniversary', line 205.

8 Greenblatt (note 1), 377.

9 Thomas De Quincey, *On Murder* (Oxford 2006), 5.

10 L. Danson, *Shakespeare's Dramatic Genres* (Oxford 2000).

11 W.B. Yeats, *Essays and Introductions* (New York 1961), 240.

12 G. Steiner in *Tragedy and the Tragic*, ed. M. Silk (Oxford 1996), 540.

13 Cf. E. Schanzer, *The Problem Plays of Shakespeare* (London 1963), 6: 'A play in which we find a concern with a moral problem which is central to it, presented in such a manner that we are unsure of our moral bearings, so that uncertain and divided responses to it in the minds of the audience are possible and even probable.'

[14] T. Hawkes, *Meaning by Shakespeare* (London 1992), 55.

[15] Cf. C. Butler, *Postmodernism* (Oxford 2002), 15: 'the basic attitude of postmodernists was a scepticism about the claims of any kind of overall, totalising explanation'; Walt Whitman, *Leaves of Grass*, 'Song of my Self', Section 51.

[16] *Letters of John Keats* ed. F. Page (London 1954), 53.

[17] D. Walsh, *Literature and Knowledge* (Middleton 1969), 136; see also M. Wood, *Literature and the Taste of Knowledge* (Cambridge 2005).

[18] O. B. Hardison, Jr. in *Aristotle's Poetics*, trans. L. Golden (Englewood Cliffs, N. J.1968), 116-20.

[19] Leech (note 4), 51; Italo Calvino, *Why Read the Classics?* (London 2000), 9.

[20] H. Bloom, *Shakespeare: The Invention of the Human* (New York 1998); W. B. Yeats, *A Vision* (London 1981), 294.

[21] Aristotle, *Poetics* 50a.

[22] For Reception Studies see L. Hardwick, *Reception Studies* (Oxford 2003); *Classics and the Uses of Reception*, eds. C. Mertindale & R. F. Thomas (Oxford 2006); *A Companion to the Classical Tradition*, ed. C. W. Kallendorf (Oxford 2007).

[23] C. Martindale, *Redeeming the Text* (Cambridge 1993), 1-34.

[24] Longinus 13; T. M. Greene, The Light in Troy: Imitation and Discovery in Renaissance Poetry (New Haven 1982), esp. 38-53.

[25] S. Goldhill, Who Needs Greek? Contests in the Cultural History of Hellenism (Cambridge 2003), 297.

[26] T. S. Eliot, *Selected Essays* (New York 1966), 182; Marina Carr, 'Talking to the Dead', *Irish University Review* 28 (1998), 19.

[27] For Cannibalism see E. R. P. Vieira in *Post-Colonial Translation*, eds. S. Bassnett & H. Trivedi (London / New York 2002), 95-113; for Du Bellay see P.Ford in Kallendorf (note 21), 160.

[28] Bloom (note 1).

[29] George Watson (ed.), John Dryden: Of Dramatic Poesie and other Critical Essays (London 1962), Vol. 1, 69.

[30] J. Shapiro, *Rival Playwrights: Marlowe, Jonson and Shakespeare* (New York 1991), 75-132; H. Bloom, *The Anxiety of Influence* (New York 1977), xl-xlvii; P. Honan, *Christopher Marlowe – Poet and Spy* (Oxford 2005), 186-96.

[31] Robert Greene, *Groatsworth of Wit*, quoted in Honan (note 6), 159. For a useful account of scholarship on Greene's attack see D. A.

Carroll, 'Greene's "Upstart crow" Passage: A Survey of Commentary', *Research Opportunities in Renaissance Drama* 28 (1985), 111-27; for further comment see Greenblatt (note 1), 203-25.

32 Greenblatt (note 1), 224.

33 *ibid*, 216-25.

Notes to Chapter One

1 Ben Jonson, verses in the First Folio; E. H. Mikhail, ed., *W. B. Yeats: Interviews and Recollections*, Vol ii (London 1977), 199-203.

2 For the Renaissance see J. Hale, *The Civilization of Europe in the Renaissance* (London 2005); *Reconceiving the Renaissance – A Critical Reader*, eds. E. Fernie, R. Wroy, M. T. Burnett, C. Mc Manus. For the impact of Greece and Rome see R. Weiss, *The Renaissance Discovery of Classical Antiquity* (Oxford 1969). M. T. Burnett in *Reconceiving the Renaissance* asserts that' Shakespeare has become inseparable from the "Renaissance" with one leading into, and being incorporated within, the other' (147).

3 P. Bourdieu, *Distinction – A Social Critique of the Judgement of Taste* (Cambridge, Mass. 2002), index s.v. Cultured Capital.

4 W.J. Ong, S.J. 'Latin Language Study as a Renaissance Puberty Rite,' *Studies in Philology* 56 (1959), 103-24.

5 Montaigne, 'On Pedantrie'.

6 For Shakespeare's education esp. T.W. Baldwin, *William Shakespeare's Small Latina and Lesse Greeke*, 2 vols. (Urbana 1944), which remains indispensable. See also P. Honan, *Shakespeare – A Life* (New York 1999), 43-59; A. Holden, *William Shakespeare – His Life and Work* (London 2005), 30-37; P. Ackroyd, *Shakespeare – The Biography* (London 2005), 50-61.

7 Bishops, quoted by Honan (note 6), 48.

8 Baldwin (note 6), II, 663; S. Wells in *The Oxford Companion to Shakespeare*, eds. M. Dobson and S. Wells (Oxford 2005), 124. Cf. R. Jenkyns in *A Companion to the Classical Tradition*, ed. C.W. Kallendorf (Oxford 2007), 271: 'the years of Latin drill at Stratford Grammar School would have given him a thorough knowledge of the language'.

8a G. V. Monitto, 'Shakespeare and Culmann's *Sententiae Pueriles*', *Notes and Queries 32* (1985), 30-1.

9 John Aubrey, *Brief Lives*, ed. R. Barber (Woodbridge 2004), 286.

10 For Shakespeare in Lancashire see esp. *Theatre and Religion – Lancastrian Shakespeare*, eds. R. Dutton, A. Findlay, R. Wilson

(Manchester 2003); R. Wilson, *Secret Shakespeare – Studies in theatre, religion and resistance* (Manchester 2004). See also Honan (note 6), 60-71; Holden (note 6), 53-62; Ackroyd (note 6), 70-78; S. Greenblatt, *Will in the World – How Shakespeare Became Shakespeare* (London 2004), 103-06. For Scepticism about Shakespeare in Lancashire see F. Kermode, *The Age of Shakespeare* (London 2004), 29-35; for scepticism about John Shakespeare's spiritual testament see R. Bearman, *SSu* 56 (2003), 184-202.

[11] M. Charney, *Shakespeare on Love and Lust* (New York 2000), 192-93.

[11a] James Joyce, *A Portrait of the Artist as a Young Man*, ed. J. Johnson (Oxford 2000), 39-41; id., *Finnegans Wake* 454.15.

[12] *Literary Essays of Ezra Pound*, ed. T. S. Eliot (London 1960), 232.

[13] For Shakespeare's reading see V. K. Whitaker, Shakespeare's Love of Learning: An Inquiry into the Growth of his Mind and Art (San Marino, California 1953); R. S. Miola, Shakespeare's Reading (Oxford 2000); L. Barkan in The Cambridge Companion to Shakespeare, eds. M. de Grazia and S. Wells (Cambridge 1988), 31-47.

[14] Thomas Nashe, quoted in Honan (note 6), 154.

Notes To Chapter Two

[1] Livy 1.10.

[2] Trevor Nunn in *Political Shakespeare*, eds. J. Dollimore & A. Sinfield (Manchester 1985), 194.

[3] H. White, Metahistory – The Historical Imagination in Nineteenth-Century Europe (Baltimore / London 1975).

[4] For Plutarch see D. Russell, *Plutarch* (London 1973); R. Lamberton, *Plutarch* (New Haven / London 2001); C. B. R. Pelling, *Plutarch and History: Eighteen Studies* (London 2002); S. Goldhill, *Who Needs Greek? Contests in the Cultural History of Hellenism* (Cambridge 2003), 246-93. For Plutarch and Rome see C. P. Jones, *Plutarch and Rome* (Oxford 1971). For the *Lives* used by Shakespeare see *Shakespeare's Plutarch*, ed. T. J. B. Spencer (Harmondsworth 1964).

[5] For North's translation see F. O. Malthiessen, *Translation: an Elizabethan Art* (Cambridge, Mass. 1931), 54-102, who describes it as 'a masterpiece in its own right' (5).

[6] T. S. Eliot, *Selected Essays* (New York 1964), 6.

[7] J. Shapiro, *1599 – A Year in the Life of William Shakespeare* (London 2005), 150. Cf. C. Marshall, Shakespeare, 'Crossing the Rubicon', *SSu* 52 (2000), 75-88.

[8] M. Neill, *William Shakespeare – The Tragedy of Antony and Cleopatra* (Oxford 2000), 7. For Shakespeare's Roman plays see M. W. MacCallum, *Shakespeare's Roman Plays and their Background* (London 1910; London 1967); T. G. B. Spencer, 'Shakespeare and the Elizabethan Romans', *SSu* 10 (1957), 39-49; R. S. Miola, *Shakespeare's Rome* (Cambridge 1983); V. Thomas, *Shakespeare's Roman World* (London 1989); G. Miles, *Shakespeare and the Constant Romans* (Oxford 1996), C. Kahn, *Roman Shakespeare: Warriors, Wounds and Women* (London 1997), A. Leggatt, *Shakespeare's Political Drama* (London 2002). For Coriolanus see also K. Burke, *Language as Symbolic Action* (Los Angeles 1966). 81-97; B. King, *Coriolanus* (London 1989); R. B. Parker, *William Shakespeare – The Tragedy of Coriolanus* (Oxford 1998), 1-148.

[9] Spencer (note 8),

[10] Coleridge, 'Marginalia and notebooks', quoted in *Shakespeare: Coriolanus*, ed. B. A. Brockman (London 1968), 31.

[11] L. Bliss, *Coriolanus* (Cambridge 2007), 11-13.

[12] R. A. Bauman, *Women and Politics in Ancient Rome* (London 1994).

[13] Kahn, (note 8), 150-8.

[14] T. P. Wiseman, 'Roman History and the Ideological Vacuum' in *Classics in Progress*, ed. T. P. Wiseman (Oxford 2006), 285-310.

[15] For Julius Caesar see *Shakespeare – Julius Caesar*, ed. P. Ure (London 1969); *William Shakespeare – Julius Caesar*, ed. A. Humphreys (Oxford 1998), 1-83; *The Arden Shakespeare – Julius Caesar*, ed. D. Daniell (London 2003), (London 2005), 1-147; *William Shakespeare – Julius Caesar*, ed. N. Sanders, intro, M. Wiggins (London 2005), xxi-lxv.

[16] For Julius Caesar see M. Grant, *Julius Caesar* (London 1972); C. Pelling, 'Judging Julius Caesar' in *Julius Caesar in Western Culture*, ed. M. Wyke (Oxford 2006), 3-26; M. Wyke, *Caesar – A Life in Western Culture* (London 2007)

[16a] Dante, *Inferno* xxxiv.

[17] R. Syme, *The Roman Revolution* (Oxford 2002), viii.

[18] Shapiro (note 7), 142-53; 172-86.

[19] D.C. Green, *Julius Caesar and its Sources* (Salzburg 1979).

[20] B. Arkins, *Hellenising Ireland – Greek and Roman Themes in Modern Irish Literature* (Newbridge 2005), 27-9.

[21] Suetonius, *Julius Caesar* 82.

22 J. Fuzier, 'Rhetoric versus Rhetoric: A Study of Shakespeare's Julius Caesar, Act III, Scene 2', *Cahiers Elizabéthans* 5 (1981), 25-65.

23 Plutarch, *Life of Caesar* 66.4.

23a For Stoic suicide see J. M. Rist, *Stoic Philosophy* (Cambridge 1969), 233-55, esp. 246-50.

23b Seneca, Letters 26.9, *Macbeth* 1.4. 8-9; Hamlet 5.2.292.

24 Bauman (note 12), who deals with Servilia at pp. 73-6.

25 Kahn (note 8), 101.

26 For Antony and Cleopatra see esp J. Adelman, *The Common Liar: An Essay on Antony and Cleopatra* (New Haven / London 1973). For this period see J. Osgard, *Caesar's Legacy* (Cambridge 2006). For Cleopatra and her image see M. Grant, *Cleopatra* (London 2003); L. Hughes-Hallett, *Cleopatra* (London 1991); M. Hamer, *Signs of Cleopatra* (London 1993), J. O'Connor, *Shakespearean Afterlives* (Oxford, Cambridge 2003), 69-94.

27 M. Foucauld, *The History of Sexuality*, Volume One: *An Introduction* (Harmondsworth 1981), 48.

28 J. Wilders, (ed), Antony and Cleopatra (London 2006, Arden), 56-61.

29 Plutarch, Antony 10.3; for Fulvia see Bauman (note 12), 83-9.

29a For Octavia see Bauman (note 12), 91-8.

30 Syme (note 17), 297; for the battle of Actium see J. Carter, *The Battle of Actium, the Rise and Triumph of Augustus Caesar* (London 1970); W. Tarn, *The Battle of Actium, Journal of Roman Studies* 21 (1931), 173-99; Osgood (note 26), 372-84.

31 B. Hodgson, 'Antony and Cleopatra in the Theatre', *The Cambridge Companion to Shakespearean Tragedy*, ed. C. Mc Eachern (Cambridge 2002), 241-63, at p. 254.

32 Bacon, 'On Love'.

33 J. Griffin, *'Propertius and Antony'* in his *Latin Poets and Roman Life* (London 1985), 32-47. For Antony as depicted in Plutarch's Antony see C. B. R. Pelling (ed.), *Plutarch, Life of Antony* (Cambridge 1988).

34 For Antony as Hercules see E. Waith, *The Herculean Hero in Marlowe, Chapman, Shakespeare and Dayden* (New York / London 1962), 113-21; B.J. Bono, *Literary Transvaluation: From Virgilian Epic to Shakespearean Tragicomedy* (Berkeley, Los Angeles / London 1984), 151-67.

35 *Four Greek Poets*, trans. E. Keeley & P. Sherrard (Harmondsworth 1966), 14.

35a P. D. Westbrook, 'Horace's Influence on Antony and Cleopatra', *PMLA* 62 (1947), 392-8.

35b O'Connor, (note 26), 88. For Shaw's marriage see J. Meyers, *Married to Genius* (Harpenden, Herts 2005), 47-70.

36 E. Jones, 'Stuart Cymbeline', *Essays in Criticism II* (1961), 84-99; T. Hawkes, *Shakespeare in the Present* (London / New York 2002), 46-65.

37 H. Nearing, 'The Legend of Julius Caesar's British Conquest', *PMLA* 64 (1949), 889-929.

38 R. Warren, *William Shakespeare – Cymbeline* (Oxford 1998), 11.

39 B. Vickers, *Shakespeare, Co-author* (Oxford 2004), 148-243.

40 Spencer (note 8), 32.

41 Eliot (note 6), 124.

42 G. Steiner, *Antigones* (Oxford 1984).

Notes To Chapter Three

1 Schopenhauer, quoted in T. Eagleton, *Sweet Violence – The Idea of the Tragic* (Oxford 2003), 4.

2 Byron, *Don Juan*, Canto III, ix.

3 G. Steiner in *Tragedy and the Tragic*, ed. M. S. Silk (Oxford 1996), 542.

4 N. T. Croally, Euripidean Polemic – The Trojan Women and the Function of Tragedy (Cambridge 1994), 43.

5 N. Rabkin, *Shakespeare and the Problem of Meaning* (Chicago / London 1981), 33-62.

6 T. S. Eliot, *Selected Essays* (London 1951), 65.

7 For Senecan tragedy see C. J. Herington, 'Senecan Tragedy', *Arion* 5 (1966), 422-71; T. G. Rosenmeyer, *Senecan Drama and Stoic Cosmology* (Berkeley 1989); A. J. Boyle, *Tragic Seneca: an Essay in the Theatrical Tradition* (London 1997).

8 C. J. Herington in *The Cambridge History of Classical Literature, II Latin Literature* (Cambridge 1982), 514.

9 The tragedy *Hercules Oetaeus* and the historical drama *Octavia* are not by Seneca, but by another author(s) of the same period.

10 W. Benjamin, *Illuminations* (London 1999), 248.

[11] Horace, *Epistles* 2.1.185-86; for bear-bating in England see T. Hawkes, *Shakespeare in the Present* (London / New York 2002), 82-106.

[12] A. Artaud, *The Theatre and its Double* (London 1999), 64-87.

[13] Artaud, quoted by G. Braden in *The Legacy of Rome*, ed. R. Jenkyns (Oxford 1992), 266.

[14] For Stoicism see J. M. Rist, *Stoic Philosophy* (Cambridge 1969); J. Sellars, *Stoicism* (Chesham 2006).

[15] G. Brendan, *Renaissance Tragedy and the Senecan Tradition: Anger's Privilege* (New Haven 1985); Boyle (note 7), 141-207.

[15a] T. S. Eliot, *Selected Essays* (New York 1964), 51-2.

[16] For Seneca and Shakespeare see esp. R. S. Miola, *Shakespeare and Classical Tragedy: The Influence of Seneca* (Oxford 1992); B. Arkins, 'Heavy Seneca: His Influence on Shakespeare's Tragedies', *Classics Ireland* 2 (1995), 1-16. For (unwarranted) scepticism see F. K. Hunter, 'Seneca and the Elizabethans' *SSu* 20 (1967), 17-26, and 'Seneca and English Tragedy' in *Seneca*, ed. C. D. N. Costa (London / Boston 1974), 166-204.

[17] R. N. Watson in *The Cambridge Companion to Shakespearean Tragedy*, ed. C. McEachern (Cambridge 2002), 163.

[18] Aeschylus, *The Libation-Bearers* 400-2; Marston, *Antonio's Revenge* 3.3.71; Shakespeare, *Macbeth* 3.4.122.

[19] For links between *The Spanish Tragedy* and *Titus Andronicus* see *Titus Andronicus*, ed. J. Bate (London 2006), 85-87.

[20] P. D. James, quoted in *The Oxford Dictionary of Literary Quotations*, ed. P. Kemp (Oxford 1999), 45.2.

[21] For *Titus Andronicus* as a Roman play, see Chapter Two, Section 7. For the play see Bate (note 19), 1-181; Waith (note 24), 1-69.

[22] For violence in Seneca and Shakespeare see G. Lloyd Evans in *Roman Drama*, eds. D. R. Dudley & T. A. Dorey (London 1965), 123-59.

[23] K. Muir, The Sources of Shakespeare's Plays (London 1977), 23.

[23a] Eliot (note 6), 67.

[24] Peter Brook, quoted by C. M. Waith, *Titus Andronicus* (Oxford 1998), 55-56, who provides comment on the production at 54-56; further comment in Bate (note 19), Index s. v. Brook, Peter; M. Kustow, *Peter Brook* (London 2006), 83-84.

[25] The quotations from Seneca's *Phaedra* in *Titus Andronicus* appear in scenes of the play – 2.1 and 4.1 – that were probably written by Peele and so can be briefly dealt with. Peele uses Hippolytus' anguish about

Phaedra's illicit love for him as analogue for Titus' anguish about Lavinia's rape: *tam lentus audis scelera, tam lentus vides?* 'do you hear of crimes so calmly, do you see them so calmly?' (*Phaedra* 672); Peele uses Phaedra's position in the Underworld as analogue for Demetrius' sense that he is already among the dead: *Per Stygia, per manes vehor*, 'I am borne through the Stygian waters, through the shades' from *per Styga, per amnes igneas amens seguer*, 'I will follow madly through the Styx, through fiery rivers' (*Phaedra* 1180).

26 M. Doran, *Endeavours of Art: A Study of Form in Elizabethan Drama* (Madison 1954), 16.

27 Thomas Lodge, quoted in Thompson & Taylor (note 28), 44.

28 *Hamlet* 3.2.380-2; all references to *Hamlet* are to the Second Quarto of 1603/4, as found in *Hamlet*, eds A. Thompson & N. Taylor (London 2006). *Seneca – Thyestes*, translated and introduced by Caryl Churchill (London 1995), vii.

29 *Elizabethan Critical Essays*, ed. G. G. Smith (Oxford 1971), vol, 1, 312.

30 For death in *Hamlet* see F. O'Toole, *Shakespeare is Hard, but so is Life* (London / New York 2002), 45-68.

31 G. R. Hibbard, *Shakespeare, Hamlet* (Oxford 1998), 29-33.

32 Seneca, *The Trojan Women* 1153-4; *Hamlet* 2.2.415-20.

33 Accordingly, Hamlet is *not* like Orestes, who does kill his mother Clytemnestra.

34 Cf. N. Rabkin, *Shakespeare and the Problem of Meaning* (Chicago / London 1981), 95: 'Richard kills his family not because he wants to be king but because he wants to kill his family'.

35 Schiller, quoted by G. Steiner, *The Death of Tragedy* (New Haven / London 1980), 158.

36 Muir (note 23), 37.

37 For these figures see A. Hammond, *King Richard III* (London / New York 1992), 99-104.

38 H. F. Brooks, '*Richard III*, Unhistorical Amplifications: The Women's Scenes and Seneca', *Modern Language Review* 75 (1980), 721-37.

39 J. Kott, Shakespeare Our Contemporary (London 1965), 35.

40 H. N. Paul, *The Royal Play of 'Macbeth'* (London 1950), 48.

41 K. Muir, *Macbeth* (London 2006), lxiii.

42 For Macbeth and Seneca see Y. Peyré. 'Confusion now hath made his masterpiece: Senecan resonances in *Macbeth* in *Shakespeare and*

the Classics, eds C. Martindale & A. B. Taylor (Cambridge 2005), 141-55.

43 C. & M. Martindale, *Shakespeare and the Uses of Antiquity* (London / New York 2005), 15-8.

44 Note too, Seneca, *Phaedra* 315-8.

45 *Macbeth* 5.3.40, 5.5.24, Seneca *Epistulae Morales* 80.7. For Shakespeare and Stoicism see C & M Martindale (note 43), 165-89

46 I & S. Ewbank, 'The Fiend-like Queen: A Note on *Macbeth* and Seneca's *Medea*', SSu 19 (1966), 82-94; reprinted in *Aspects of Macbeth*, eds. K. Muir & P. Edwards (Cambridge 1977), 53-65.

47 H. Wilamowitz-Moellendorff, *Griechische Tragödie* (Berlin 1919), III, 162

48 Corneille, *Médée* 319-21.

49 Kyd, The Spanish Tragedy 4.4.83; Middleton, The Revenger's Tragedy 3.5.167; Webster, The Duchess of Malfi 4.2.139; Shakespeare, 3 Henry VI 5.6.83; Antony and Cleopatra 3.13.92-3, 187.

50 Jonson, *Catiline*; Marston, *The Malcontent* 5.4.14-5; Shakespeare, *Macbeth* 3.2.58, 3.4.137-9; *Richard III* 4.2.63-4; *Hamlet* 3.3.88.

51 Miola, (note 16), 177-87.

52 For parody see M. A. Rose, *Parody: Ancient, Modern, and Post-Modern* (Cambridge 1993); for parody on the Elizabethan and Jacobean stage see S. Dentith *Parody* (London 2000), 123-34, for this passage see *A Midsummer Night's Dream*, ed. R. A. Foakes (Cambridge 1990), 58.

53 Steiner (note 35), 21.

54 Tom Stoppard, *Rosenkrantz and Guildenstern Are Dead* (London 2000), 23.

55 Ted Hughes, *Oedipus* (London 1969); for comment see M. Kustow, (note 24), 172-6; Churchill (note 28).

Notes to Chapter Four

1 For comedy see *Comedy: Developments in Criticism*, ed. D. J. Palmer (London 1984); E. Segal, *The Death of Comedy* (Cambridge, Mass. / London 2001); A. Stott, *Comedy* (New York / London 2005).

2 Byron, *Don Juan*, Canto III, ix.

3 Samuel Beckett, quoted by V. Abbott in *Desmond Egan – The Poet and his Work*, ed. H. Kenner (Orono 1990), 52.

4 Plato, *Symposium* 223 d.

5 Freud, *Jokes and their Relation to the Unconscious*, Vol. 8, Standard edition, ed. J. Strachey (London 2001), 222.

6 For Plautus and Terence see G. E. Duckworth, *The Nature of Roman Comedy* (Princeton 1967); for Plautus see further E. Segal, *Roman Laughter – The Comedy of Plautus* (Cambridge, Mass. 1970). For New Comedy in Shakespeare see R. S. Miola, *Shakespeare and Classical Comedy* (Oxford 1997); W. Richle, *Shakespeare, Plautus and the Humanist Tradition* (Cambridge 1990).

7 M. Bakhtin in *Modern Criticism and Theory* ed. D. Lodge (London / New York 1993), 138.

8 G. Rubin ' "The Traffic in Women": Notes on the Political Economy of Sex' in *Literary Theory: An Anthology*, eds. J. Rivkin & M. Ryan (Oxford 2004), 770-94.

9 Terence, *Eunuchus* 36-38.

10 For Shakespeare's comedies see C. L. Barber, *Shakespeare's Festive Comedy* (Princeton 1959); A. Leggatt, *Shakespeare's Comedy of Love* (London 1974); L. Salinger, *Shakespeare and the Traditions of Comedy* (Cambridge 1974); *The Cambridge Companion to Shakespearean Comedy*, ed. A. Leggatt (Cambridge 2002), in which L. G. Clubb deals with the Italian background at pp. 32-46. The Yeats quotation is from *W. B.Yeats – The Poems*, ed. R. J. Finneran (Dublin 1964), 107.

11 N. Frye in Palmer (note 1), 79-84.

12 Francis Meres, quoted in P. Honan, *Shakespeare – A Life* (Oxford 1999), 264.

13 Julius Caesar in Suetonius, *Life of Terence* 5.

14 Horace, *Epistles* 2.1.170-76; for Jonson's statement and comment see H. Grady in *The Cambridge Companion to Shakespeare*, eds. M. de Grazia and S. Wells (Cambridge 2002), 267; Cicero, *De Officiis* 1.104.

15 For *The Comedy of Errors* see esp. *The Comedy of Errors – Critical Essays*, ed. R. S. Miola (New York / London 2001); also T. W. Baldwin, *On the Compositional Genetics of 'The Comedy of Errors'* (Urbana 1965).

16 A. Burgess, *Shakespeare* (London 2002), 45.

17 Baldwin (note 15), 47-8.

18 Coleridge in Miola (note 15), 55.

19 C. Whitworth in *William Shakespeare – The Comedy of Errors* ed. C. Whitworth (Oxford 2002), 42-59.

20 E. Segal, *The Menaechmi*: 'Roman Comedy of Errors', *Yale Classical Studies* 21 (1969), 77-93.

21 Miola (note 6), 22.

22 H. Levin in Miola (note 15), 124.

22a For Ephesus see L. Maguire in Miola (note 15), 360-66.

23 N. Frye, *Anatomy of Criticism* (Princeton 1957), 185.

24 A. W. Schlegel, quoted in Miola (note 15), 118.

25 Manningham, quoted in *Twelfth Night Or What You Will*, ed. E. S. Donno & P. Gay (Cambridge 2004), 1.

26 N. K. Hayles, 'Sexual Disguise in 'As You Like It' and 'Twelfth Night'', *SSu* 32 (1979), 63-72; B. Hayden in Leggatt (not 10), 179-97.

27 C. Paglia, *Sexual Personae* (London 1992), 212.

28 Dr. Johnson in *William Shakespeare: The Critical Heritage*, ed. B. Vickers, Volume 5, 1765-1774 (London / New York 1979), 110.

29 For comment on this controversial issue see A. Thompson in *The Taming of the Shrew*, ed. A. Thompson (Cambridge 2006), 25-41.

30 Dr. Johnson in Vickers (note 28), 124.

31 Seneca, *Apocolyntosis* 8.2.

32 Terence, *Eunuchus* 591; *The Merry Wives of Windsor* 5.5.12.

33 For the theme of the braggart soldier see J.A. Henson, 'The Glorious Military' in *Roman Drama*, eds. D. R. Dudley and T. A. Doray (London 1965), 51-85; D. D. Boughner, *The Braggart in Renaissance Comedy* (Minneapolis 1954).

34 *Love's Labour's Lost* 5.1.12; *As You Like It* 5.2.31/

35 A. Leggatt, *Shakespeare's Political Drama* (London / NewYork 2002) 99-100.

36 R. Dutton, 'The *C of E – The Columny of Apelles*: An Exercise Source Study' in *A Companion to I's Works, Vol. 3: The Comedies*, eds. R. Dutton & J. E. Howard (Oxford 2003), 307-19.

37 B. Knox, '"The Tempest" and Ancient Comic Tradition' in *English Stage Comedy*, ed. W. K. Wimsatt (New York 195), 52-73; reprinted in *William Shakespeare – The Tempest*, ed. R. Langbaum (New York / Toronto / London 1964), 163-81.

38 F. Teague, 'Othello and New Comedy' in *Acting Funny: Comic Theory and Practice*, ed. F. Teague (Rutherford 1994), 29-39.

39 For New Comedy in *King Lear* see Miola (note 6), 187-201.

⁴⁰ Patrick Kavanagh in Patrick Kavanagh, *Collected Poems* (London 1973), xiv.

Notes to Chapter Five

¹ For Ovid see, e.g., *The Cambridge Companion to Ovid*, ed. P. Hardie (Cambridge 2002). For Shakespeare and Ovid see esp. J. Bate, *Shakespeare and Ovid* (Oxford 2001). See also L. Barkan, *The Gods Made Flesh. Metamorphosis and the Pursuit of Paganism* (New Haven / London 1986), 243-88; C. & M. Martindale, *Shakespeare and the Uses of Antiquity* (London 1994), 45-90; S. A. Brown, *The Metamorphoses of Ovid: Chaucer to Ted Hughes* (London 1999), 57-84; *Shakespeare's Ovid: The Metamorphoses in the Plays and Poems*, ed. A. B. Taylor (Cambridge 2006); 'the poet' comes from *The Merchant of Venice* 5.1.79.

² Francis Meres, quoted in Bate (note 1), 2-3.

³ For Ovid's *Metamorphoses* see B. Otis, *Ovid as an Epic Poet* (Cambridge 1970); J. B. Solodow, *The World of Ovid's Metamorphoses*; E. Fantham, *Ovid's Metamorphoses* (Oxford 2004).

⁴ A. Feldherr in Hardie (note 1), 173-4.

⁵ *After Ovid – New Metamorphoses*, eds. M. Hoffmann & J. London (London 1996); the editors, ix.

⁶ J. Shapiro, *1599 – A Year in the Life of William Shakespeare* (London 2005), 133-55, esp 153-55.

⁷ R. K. Root, *Classical Mythology in Shakespeare* (New York 1965), 3.

⁸ M. Heidegger, quoted in G. Steiner, *Antigones* (Oxford 1984), 301; Wallace Stevens, *Opus Posthumus*, ed. S. F. Morse (London 1959), 178; R. Calasso, *The Marriage of Cadmus and Harmony* (London 1994), 383.

⁹ B. Arkins, *Irish Appropriation of Greek Tragedy* (Dublin 2010).

¹⁰ Ted Hughes, *Tales from Ovid* (London 1997), ix.

¹¹ For Ovid's style see E. J. Kenney, 'The style of the *Metamorphoses*' in *Ovid*, ed. J. W. Burns (London / Boston 1973), 116-53.

¹² C.P. Segal, *Landscape in Ovid's Metamorphoses* (Wiesbaden 1969), 93.

¹³ T.S. Eliot, *Collected Poems* (London 1974), 66.

¹³ᵃ S. Dixon, *Cornelia – Mother of the Gracchi* (Abingdon 2007), 18-9, 41-3, 52-3.

¹⁴ Tranio is the name of the clever urban slave in Plautus' comedy *Mostellaria*; Grumio is the name of the rustic slave in that play.

15 For Giulio Romano and his statue of Hermione see S. Orgel, *William Shakespeare – The Tempest* (Oxford 1998), 57-79.

15a Helena Faucit, quoted in *Shakespeare – The Winter's Tale*, ed. K. Muir (London 1982), 49.

16 Bate (note 1), 238. For the Pygmalion theme see V. I. Stoichita, *The Pygmalion Effect* (Chicago / London 2008), who deals with *The Winter's Tale* at pp. 101-10.

17 *ibid.*, 8.

18 For dreams see P. Holland, *William Shakespeare – A Midsummer Night's Dream* (Oxford 1998), 3-21.

19 For Apuleius see J. J. M. Tobin, *Shakespeare's Favourite Novel* (Lanham 1984), 32-40; the remainder of this book fails to convince.

20 For Pyramus and Thisbe in *Dream* see Bate (note 1), 129-44; N. Rudd in Taylor (note 1), 113-25.

21 Samuel Pepys, quoted in Holland (note 18), 99.

22 Peter Brook, quoted in M. Kustow, *Peter Brook – A Biography* (London 2005), 157.

23 Rudd (note 20), 125. Cf. Bate (note 1), 132: 'Shakespeare's most luminous *imitatio* of Ovid'.

24 W. Keach, *Elizabethan Erotic Narratives* (New Brunswick 1977); C. Hulse, *Metamorphic Verse: The Elizabethan Miniature Epic* (Princeton 1981). For an edition of Chapham's *Narcissus* see C. Martindale & C. Burrow, *English Literary Renaissance* 22 (1992), 147-76.

25 Carew, quoted by C. Burrow (ed.) in *William Shakespeare – The Complete Sonnets and Poems* (Oxford 2002), 16. Note too Nashe's most popular poem *The Choice of Valentines*, a pornographical pastiche of poems like *Venus and Adonis*.

26 For *Venus and Adonis* see P. C. Kolin (ed.), *Venus and Adonis : Critical Essays* (New York / London 1997); J. Roe (ed.) *Shakespeare – The Poems* (Cambridge 1992), 3-2; Burrow (note 25), 6-40.

27 Burrow (note 25), 36. For Venus's sexual desire see C. Kahn in Kolin (note 26), 111-202.

28 R. T. Simone, *Shakespeare and Lucrece: A Study of the Poem and its Relation to the Plays* (Salzburg 1974); Roe (note 26), 22-41; Burrow (note 25), 40-73. For adverse comment see C. & M. Martindale (note 1), 61-4.

28a Gabriel Harvey, quoted in Simone (note 28), 210.

29 I. Donaldson, *The Rapes of Lucretia: A Myth and its Transformations* (Oxford 2001), who deals with Shakespeare at pp. 40-51, 115-17.

30 C. Kahn, 'The Rape in Shakespeare's Lucrece', *SSt* 9 (1976), 45-72.

31 Burrow (note 25), 58.

32 Augustine, *The City of God* 1.19.

33 For the *Sonnets* see J. Kerrigan (ed.), *William Shakespeare – The Sonnets and A Lover's Complaint* (London 2005), 7-63; H. Vendler, *The Art of Shakespeare's Sonnets* (Cambridge, Mass. 1997); K. Duncan-Jones (ed.), *Shakespeare's Sonnets* (London 2007), 1-105; Burrow (note 25), 91-138.

34 For the later impact of Ovid see M. L. Stapleton, *Harmful Eloquence: Ovid's 'Amores' from Antiquity to Shakespeare* (Michigan 1996).

35 See A. F. Marotti, '"Love is not Love": Elizabethan Sonnet Sequences and the Social Order', *English Literary History* 49 (1982), 396-428.

36 Kerrigan (note 33), 11.

37 Ovid's Metamorphoses, Translated by Arthur Golding, ed. M. Foley (London 2002), 463; cf. Horace Odes 3.30. For comment on Golding see G. Braden, The Classics and English Renaissance Poetry: Three Case Studies (New Haven 1978), 1-54; R. Lyne, Ovid's Changing Worlds (Oxford 2001), 27-79.

38 *ibid.*, 444.

39 *ibid.*, 441.

40 Ovid, *Metamorphoses* 15. 878.

Notes to Chapter Six

1 T. S. Eliot, *On Poetry and Poets* (London 1969), 68. For comment see B. Arkins, 'Eliot as Critic: The Case of Latin Literature', *Yeats-Eliot Review* 17,3 (2001), 10-14.

2 M. Tudeau-Clayton, Jonson, Shakespeare and Early Modern Virgil (Cambridge 1998).

3 The large amount of work on Shakespeare and Virgil often fails to convince; for a suitably astringent view of the topic see C. Martindale, 'Shakespeare and Virgil' in *Shakespeare and the Classics*, eds C. Martindale & A. B. Taylor (Cambridge 2005), 89-106.

4 J. Pitcher, ' "A Theatre of the Future": The *Aeneid* and *The Tempest*, *Essays in Criticism*' 34 (1984), 197.

5 For Dido see, eg., W. A. Camps, *An Introduction to Virgil's Aeneid* (Oxford 1969), 31-35; for later views of her see *A Woman Scorn'd: Responses to the Dido Myth*, ed. M. Burden (London 1998).

6 Eliot (note 1), 62.

7 William Shakespeare, *The Tempest*, ed. S. Orgel (Oxford 1995), 40-42.

8 C. Martindale (note 3), 90-91.

9 H. James, *Shakespeare's Troy: Drama, Politics, and the Translation of Empire* (Cambridge 1997).

10 R. S. Miola, *Shakespeare's Rome* (Cambridge 1983), 82-85.

11 William Shakespeare, *Hamlet*, ed. G. R. Hibbard (Oxford 1998), 227.

12 For *The Tempest* and the *Aeneid* see D. B. Hamilton, *Virgil and 'The Tempest'* (Columbus 1980); James (note 9), 189-221; Tudeau-Clayton (note 2), 184-244; J. Kott, 'The *Aeneid* and *The Tempest*', *Arion* 3 (1978), 425-52; Pitcher (note 4), 194-215. It is difficult to feel that these ingenious works establish a convincing relationship between the two texts.

13 For the masque see Orgel (note 7), 43-50.

14 *ibid.*, 48.

15 For these themes see *The Tempest*, eds. V. M. Vaughan & A. T. Vaughan (London 2007), 98-108.

16 Mannoni, cited in Vaughan & Vaughan (note 15), 337.

Notes to Chapter Seven

1 For recent accounts of Latin see F. Waquet, *Latin or the Empire of a Sign* (London / New York 2001), T. Jonson, *A Natural History of Latin* (Oxford 2004). For Latin in Shakespeare see J. W. Binns, *SSu* 35 (1982), 11-28.

2 Waquet (note 1), 80-88.

3 For Cade see William Shakespeare, *Henry VI, Part Two*, ed. R. Warren (Oxford 2003), 50-57.

4 F. Palmer, *Grammar* (Harmondsworth 1978), 62.

5 Cf. A. C. Bough & T. Cable, *A History of the English Language* (Abingdon 2006), 11: 'more than half its vocabulary is derived from Latin'; this book deals with Renaissance English at pp. 214-35. Estimates of the amount of Latin in English can be much higher or much lower: Jonson (note 1), 173 says 'The words that come from Latin or Greek, either directly or via French, are the great majority. Estimates vary between three quarters and nine tenths'; R. Posner in

The Legacy of Rome, ed. R. Jenkyns (Oxford 1992), 391: 'As a result of borrowing, it has been estimated that a quarter of English vocabulary, taken broadly in the sense of words listed in a large dictionary, is ultimately of Latin origin'.

6 For Shakespeare's language see esp. F. Kermode, *Shakespeare's Language* (London 2000). For his vocabulary see J. Schaefer, *Shakespeare's Stil: Germanisches und Romanisches Vocabular* (Frankfurt-am-Main 1973). For new Latin-based words in Shakespeare see B. A. Gerner, 'Shakespeare's Latinate Neologisms', *Shakespeare Studies* 15 (1982), 149-70.

7 Defne, quoted in Bough & Cable (note 5), 287.

8 W. Pater, quoted in *William Shakespeare – Love's Labour's Lost*, ed. J. Kerrigan (London 1982), 22.

9 For Mantuan see R. Jenkyns in Jenkyns (note 5), 157-59.

9a Binns (note 1), 126.

10 For a list of these see Gerner (note 6), 158-67.

11 T.S. Eliot, *Collected Poems 1909-1962* (London 1974), 131; W. B. Yeats, *The Poems*, ed. R. J. Finneran (Dublin 1984), 338.

12 For compound words in English see D. J. Allerton & M. A. French in *The English Language*, eds. W. F. Bolton & D. Crystal (London 1993), 121-32; for compound adjectives in Hopkins see B. Arkins, 'Style in the Poetry of Hopkins', *Rivisto di studi Vittoriani* 2, 4 (1997), 65-66.

13 For hendiadys in *Hamlet* see G. T. Wright, 'Hendiadys in *Hamlet*', *PMLA* 96 (1981), 168-93, Kermode (note 6), 100-25.

14 Carew, quoted in Schaefer (note 6), 49; for this passage in *Macbeth* see W. Empson, *Seven Types of Ambiguity* (Harmondsworth 1977), 69-71.

15 For these synonyms see Schaefer (note 6), 116-51.

16 Jonson, quoted in William Shakespeare, *Henry IV, Part 2*, ed. R. Weiss (Oxford 1998), 177.

17 For the impact of Greek and Latin on English literature since the Renaissance see K. Haynes, *English Literature and Ancient Languages* (Oxford 2003).

18 *Hamlet* 1.2.146; 1.4.90; 2.2.90; 2.2.467-8; 2.2.202-3; 3.4.158; 1.5.165-6; 2.3.373-4.

19 *Poetical Works of Alfred Lord Tennyson* (London 1899), 571.

20 Pinker, quoted in *The Oxford Dictionary of Literary Quotations*, ed. P. Kemp (Oxford 1997), 123.8.

Notes to Chapter Eight

1. E. J. Kenney in *The Cambridge History of Classical Literature, IV Latin Literature* (Cambridge 1982), 456.

2. For derogatory views of the Greeks in early modern England see T. Spencer, *Fair Greece Sad Relic* (London 1954), 32-47; for these views in Rome see J. P. V. D. Balsdon, *Romans and Aliens* (London 1979), 30-58.

3. Horace, *Epistles* 2.1.156-7; Plautus, *Mostellaria* 1.1.22, Juvenal 3.60-1. Robert Greene, quoted in P. Honan, (Oxford 1999), 159.

4. For Shakespeare and Greek tragedy see M. Silk in *Shakespeare and the Classics*, eds C. Martindale & A. B. Taylor (Cambridge 2005), 247-57; see also A. Poole, *Tragedy: Shakespeare and the Greek Example* (Oxford 1987).

5. It is argued for strongly by E. Jones, *The Origins of Shakespeare* (Oxford 1977), 85-118.

6. C. & M. Martindale, *Shakespeare and the Uses of Antiquity* (London / New York 1994), 44.

7. M. S. Silk, 'Tragic Language: The Greek Tragedians and Shakespeare' in *Tragedy and the Tragic*, ed. M. S. Silk (Oxford 1996), 458-96.

8. For Platonism in Shakespeare see J. Roe, 'Italian Neoplatonism and the Poetry of Sidney, Shakespeare, Chapman and Donne' in *Platonism and the English Imagination*, eds. A. Baldwin & S. Hutton (Cambridge 1994), 100-16; S. Metcalf, 'Shakespeare on Beauty, Truth and Transcendence', *ibid*, 117-25.

9. Roe (note 8), 107-10.

10. Metcalf (note 8), 119-22.

11. For this epigram and various translations and versions of it see J. Hutton, 'Analogues of Shakespeare's Sonnets 153-54', *Modern Philology* 38 (1941), 385-403.

12. J. Kerrigan, *William Shakespeare – The Sonnets and A Lover's Complaint* (London 2005), 13-15; 61-2.

13. For the text of *Pericles* and comment on it see R. Warren (ed), *William Shakespeare and George Wilkins, Pericles, Prince of Tyre* (Oxford 2004); for further comment see *Pericles – Critical Essays*, ed. D. Skeele (New York / London 2000), G. Wilson Knight, *The Crown of Life* (London 1985), 32-75. For the collaboration with Wilkins, see B. Vickers, *Shakespeare, Co-author* (Oxford 2004), 291-332.

14. Ben Jonson, *Ode to Himself*, 21-2.

¹⁴ᵃ C. Nicholl, *The Lodger – Shakespeare on Silver Street* (London 2007), 197-226.

¹⁵ K. Muir, *Shakespeare as Collaborator* (London 1960), 88-9.

¹⁶ For the Greek and Roman novel see M. Doody, *The True History of the Novel* (New Brunswick, NJ 1957); *Twelfth Night* 5.1.106-9; for narrative devices in Pericles see D. Delvecchio & A. Hammond, *Pericles, Prince of Tyre* (Cambridge 2006), 27-36.

¹⁷ N. Frye, *Anatomy of Criticism* (Princeton 1954), 57.

¹⁷ᵃ Louis MacNeice, *Collected Poems*, ed. P. McDonald (London 2007), 274.

¹⁸ Cf. Basola in Webster, *The Duchess of Malfi* (5.4.53-4): 'We are merely the stars' tennis-balls, struck and bandied / Which may please them'.

¹⁹ T.S. Eliot, quoted in Skeale (note 13), 6.

²⁰ *Acts* 19. For Diana in *Pericles* see C. Bicks in Skeale (note 13), 205-27.

²⁰ᵃ Henry James in *The Oxford Book of Literary Quotations*, ed. P. Kemp (Oxford 1999), 17.5.

²¹ For the collaboration between Middleton and Shakespeare see J. Jowett (ed.), *William Shakespeare and Thomas Middleton, The Life of Timon of Athens* (Oxford 2004); Vickers (note 13), 244-90.

²² Steiner in Silk (note 7), 540-41.

²³ 1 Timothy 6:10.

²⁴ G. Egan, *Shakespeare and Marx* (Oxford 2000, 106-15.

²⁵ Aristotle, *Nicomachean Ethics II*

²⁶ W.B. Yeats, *The Poems*, ed. R. J. Finneran (Dublin 1984), 286.

²⁷ P. Masterson, 'The concept of resentment', *Studies* 68 (1979), 157-72; for Apemantus as Cynic philosopher see R. B. Pierce, *Classical and Modern Literature* 25 (2005), 77-88; Hazlitt, quoted in Jowett (note 21), 76.

²⁸ Plutarch, *Life of Antony*, ed. C. B. R. Pelling (Cambridge 1999), 293.

²⁹ For Alcibiades see S. Forde, *The Ambition to Rule: Alcibiades and the Politics of Imperialism in Thucydides* (Ithaca / London 989); W. Ellis, *Alcibiades* (London / New York 1989); D. Gribble, *Alcibiades and Athens: A Study in Literary Presentation* (Oxford 1999).

³⁰ Aristophanes, *Frogs*, 1431 b-2.

³¹ For Alcibiades in *Timon of Athens* see S. Henna, *Classical and Modern Literature* 23 (2003), 77-94.

31a E. M. Waith, *The Twin Noble Kinsmen* (Oxford 1998), 43.

32 For Troilus and Cressida see K. Muir (ed.) William Shakespeare – Troilus and Cressida (Oxford 1998), 1-40; C. Burrow in *William Shakespeare – Troilus and Cressida*, ed. R. A. Foches (London 2006), xxi-lxxiv.

33 Chaucer.

34 *Chapman's Homer – The Iliad, The Odyssesy*, Introduction by J. Parker (Were, Hertfordshire 2002); quotation on p. 418. For comment on Chapman see R. A. Brower, *Hero and Saint – Shakespeare and the Greco-Roman Heroic Tradition* (Oxford 1971), 50-81.

35 *Homer in English*, ed. G. Steiner (London 1956), 126.

36 S. Freud, *Collected Papers* (London 1950), IV 214.

37 D. M. Halperin, *One Hundred Years of Homosexuality* (New York / London 1990), 75-87.

38 For language see P. Thompson, 'Rant and Cant in Troilus and Cressida', *Essays and Studies* 22 (1969), 33-56, T. McAlindon, 'Language, Style and Meaning in *Troilus and Cressida*', *PMLA* 84 (1969), 29-43.

39 C. Spurgeon, *Shakespeare's Imagery and What it Tells Us* (Cambridge 1935).

40 For possible further use of Aristotle in this play se *Troilus and Cressida*, ed. K. Palmer (London 1982), 311-20.

41 C. Burrow in Martindale & Taylor (note 4), 21.

42 G. Steiner, *The Death of Tragedy* (New Haven / London 1996), 24.

Notes To Conclusion

1 Ezra Pound, *The Cantos* (London 1987), 796.

2 L.A. Hitchcock, *Theory for Classics* (New York / London 2008), 51.

3 Racine, Preface to *Bérénice*; R. W. Emerson, *Representative Men* (London 1012), 89.

4 Shakespeare, *Henry V*, Prologue 2.

5 Quintilian 10. 2. 4, 1.

6 W.B. Yeats, *Essays and Introductions* (New York 1961), 522.

7 E. Auerbach, *Mimesis* (Princeton 1968), 278.

Select Bibliography

GENERAL WORKS ON SHAKESPEARE AND HIS ERA

Ackroyd, P., *Shakespeare – the Biography* (London 2005).

Adelman, J., *The Common Liar: An Essay on Antony and Cleopatra* (New Haven / London 1973).

Barber, C. L., *Shakespeare's Festive Comedy* (Princeton 1959).

Barkan, L., 'What did Shakespeare read?' in *The Cambridge Companion to Shakespeare*, eds. M. de Grazia & S. Wells (Cambridge 2001), 31-47.

Bate, J., *The Genius of Shakespeare* (London 1997).

Beer, A., *Milton* (London 2008).

Bell, M., *Shakespeare's Tragic Scepticism* (New Haven / London 2002).

Bloom, H., *Shakespeare: The Invention of the Human* (New York 1998).

Bradshaw, G., *Shakespeare's Scepticism* (Ithaca 1990).

Burgess, A, *Shakespeare* (London 2002).

Carroll, D. A., 'Greene's "Upstart Crow" Passage: A Survey of Commentary', *Research Opportunities in Renaissance Drama* 28 (1985), 111-27.

Danson, L., *Shakespeare's Dramatic Genres* (Oxford 2002).

Dobson, M & Wells. S. (eds), *The Oxford Companion to Shakespeare* (Oxford 2005).

Doran, M., *Endeavours of Art: A Study of Form in Elizabethan Drama* (Madison 1954).

Dutton, R. et al (eds), *Theatre and Religion – Lancastrian Shakespeare* (Manchester 2003).

Dollimore, J. & Sinfield, A., (eds), *Political Shakespeare* (Manchester 1985).

Egan, G., *Shakespeare and Marx* (Oxford 2004).

Fernie, E. et al (eds.), *Recovering the Renaissance – A Critical Reader* (Oxford 2005).

Fuzier, J., 'Rhetoric Versus Rhetoric: A Study of Shakespeare's Julius Caesar, Act III, Scene 2', *Cahiers Elizabéthans* 5 (1981), 25-65.

Greenblatt, S., *Will in the World* (London 2004).

Greene, T. M., *The Light in Troy: Imitation and Discovery in Renaissance Poetry* (New Haven 1982).

Hale, J., *The Civilization of Europe in the Renaissance* (London 2005).

Hayles, N. K., 'Sexual Disguise in *As You Like It* and *Twelfth Night*', *SSu* 32 (1979), 63-72.

Hawkes, T., *Meaning by Shakespeare* (London 1992).

---, *Shakespeare in the Present* (London / New York 2002).

Hodgson, B., 'Antony and Cleopatra in the Theatre' in *The Cambridge Companion to Shakespearean Tragedy* ed. C. McEachern, (Cambridge 2002), 241-63.

Hoffenden, J. (ed.), *Berryman on Shakespeare* (New York 2001).

Holden, A., *William Shakespeare – His Life and Work* (London 2005).

Honan, P., *Shakespeare – A Life* (New York 1999).

---, *Christopher Marlowe – Poet and Spy* (Oxford 2005).

Hulse, C., *Metamorphic Verse: The Elizabethan Minor Epic* (Princeton 1981).

Jenkyns, R., 'Pastoral' in *The Legacy of Rome*, ed. R. Jenkyns (Oxford 1992), 151-75.

Jones, E., 'Stuart Cymbeline', *Essays in criticism* 11 (1961), 84-99.

Jones, E., *The Origins of Shakespeare* (Oxford 1977).

Kahn, C., 'The Rape in Shakespeare's Lucrece', *SSt* 9 (1976), 45-72.

Keach, W., *Elizabethan Erotic Narrative* (New Brunswick 1977)

Kermode, F., *Shakespeare's Language* (London 2000).

---, *The Age of Shakespeare* (London 2004).

Kolin, P. C. (ed.), *Venus and Adonis: Critical Essays* (New York / London 1977).

Kott, J., *Shakespeare Our Contemporary* (London 1965).

Legatt, A., *Shakespeare's Comedy of Love* (London 1974).

---, *Shakespeare's Political Drama* (London / New York 2002).

---, (ed.), *The Cambridge Companion to Shakespearean Comedy* (Cambridge 2002).

McAlindon, T., 'Language, Style and Meaning in Troilus and Cressida', *PMLA* 84 (1969), 29-43.

Matthiessen, F. O., *Translation: An Elizabethan Art* (Cambridge, Mass 1931).

Miola, R. S., *Shakespeare's Reading* (Oxford 2000).

Muir, K., *Shakespeare as Collaborator* (London 1960).

Nicholl, C., *The Lodger – Shakespeare on Silver Street* (London 2007).

Ong, W. J., S. J., 'Latin Language Study as a Renaissance Puberty Rite', *Studies in Philology* 56 (1959), 103-24.

O'Toole, F., *Shakespeare is Hard, but so is life* (London / New York 2002).

Rabkin, N., *Shakespeare and the Problem of Meaning* (Chicago / London 1981).

Salinger, L., *Shakespeare and the Traditions of Comedy* (Cambridge 1974).

Schanzer, E., *The Problem Plays of Shakespeare* (London 1963).

Shapiro, J., Rival Playwrights: Marlow, Jonson and Shakespeare (New York 1991).

---, *1599 – A Year in the Life of William Shakespeare* (London 2005).

Simone, R. T., *Shakespeare and Lucrece: A Study of the Poem and its Relation to the Plays* (Salzburg 1974).

Skeele, D. (ed.), *Pericles – Critical Essays* I (New York / London 2000).

Smith, G. G., *Elizabethan Critical Essays* I (Oxford 1971).

Spurgeon, C., *Shakespeare's Imagery and What it Tells Us* (Cambridge 1935).

Thompson, P., 'Rant and Cant in Troilus and Cressida', *Essays and Studies* 22 (1969), 33-56.

Vendler, H., *The Art of Shakespeare's Sonnets* (Cambridge, Mass. 1997).

Vickers, B., *Shakespeare, Co-author* (Oxford 2004).

Wells, S., *Shakespeare – The Poet and his Plays* (London 2001).

Whitaker, V. K., *Shakespeare's Use of Learning* (San Marino, Cal. 1953).

Wilson, R., *Secret Shakespeare – Studies in theatre, religion and resistance* (Manchester 2004).

Wright, G. T., 'Hendiadys in *Hamlet*, *PMLA* 96 (1981), 168-93.

SHAKESPEARE, WILLIAM – EDITIONS OF HIS WORKS

Bate, J., *The Arden Shakespeare – Titus Andronicus* (London 2006).

Bliss, L., *The New Cambridge Shakespeare – Coriolanus* (Cambridge 2007).

Burrow, C., *William Shakespeare – The Complete Sonnets and Poems* (Oxford 2002).

Delvecchio, D. & Hammond, A., *The New Cambridge Shakespeare – Pericles, Prince of Tyre* (Cambridge 2006).

Donno, E. S. & Gay, P., *The New Cambridge Shakespeare – Twelfth Night or What You Will* (Cambridge 2004).

Foakes, R. A., *Troilus and Cressida* (London 2006).

---, *The New Cambridge Shakespeare – A Midsummer Night's Dream* (Cambridge 1990).

Hammond, A., *The Arden Shakespeare – King Richard III* (London 1992).

Hibberd, G. R., *William Shakespeare – Hamlet* (Oxford 1998).

Holland, P., William Shakespeare – A Midsummer Night's Dream (Oxford 1998).

Jowett, J., *William Shakespeare & Thomas Middleton, The Life of Timon of Athens* (Oxford 2004).

Kerrigan, J., *William Shakespeare – The Sonnets and A Lover's Complaint* (London 2005).

Muir, K., *William Shakespeare – Troilus and Cressida* (Oxford 1998).

Neill, M., *William Shakespeare – The Tragedy of Antony and Cleopatra* (Oxford 2000).

Orgel, S., *William Shakespeare – The Tempest* (Oxford 1998).

Palmer, K., *The Arden Shakespeare: Troilus and Cressida* (London 1992).

Parker, R. B., *William Shakespeare – The Tragedy of Coriolanus* (Oxford 1998).

Roe, J., *The New Cambridge Shakespeare: The Poems* (Cambridge 1992).

Thompson, A., *The New Cambridge Shakespeare – The Taming of the Shrew* (Cambridge 2006).

Thompson, A. & Taylor, N., *The Arden Shakespeare, Hamlet* (London 2006).

Vaughan, V. M., & Vaughan, A. T., *The Arden Shakespeare – The Tempest* (London 2007).

Waith, E. M., *William Shakespeare – Titus Andronicus* (Oxford 1998).

Warren, R., *William Shakespeare – Cymbeline* (Oxford 1998).

---, *William Shakespeare & George Wilkins, Pericles, Prince of Tyre* (Oxford 2004).

Weiss, R., *William Shakespeare – Henry IV, Part Two* (Oxford 1998).

Whitworth, C., William Shakespeare – The Comedy of Errors (Oxford 2002).

Wilders, J., *The Arden Shakespeare – Antony and Cleopatra* (London 2006).

GENERAL WORKS ON ROMAN AND GREEK THEMES

Arkins, B., *Hellenising Ireland: Greek and Roman Themes in Modern Irish Literature* (Newbridge 2005).

---, *Irish Appropriation of Greek Tragedy* (Dublin 2010).

Barkan, L., *The Gods Made Flesh: Metamorphosis and the Pursuit of Paganism* (New Haven / London 1986).

Bauman, R. A., *Women and Politics in Ancient Rome* (London 1994).

Boyle, A. J., *Tragic Seneca – an Essay in the Theatrical Tradition* (London 1997).

Brown, S. A., *The Metamorphoses of Ovid: Chaucer to Ted Hughes* (London 1999).

Burden, M. (ed.), *A Woman Scorn'd: Responses to the Dido Myth* (London 1998).

Balsdon, J. P. V. D., *Romans and Aliens* (London 1978).

Calasso, R., *The Marriage of Cadmus and Harmony* (London 1994).

Camps, W. A., *An Introduction to Virgil's Aeneid* (Oxford 1969).

Carter, J., *The Battle of Actium* (London 1970).

Croally, N. T., *Euripidean Polemic: The Trojan Women and the Function of Tragedy* (Cambridge 1994).

Dixon, S., *Cornelia – Mother of the Gracchi* (Abingdon 2007).

Donaldson, I., *The Rapes of Lucretia: A Myth and its Transformations* (Oxford 1982).

Doody, M., *The True History of the Novel* (New Brunswick, NJ 1997).

Duckworth, G. E., *The Nature of Roman Comedy* (Princeton 1967).

Fantham, E., *Ovid's Metamorphoses* (Oxford 2004).

Forde, S., *The Ambition to Rule: Alcibiades and the Politics of Imperialism* (Ithaca / London 1989).

Golding, Arthur, *Ovid's Metamorphoses*, ed. M. Foley (London 2002).

Grant, M., *Julius Caesar* (London 1972).

---, *Cleopatra* (London 2003).

Gribble, D., *Alcibiades and Athens: A Study in Literary Presentation* (Oxford 1999).

Halperin, D. M., *One Hundred Years of Homosexuality* (New York / London 1990).

Hamer, M., *Signs of Cleopatra* (London 1993).

Hardie, P. (ed.), *The Cambridge Companion to Ovid* (Cambridge 2002).

Hardwick, L., *Reception Studies* (Oxford 2003).

Haynes, K., *English Literature and Ancient Languages* (Oxford 2003).

Herington, C. J., 'Senecan Tragedy', *Arion* 5 (1966), 422-71.

---, 'The Younger Seneca' in *The Cambridge History of Classical Literature, II, Latin Literature*, ed. E. J. Kenney (Cambridge 1982), 511-32.

Hofmann, M. & Lasdeen, J. (eds.), *After Ovid – New Metamorphoses* (London 1996).

Hughes, Ted, *Oedipus* (London 1969).

---, *Tales from Ovid* (London 1997).

Hughes-Hallett, L., *Cleopatra* (London 1991).

Jansen, T., *A Natural History of Latin* (Oxford 2004).

Kenney, E. J., 'The Style of the Metamorphoses' in *Ovid*, ed. J. W. Binns (London / Boston 1973), 116-53.

Lamberton, R., *Plutarch* (New Haven / London 2001).

Martindale, C. & Thomas, R. F., *Classics and the Uses of Reception* (Oxford 2006).

Morgan, K., *Ovid's Art of Imitation: Propertius in the Amores* (Leiden 1979).

Neering, H., 'The Legend of Julius Caesar's British Conquest', *PMLA* 64 (1949), 889-929.

Osgood, J., *Caesar's Legacy* (Cambridge 2006).

Otis, B., *Ovid as an Epic Poet* (Cambridge 1970).

Pelling, C. B. R. (ed.), *Plutarch – Life of Antony* (Cambridge 1999).

Rist, J. M., *Stoic Philosophy* (Cambridge 1969).

Russell, D., *Plutarch* (London 1973).

Segal, C., *Landscape in Ovid's Metamorphoses* (Wiesbaden 1969).

Segal, E., *Roman Laughter – The Comedy of Plautus* (Cambridge, Mass. 1970).

Segal, E., 'The *Menaechmi*: Roman Comedy of Errors', *Yale Classical Studies* 21 (1969), 77-93.

Steiner, G., *Antigones* (Oxford 1984).

---, (ed.) *Homer in English* (London 1996).

Syme, R., *The Roman Revolution* (Oxford 2002).

Tarn, W., 'The Battle of Actium', *Journal of Roman Studies* 21 (1931), 173-99.

Waith, E., *The Herculean Hero in Marlowe, Chapman, Shakespeare and Dryden* (New York / London 1962).

Waquet. F., *Latin or the Empire of a Sign* (London / New York 2001).

Weiss, R., *The Renaissance Discovery of Classical Antiquity* (Oxford 1969).

Wilamowitz-Moellendorff, U., *Griechische Tragödie*, III (Berlin 1919).

Wiseman, T. P., 'Roman History and the Ideological Vacuum' in *Classics in Progress*, ed. T. P. Wiseman (Oxford 2006), 285-310.

Wyke, M. (ed.), *Julius Caesar in Western Culture* (Oxford 2006).

---, *Caesar – A Life in Western Culture* (London 2007).

ON ROMAN AND GREEK THEMES IN SHAKESPEARE

Arkins, B., 'Heavy Seneca: His Influence on Shakespeare's Tragedies', *Classics Ireland* 2 (1995), 1-16.

Bate, J., *Shakespeare and Ovid* (Oxford 2001).

Bicks, C., 'Backsliding at Ephesus; Shakespeare's Diana and the churching of women' in *Pericles – Critical Essays*, ed. D. Skeele (New York/London 2000), 205-27.

Bono, B. J., *Literary Transvaluations: From Virgilian Epic to Shakespearean Tragicomedy* (Berkeley 1984).

Borrow, C., 'Shakespeare and Humanistic culture' in Martindale & Taylor, 9-27.

Boughner, D. D., *The Braggart in Renaissance Comedy* (Minneapolis 1954).

Braden, G., *Renaissance Tragedy and the Senecan Tradition: Anger's Privilege* (New Haven 1985).

Brooks, H. F., 'Richard III, Unhistorical Amplifications: The Women's Scenes and Seneca', *Modern Language Review* 75 (1980), 721-37.

Brower, R. A., *Hero and Saint: Shakespeare and the Graeco-Roman Heroic Tradition* (Oxford 1971).

Ewben, I-S, 'The Fiend-like Queen: A Note on *Macbeth* and Seneca's *Medea*', *SSu* 19 (1966), 82-94.

Garner, B. A., 'Shakespeare's Latinate Neologisms', *SSt* 15 (1982), 70-149.

Green, D. C., *Julius Caesar and its Sources* (Salzburg 1979).

Hamilton, D. B., *Virgil and 'The Tempest'* (Columbus 1980).

Hanna, S., 'The Trial of Alcibiades in Shakespeare's *Timon of Athens*', *Classical and Modern Literature* 23 (2003), 77-94.

Hanson, J. A., 'The Glorious Military' in *Roman Drama*, eds. D. R. Dudley & T. A. Dorey (London 1965), 51-85.

Hart, F. E., ' "Great is Diana" of Shakespeare's Ephesus', *Studies in English Literature* 43 (2003), 347-74.

Hulme, H. M., Explorations in Shakespeare's Language (London 1962).

Hulton, J., 'Analogues of Shakespeare's Sonnets 153-54', *Modern Philology* 38 (1941), 385-403.

Hunter, G. K., 'Seneca and the Elizabethans', *SSu* 20 (1967), 17-26.

---, 'Seneca and English Tragedy' in *Seneca*, ed. C. N. D. Costa (London 1974), 166-204.

James, H., *Shakespeare's Troy: Drama, Politics, and the Translation of Empire* (Cambridge 1997).

Kahn, C., *Roman Shakespeare: Warriors, Wounds and Women* (London 1997).

Knox, B., '"The Tempest" and Ancient Comic Tradition' in *William Shakespeare – The Tempest*, ed. R. Langbaum (New York 1964), 163-81.

Kott, J., 'The Aeneid and The Tempest', *Arion* 3 (1978), 425-52.

Levin, H, 'Two Comedies of Errors' in *The Comedy of Errors*, ed. R. S. Miola (New York 2001), 113-33.

Lloyd-Evans, G., 'Shakespeare, Seneca, and the Kingdom of Violence' in *Roman Drama*, eds. D. R. Dudley & T. A. Dorey (London 1965), 123-59.

Lyne, R., *Ovid's Changing Worlds: English Metamorphoses 1567-1632* (Cambridge 2001).

MacCallum, M. W., *Shakespeare's Roman Plays and their Background* (London 1910; 1967).

Martindale, C. & M., *Shakespeare and the Uses of Antiquity* (London 1994)/

Martindale, C. & Taylor, A. B., (eds.) *Shakespeare and the Classics* (Cambridge 2005).

Martindale, C., 'Shakespeare and Virgil' in Martindale & Taylor, 89-106.

Metcalf, 'Shakespeare on Beauty, Truth and Transcendence' in *Platonism and the English Imagination*, eds. A. Baldwin & S. Hulton (Cambridge 1994), 117-25.

Miles, G., *Shakespeare and the Constant Romans* (Oxford 1996).

Miola, R. S., *Shakespeare's Rome* (Cambridge 1983).

---, *Shakespeare and Classical Tragedy*: The Influence of Seneca (Oxford 1992).

---, *Shakespeare and Classical Comedy* (Oxford 1997).

---, (ed.) *The Comedy of Errors – Critical Essays* (New York / London 2001).

O'Connor, J., *Shakespearean Afterlives* (Duxford, Camb. 2003).

Paul, H. N., *The Royal Play of 'Macbeth'* (London 1950).

Peyré, Y., 'Confusion now hath made his masterpiece: Senecan resonances in *Macbeth*' in Martindale & Taylor, 141-55.

Pierce, R. B., 'From Anecdotal Philosophy to Drama: Shakespeare's Apemantus as Cynic', *Classical and Modern Literature* 25 (2005), 77-88.

Pitcher, J., ' "A Theatre of the Future": The *Aeneid* and *The Tempest*', *Essays in Criticism* 34 (1984), 194-215.

Poole, A., *Tragedy and the Greek Experience* (Oxford 1987).

Riehle, W., *Shakespeare, Plautus and the Humanist Tradition* (Cambridge 1990).

Roe, J., 'Italian Neoplatonism and the Poetry of Sidney, Shakespeare, Chapman and Donne' in Baldwin & Hutton (above, Metcalf), 100-16.

Root, R. K., *Classical Mythology in Shakespeare* (New York 1965).

Schaefer, J., *Shakespeares Stil: Germanisches and Romanisches Vokabular* (Frankfirt 1973).

Silk, M., 'Tragic Language: The Greek Tragedians and Shakespeare in *Tragedy and the Tragic*, ed. M. S. Silk (Oxford 1996), 458-96.

Spencer, T. J. B., 'Shakespeare and the Elizabethan Romans', *SSu* 10 (1957), 39-49.

---, (ed.) *Shakespeare's Plutarch* (Harmondsworth 1964).

Taylor, A. B. (ed.), *Shakespeare's Ovid: The Metamorphoses in the Plays and Poems* (Cambridge 2006).

Tobin, J. J. M., *Shakespeare's Favorite Novel* (Lanham 1984).

Tudeau-Clayton, M., Jonson, *Shakespeare and Early Modern Virgil* (Cambridge 1998).

REMAINING WORKS CITED

Abbott, V., 'How It Was: Egan and Beckett' in *Desmond Egan – The Poet and his Work*, ed. H. Kenner (Orono 1990), 45-53.

Allerton, D. J. & French, M. A., 'Morphology: The Forms of English' in *The English Language* eds. W. F. Bolton & D. Crystal (London 1993), 121-32.

Arkins, B., 'Style in the Poetry of Hopkins', *Rivista di Studi Vittoriani* 2 (1997), 51-71.

---, 'Eliot as Critic: The Case of Latin Literature', *Yeats-Eliot Review* 17, 3 (2001), 10-14.

Artaud, A., *The Theatre and its Double* (London 1999).

Bakhtin, M., 'From the prehistory of novelistic discourse' in *Modern Criticism and Theory*, ed. D. Lodge (London 1993), 125-56.

Benjamin, W., *Illuminations* (London 1999).

Berst, C. A., 'New Theatres for Old in *The Cambridge Companion to Shaw*, ed. C. Innes (Cambridge 2004), 55-75.

Bloom, H., *The Anxiety of Influence* (New York / Oxford 1997).

Bough, A. C. & Cable, T., *A History of the English Language* (Abingdon 2006).

Bourdieu, P., *Distinction – A Social Critique of the Judgment of Taste* (Cambridge Mass. 2002).

Butler, C., *Postmodernism* (Oxford 2002).

Calvino, I., *Why Read the Classics?* (London 2000).

Denteith, S., *Parody* (London 2000).

De Quincey, Thomas, *On Murder* (Oxford 2006).

Eagleton, T., *Sweet Violence - The Idea of the Tragic* (Oxford 2003).

Eliot, T. S. (ed.), *Literary Essays of Ezra Pound* (London 1960).

---, *On Poetry and Poets* (London 1969).

---, *Collected Poems* (London 1974)

---, *Selected Essays* (New York 1966).

Empson, W., *Seven Types of Ambiguity* (Harmondsworth 1977).

Foucauld, M., *The History of Sexuality, Volume One: An Introduction* (Harmondsworth 1981).

Freud, S., *Jokes and their Relation to the Unconscious* (London 2001).

Frye, N., 'The Argument of Comedy' in *Comedy: Developments in Criticism*, ed. D. J., Palmer (London 1984), 74-84.

---, *Anatomy of Criticism* (Princeton 1957).

Housman, A. E., *Selected Prose*, ed. J. Carter (Cambridge 1961).

Joyce, James, *A Portrait of the Artist as a Young Man*, ed. J. Johnson (Oxford 2000).

---, *Finnegans Wake* (London 1992).

Kavanagh, Patrick, *Collected Poems* (London 1973).

Keeley, E. & Sherrard, P. (trans.), *Four Greek Poets* (Harmonsworth 1966).

Kemp, P. (ed.), *Oxford Dictionary of Literary Quotations* (Oxford 1999).

Kustow, M., *Peter Brook* (London 2006).

Leech, C., *Tragedy* (London 1969).

Masterson, P., 'The Concept of Resentment', *Studies* 68 (1979), 157-72.

Meyers, J., *Married to Genius* (Harpenden, Herts. 2005).

Miklail, E. H. (ed.), *W. B. Yeats: Interviews and Recollections* Vol. Ii (London 1977).

Paglia, C., *Sexual Personae* (London 1992).

Palmer, F., *Grammar* (Harmondsworth 1978).

Pater, W., *Appreciations* (London   ).

Pound, Ezra, *The Cantos* (London 1987).

Rose, M. A., *Parody: Ancient, Modern and Postmodern* (Cambridge 1993).

Rubin, G., ' "The Traffic in Women": Notes on the Political Economy of Sex' in *Towards an Anthropology of Women*, ed. R. R. Reiter (New York 1975), 157-210.

Segal, E., *The Death of Comedy* (Cambridge, Mass / London 2001).

Steiner, G., *The Death of Tragedy* (New Haven / London 1996).

---, 'Tragedy, Pure and Simple' in *Tragedy and the Tragic*, ed. M. Silk (Oxford 1996), 534-46.

Stevens, Wallace, *Opus Posthumus*, ed. S. F. Morse (London 1959).

Stoppard, Tom, *Rosenkrantz and Guildenstern are Dead* (London 2000).

Stott, A., *Comedy* (New York / London 2005).

Tennyson, Lord Alfred, 'To Virgil' in *Poetical Works of Alfred Lord Tennyson* (London 1899), 570-71.

Vieira, E. R. P., 'Liberating Calibans: Reading of Anthropofagia and Haraldo de Campos's *Poetics of Transcreation* in *Post-Colonial Translation*, eds. S. Bassnett & H. Trivedi (London / New York 2002), 95-113.

Walsh, D., *Literature and Knowledge* (Middletown 1969).

White, H., *Metahistory – The Historical Imagination in Nineteenth-Century Europe* (Baltimore / London 1975).

Wood, M., *Literature and the Taste of Knowledge* (Cambridge 2005).

Yeats, W.B., *The Poems*, ed. R. J. Finneran (Dublin 1984).
---, *Essays and Introductions* (New York 1961).
---, *A Vision* (London 1981).

Carysfort Press was formed in the summer of 1998. It receives annual funding from the Arts Council.

The directors believe that drama is playing an ever-increasing role in today's society and that enjoyment of the theatre, both professional and amateur, currently plays a central part in Irish culture.

The Press aims to produce high quality publications which, though written and/or edited by academics, will be made accessible to a general readership. The organisation would also like to provide a forum for critical thinking in the Arts in Ireland, again keeping the needs and interests of the general public in view.

The company publishes contemporary Irish writing for and about the theatre.

Editorial and publishing inquiries to:
Carysfort Press Ltd.,
58 Woodfield,
Scholarstown Road,
Rathfarnham,
Dublin 16,
Republic of Ireland.

T (353 1) 493 7383
F (353 1) 406 9815
E: info@carysfortpress.com
www.carysfortpress.com

HOW TO ORDER

TRADE ORDERS DIRECTLY TO:
Irish Book Distribution
Unit 12, North Park, North Road,
Finglas, Dublin 11.

T: (353 1) 8239580
F: (353 1) 8239599
E: mary@argosybooks.ie
www.argosybooks.ie

INDIVIDUAL ORDERS DIRECTLY TO:
eprint Ltd.
35 Coolmine Industrial Estate,
Blanchardstown, Dublin 15.
T: (353 1) 827 8860
F: (353 1) 827 8804 Order online @
E: books@eprint.ie
www.eprint.ie

FOR SALES IN NORTH AMERICA AND CANADA:
Dufour Editions Inc.,
124 Byers Road,
PO Box 7,
Chester Springs,
PA 19425,
USA

T: 1-610-458-5005
F: 1-610-458-7103

Polite Forms

Harry White

Polite Forms is a sequence of poems that meditates on family life. These poems remember and reimagine scenes from childhood and adolescence through the formal composure of the sonnet, so that the uniformity of this framing device promotes a tension as between a neatly arranged album of photographs and the chaos and flow of experience itself. Throughout the collection there is a constant preoccupation with the difference between actual remembrance and the illumination or meaning which poetry can afford. Some of the poems 'rewind the tapes of childhood' across two or three generations, and all of them are akin to pictures at an exhibition which survey individual impressions of childhood and parenthood in a thematically continuous series of portraits drawn from life.

Harry White was born in Dublin in 1958. He is Professor of Music at University College Dublin and widely known for his work in musicology and cultural history. His publications include "Music and the Irish Literary Imagination" (Oxford, 2008), which was awarded the Michael J. Durkan prize of the American Conference for Irish Studies in 2009. "Polite Forms" is his first collection of poems

ISBN: 978 1-904505-55-6 €10

Ibsen and Chekhov on the Irish Stage

Edited by Ros Dixon and Irina Ruppo Malone

Ibsen and Chekhov on the Irish Stage presents articles on the theories of translation and adaptation, new insights on the work of Brian Friel, Frank McGuinness, Thomas Kilroy, and Tom Murphy, historical analyses of theatrical productions during the Irish Revival, interviews with contemporary theatre directors, and a round-table discussion with the playwrights, Michael West and Thomas Kilroy.

Ibsen and Chekhov on the Irish Stage challenges the notion that a country's dramatic tradition develops in cultural isolation. It uncovers connections between past productions of plays by Ibsen and Chekhov and contemporary literary adaptations of their works by Irish playwrights, demonstrating the significance of international influence for the formation of national cannon.

Conceived in the spirit of a round-table discussion, *Ibsen and Chekhov on the Irish Stage* is a collective study of the intricacies of trans-cultural migration of dramatic works and a re-examination of Irish theatre history from 1890 to the present day.

ISBN: 978-1-904505-57-0   €20

Tom Swift Selected Plays

With an introduction by Peter Crawley.

The inaugural production of Performance Corporation in 2002 matched Voltaire's withering assault against the doctrine of optimism with a playful aesthetic and endlessly inventive stagecraft.

Each play in this collection was originally staged by the Performance Corporation and though Swift has explored different avenues ever since, such playfulness is a constant. The writing is precise, but leaves room for the discoveries of rehearsals, the flesh of the theatre. All plays are blueprints for performance, but several of these scripts – many of which are site-specific and all of them slyly topical – are documents for something unrepeatable.

ISBN: 978-1-904505-56-3   €20

Synge and His Influences: Centenary Essays from the Synge Summer School

Edited by Patrick Lonergan

The year 2009 was the centenary of the death of John Millington Synge, one of the world's great dramatists. To mark the occasion, this book gathers essays by leading scholars of Irish drama, aiming to explore the writers and movements that shaped Synge, and to consider his enduring legacies. Essays discuss Synge's work in its Irish, European and world contexts – showing his engagement not just with the Irish literary revival but with European politics and culture too. The book also explores Synge's influence on later writers: Irish dramatists such as Brian Friel, Tom Murphy and Marina Carr, as well as international writers like Mustapha Matura and Erisa Kironde. It also considers Synge's place in Ireland today, revealing how *The Playboy of the Western World* has helped to shape Ireland's responses to globalisation and multiculturalism, in celebrated productions by the Abbey Theatre, Druid Theatre, and Pan Pan Theatre Company.

Contributors include Ann Saddlemyer, Ben Levitas, Mary Burke, Paige Reynolds, Eilís Ní Dhuibhne, Mark Phelan, Shaun Richards, Ondřej Pilný, Richard Pine, Alexandra Poulain, Emilie Pine, Melissa Sihra, Sara Keating, Bisi Adigun, Adrian Frazier and Anthony Roche.

ISBN: 978-1-904505-50-1   €20.00

Constellations - The Life and Music of John Buckley

Benjamin Dwyer

Benjamin Dwyer provides a long overdue assessment of one of Ireland's most prolific composers of the last decades. He looks at John Buckley's music in the context of his biography and Irish cultural life. This is no hagiography but a critical assessment of Buckley's work, his roots and aesthetics. While looking closely at several of Buckley's compositions, the book is written in a comprehensible style that makes it easily accessible to anybody interested in Irish musical and cultural history.   *Wolfgang Marx*

As well as providing a very readable and comprehensive study of the life and music of John Buckley, Constellations also offers an up-to-date and informative catalogue of compositions, a complete discography, translations of set texts and the full libretto of his chamber opera, making this book an essential guide for both students and professional scholars alike.

ISBN: 978-1-904505-52-5   €20.00

'Because We Are Poor': Irish Theatre in the 1990s

Victor Merriman

"Victor Merriman's work on Irish theatre is in the vanguard of a whole new paradigm in Irish theatre scholarship, one that is not content to contemplate monuments of past or present achievement, but for which the theatre is a lens that makes visible the hidden malaises in Irish society. That he has been able to do so by focusing on a period when so much else in Irish culture conspired to hide those problems is only testimony to the considerable power of his critical scrutiny." Chris Morash, NUI Maynooth.

ISBN: 978-1-904505-51-8   €20.00

'Buffoonery and Easy Sentiment':
Popular Irish Plays in the Decade Prior to the Opening of The Abbey Theatre

Christopher Fitz-Simon

In this fascinating reappraisal of the non-literary drama of the late 19th - early 20th century, Christopher Fitz-Simon discloses a unique world of plays, players and producers in metropolitan theatres in Ireland and other countries where Ireland was viewed as a source of extraordinary topics at once contemporary and comfortably remote: revolution, eviction, famine, agrarian agitation, political assassination.

The form was the fashionable one of melodrama, yet Irish melodrama was of a particular kind replete with hidden messages, and the language was far more allusive, colourful and entertaining than that of its English equivalent.

ISBN: 978-1-9045505-49-5   €20.00

The Fourth Seamus Heaney Lectures, 'Mirror up to Nature':

Ed. Patrick Burke

What, in particular, is the contemporary usefulness for the building of societies of one of our oldest and culturally valued ideals, that of drama? The Fourth Seamus Heaney Lectures, 'Mirror up to Nature': Drama and Theatre in the Modern World, given at St Patrick's College, Drumcondra, between October 2006 and April 2007, addressed these and related questions. Patrick Mason spoke on the essence of theatre, Thomas Kilroy on Ireland's contribution to the art of theatre, Cecily O'Neill and Jonothan Neelands on the rich potential of drama in the classroom. Brenna Katz Clarke examined the relationship between drama and film, and John Buckley spoke on opera and its history and gave an illuminating account of his own *Words Upon The Window-Pane*.

ISBN 978-1-9045505-48-8   €12

The Theatre of Tom Mac Intyre: 'Strays from the ether'

Eds. Bernadette Sweeney and Marie Kelly

This long overdue anthology captures the soul of Mac Intyre's dramatic canon – its ethereal qualities, its extraordinary diversity, its emphasis on the poetic and on performance – in an extensive range of visual, journalistic and scholarly contributions from writers, theatre practitioners.

ISBN 978-1-904505-46-4 €25

Irish Appropriation Of Greek Tragedy

Brian Arkins

This book presents an analysis of more than 30 plays written by Irish dramatists and poets that are based on the tragedies of Sophocles, Euripides and Aeschylus. These plays proceed from the time of Yeats and Synge through MacNeice and the Longfords on to many of today's leading writers.

ISBN 978-1-904505-47-1 €20

Alive in Time: The Enduring Drama of Tom Murphy

Ed. Christopher Murray

Almost 50 years after he first hit the headlines as Ireland's most challenging playwright, the 'angry young man' of those times Tom Murphy still commands his place at the pinnacle of Irish theatre. Here 17 new essays by prominent critics and academics, with an introduction by Christopher Murray, survey Murphy's dramatic oeuvre in a concerted attempt to define his greatness and enduring appeal, making this book a significant study of a unique genius.

ISBN 978-1-904505-45-7 €25

Performing Violence in Contemporary Ireland

Ed. Lisa Fitzpatrick

This interdisciplinary collection of fifteen new essays by scholars of theatre, Irish studies, music, design and politics explores aspects of the performance of violence in contemporary Ireland. With chapters on the work of playwrights Martin McDonagh, Martin Lynch, Conor McPherson and Gary Mitchell, on Republican commemorations and the 90th anniversary ceremonies for the Battle of the Somme and the Easter Rising, this book aims to contribute to the ongoing international debate on the performance of violence in contemporary societies.

ISBN 978-1-904505-44-0 (2009) €20

Ireland's Economic Crisis - Time to Act. Essays from over 40 leading Irish thinkers at the MacGill Summer School 2009

Eds. Joe Mulholland and Finbarr Bradley

Ireland's economic crisis requires a radical transformation in policymaking. In this volume, political, industrial, academic, trade union and business leaders and commentators tell the story of the Irish economy and its rise and fall. Contributions at Glenties range from policy, vision and context to practical suggestions on how the country can emerge from its crisis.

ISBN 978-1-904505-43-3 (2009) €20

Deviant Acts: Essays on Queer Performance

Ed. David Cregan

This book contains an exciting collection of essays focusing on a variety of alternative performances happening in contemporary Ireland. While it highlights the particular representations of gay and lesbian identity it also brings to light how diversity has always been a part of Irish culture and is, in fact, shaping what it means to be Irish today.

ISBN 978-1-904505-42-6 (2009) €20

Seán Keating in Context: Responses to Culture and Politics in Post-Civil War Ireland

Compiled, edited and introduced by Éimear O'Connor

Irish artist Seán Keating has been judged by his critics as the personification of old-fashioned traditionalist values. This book presents a different view. The story reveals Keating's early determination to attain government support for the visual arts. It also illustrates his socialist leanings, his disappointment with capitalism, and his attitude to cultural snobbery, to art critics, and to the Academy. Given the national and global circumstances nowadays, Keating's critical and wry observations are prophetic – and highly amusing.

ISBN 978-1-904505-41-9 €25

Dialogue of the Ancients of Ireland: A new translation of Acallam na Senorach

Translated with introduction and notes by Maurice Harmon

One of Ireland's greatest collections of stories and poems, The Dialogue of the Ancients of Ireland is a new translation by Maurice Harmon of the 12th century *Acallam na Senorach*. Retold in a refreshing modern idiom, the *Dialogue* is an extraordinary account of journeys to the four provinces by St. Patrick and the pagan Cailte, one of the surviving Fian. Within the frame story are over 200 other stories reflecting many genres – wonder tales, sea journeys, romances, stories of revenge, tales of monsters and magic. The poems are equally varied – lyrics, nature poems, eulogies, prophecies, laments, genealogical poems. After the *Tain Bo Cuailnge*, the *Acallam* is the largest surviving prose work in Old and Middle Irish.

ISBN: 978-1-904505-39-6 (2009) €20

Literary and Cultural Relations between Ireland and Hungary and Central and Eastern Europe

Ed. Maria Kurdi

This lively, informative and incisive collection of essays sheds fascinating new light on the literary interrelations between Ireland, Hungary, Poland, Romania and the Czech Republic. It charts a hitherto under-explored history of the reception of modern Irish culture in Central and Eastern Europe and also investigates how key authors have been translated, performed and adapted. The revealing explorations undertaken in this volume of a wide array of Irish dramatic and literary texts, ranging from *Gulliver's Travels* to *Translations* and *The Pillowman*, tease out the subtly altered nuances that they acquire in a Central European context.

ISBN: 978-1-904505-40-2 (2009) €20

Plays and Controversies: Abbey Theatre Diaries 2000-2005

Ben Barnes

In diaries covering the period of his artistic directorship of the Abbey, Ben Barnes offers a frank, honest, and probing account of a much commented upon and controversial period in the history of the national theatre. These diaries also provide fascinating personal insights into the day-to- day pressures, joys, and frustrations of running one of Ireland's most iconic institutions.

ISBN: 978-1-904505-38-9 (2008) €35

Interactions: Dublin Theatre Festival 1957-2007. Irish Theatrical Diaspora Series: 3

Eds. Nicholas Grene and Patrick Lonergan with Lilian Chambers

For over 50 years the Dublin Theatre Festival has been one of Ireland's most important cultural events, bringing countless new Irish plays to the world stage, while introducing Irish audiences to the most important international theatre companies and artists. Interactions explores and celebrates the achievements of the renowned Festival since 1957 and includes specially commissioned memoirs from past organizers, offering a unique perspective on the controversies and successes that have marked the event's history. An especially valuable feature of the volume, also, is a complete listing of the shows that have appeared at the Festival from 1957 to 2008.

ISBN: 978-1-904505-36-5 €25

The Informer: A play by Tom Murphy based on the novel by Liam O'Flaherty

The Informer, Tom Murphy's stage adaptation of Liam O'Flaherty's novel, was produced in the 1981 Dublin Theatre Festival, directed by the playwright himself, with Liam Neeson in the leading role. The central subject of the play is the quest of a character at the point of emotional and moral breakdown for some source of meaning or identity. In the case of Gypo Nolan, the informer of the title, this involves a nightmarish progress through a Dublin underworld in which he changes from a Judas figure to a scapegoat surrogate for Jesus, taking upon himself the sins of the world. A cinematic style, with flash-back and intercut scenes, is used rather than a conventional theatrical structure to catch the fevered and phantasmagoric progression of Gypo's mind. The language, characteristically for Murphy, mixes graphically colloquial Dublin slang with the haunted intricacies of the central character groping for the meaning of his own actions. The dynamic rhythm of the action builds towards an inevitable but theatrically satisfying tragic catastrophe. ' [The Informer] is, in many ways closer to being an original Murphy play than it is to O'Flaherty...' Fintan O'Toole.

ISBN: 978-1-904505-37-2 (2008) €10

Shifting Scenes: Irish theatre-going 1955-1985

Eds. Nicholas Grene and Chris Morash

Transcript of conversations with John Devitt, academic and reviewer, about his lifelong passion for the theatre. A fascinating and entertaining insight into Dublin theatre over the course of thirty years provided by Devitt's vivid reminiscences and astute observations.

ISBN: 978-1-904505-33-4 (2008) €10

Irish Literature: Feminist Perspectives

Eds. Patricia Coughlan and Tina O'Toole

The collection discusses texts from the early 18th century to the present. A central theme of the book is the need to renegotiate the relations of feminism with nationalism and to transact the potential contest of these two important narratives, each possessing powerful emancipatory force. Irish Literature: Feminist Perspectives contributes incisively to contemporary debates about Irish culture, gender and ideology.

ISBN: 978-1-904505-35-8 (2008) €25

Silenced Voices: Hungarian Plays from Transylvania

Selected and translated by Csilla Bertha and Donald E. Morse

The five plays are wonderfully theatrical, moving fluidly from absurdism to tragedy, and from satire to the darkly comic. Donald Morse and Csilla Bertha's translations capture these qualities perfectly, giving voice to the 'forgotten playwrights of Central Europe'. They also deeply enrich our understanding of the relationship between art, ethics, and politics in Europe.

ISBN: 978-1-904505-34-1 (2008) €25

**A Hazardous Melody of Being:
Seóirse Bodley's Song Cycles on the poems of Micheal O'Siadhail**

Ed. Lorraine Byrne Bodley

This apograph is the first publication of Bodley's O'Siadhail song cycles and is the first book to explore the composer's lyrical modernity from a number of perspectives. Lorraine Byrne Bodley's insightful introduction describes in detail the development and essence of Bodley's musical thinking, the European influences he absorbed which linger in these cycles, and the importance of his work as a composer of the Irish art song.

ISBN: 978-1-904505-31-0 (2008)   €25

Irish Theatre in England: Irish Theatrical Diaspora Series: 2

Eds. Richard Cave and Ben Levitas

Irish theatre in England has frequently illustrated the complex relations between two distinct cultures. How English reviewers and audiences interpret Irish plays is often decidedly different from how the plays were read in performance in Ireland. How certain Irish performers have chosen to be understood in Dublin is not necessarily how audiences in London have perceived their constructed stage personae. Though a collection by diverse authors, the twelve essays in this volume investigate these issues from a variety of perspectives that together chart the trajectory of Irish performance in England from the mid-nineteenth century till today.

ISBN: 978-1-904505-26-6 (2007)   €20

Goethe and Anna Amalia: A Forbidden Love?

Ettore Ghibellino, Trans. Dan Farrelly

In this study Ghibellino sets out to show that the platonic relationship between Goethe and Charlotte von Stein – lady-in-waiting to Anna Amalia, the Dowager Duchess of Weimar – was used as part of a cover-up for Goethe's intense and prolonged love relationship with the Duchess Anna Amalia herself. The book attempts to uncover a hitherto closely-kept state secret. Readers convinced by the evidence supporting Ghibellino's hypothesis will see in it one of the very great love stories in European history – to rank with that of Dante and Beatrice, and Petrarch and Laura.

ISBN: 978-1-904505-24-2 €20

Ireland on Stage: Beckett and After

Eds. Hiroko Mikami, Minako Okamuro, Naoko Yagi

The collection focuses primarily on Irish playwrights and their work, both in text and on the stage during the latter half of the twentieth century. The central figure is Samuel Beckett, but the contributors freely draw on Beckett and his work provides a springboard to discuss contemporary playwrights such as Brian Friel, Frank McGuinness, Marina Carr and Conor McPherson amongst others. Contributors include: Anthony Roche, Hiroko Mikami, Naoko Yagi, Cathy Leeney, Joseph Long, Noreem Doody, Minako Okamuro, Christopher Murray, Futoshi Sakauchi and Declan Kiberd

ISBN: 978-1-904505-23-5 (2007) €20

'Echoes Down the Corridor': Irish Theatre - Past, Present and Future

Eds. Patrick Lonergan and Riana O'Dwyer

This collection of fourteen new essays explores Irish theatre from exciting new perspectives. How has Irish theatre been received internationally - and, as the country becomes more multicultural, how will international theatre influence the development of drama in Ireland? These and many other important questions.

ISBN: 978-1-904505-25-9 (2007) €20

Musics of Belonging: The Poetry of Micheal O'Siadhail

Eds. Marc Caball & David F. Ford

An overall account is given of O'Siadhail's life, his work and the reception of his poetry so far. There are close readings of some poems, analyses of his artistry in matching diverse content with both classical and innovative forms, and studies of recurrent themes such as love, death, language, music, and the shifts of modern life.

ISBN: 978-1-904505-22-8 (2007) €25 (Paperback)
ISBN: 978-1-904505-21-1 (2007) €50 (Casebound)

Brian Friel's Dramatic Artistry: 'The Work has Value'

Eds. Donald E. Morse, Csilla Bertha and Maria Kurdi

Brian Friel's Dramatic Artistry presents a refreshingly broad range of voices: new work from some of the leading English-speaking authorities on Friel, and fascinating essays from scholars in Germany, Italy, Portugal, and Hungary. This book will deepen our knowledge and enjoyment of Friel's work.

ISBN: 978-1-904505-17-4 (2006) €30

The Theatre of Martin McDonagh: 'A World of Savage Stories'

Eds. Lilian Chambers and Eamonn Jordan

The book is a vital response to the many challenges set by McDonagh for those involved in the production and reception of his work. Critics and commentators from around the world offer a diverse range of often provocative approaches. What is not surprising is the focus and commitment of the engagement, given the controversial and stimulating nature of the work.

ISBN: 978-1-904505-19-8 (2006) €35

Edna O'Brien: New Critical Perspectives

Eds. Kathryn Laing, Sinead Mooney and Maureen O'Connor

The essays collected here illustrate some of the range, complexity, and interest of Edna O'Brien as a fiction writer and dramatist. They will contribute to a broader appreciation of her work and to an evolution of new critical approaches, as well as igniting more interest in the many unexplored areas of her considerable oeuvre.

ISBN: 978-1-904505-20-4 (2006) €20

Irish Theatre on Tour

Eds. Nicholas Grene and Chris Morash

'Touring has been at the strategic heart of Druid's artistic policy since the early eighties. Everyone has the right to see professional theatre in their own communities. Irish theatre on tour is a crucial part of Irish theatre as a whole'. Garry Hynes

ISBN 978-1-904505-13-6 (2005) €20

Poems 2000-2005 by Hugh Maxton

Poems 2000-2005 is a transitional collection written while the author – also known to be W.J. Mc Cormack, literary historian – was in the process of moving back from London to settle in rural Ireland.

ISBN 978-1-904505-12-9 (2005) €10

Synge: A Celebration

Ed. Colm Tóibín

A collection of essays by some of Ireland's most creative writers on the work of John Millington Synge, featuring Sebastian Barry, Marina Carr, Anthony Cronin, Roddy Doyle, Anne Enright, Hugo Hamilton, Joseph O'Connor, Mary O'Malley, Fintan O'Toole, Colm Toibin, Vincent Woods.

ISBN 978-1-904505-14-3 (2005) €15

East of Eden: New Romanian Plays

Ed. Andrei Marinescu

Four of the most promising Romanian playwrights, young and very young, are in this collection, each one with a specific way of seeing the Romanian reality, each one with a style of communicating an articulated artistic vision of the society we are living in. Ion Caramitru, General Director Romanian National Theatre Bucharest.
ISBN 978-1-904505-15-0 (2005) €10

George Fitzmaurice: 'Wild in His Own Way', Biography of an Irish Playwright

Fiona Brennan

'Fiona Brennan's introduction to his considerable output allows us a much greater appreciation and understanding of Fitzmaurice, the one remaining under-celebrated genius of twentieth-century Irish drama'. Conall Morrison

ISBN 978-1-904505-16-7 (2005) €20

Out of History: Essays on the Writings of Sebastian Barry

Ed. Christina Hunt Mahony

The essays address Barry's engagement with the contemporary cultural debate in Ireland and also with issues that inform postcolonial critical theory. The range and selection of contributors has ensured a high level of critical expression and an insightful assessment of Barry and his works.

ISBN: 978-1-904505-18-1 (2005) €20

Three Congregational Masses

Seoirse Bodley

'From the simpler congregational settings in the Mass of Peace and the Mass of Joy to the richer textures of the Mass of Glory, they are immediately attractive and accessible, and with a distinctively Irish melodic quality.' Barra Boydell

ISBN: 978-1-904505-11-2 (2005) €15

Georg Büchner's Woyzeck,

A new translation by Dan Farrelly

The most up-to-date German scholarship of Thomas Michael Mayer and Burghard Dedner has finally made it possible to establish an authentic sequence of scenes. The wide-spread view that this play is a prime example of loose, open theatre is no longer sustainable. Directors and teachers are challenged to "read it again".

ISBN: 978-1-904505-02-0 (2004) €10

Playboys of the Western World: Production Histories

Ed. Adrian Frazier

'The book is remarkably well-focused: half is a series of production histories of Playboy performances through the twentieth century in the UK, Northern Ireland, the USA, and Ireland. The remainder focuses on one contemporary performance, that of Druid Theatre, as directed by Garry Hynes. The various contemporary social issues that are addressed in relation to Synge's play and this performance of it give the volume an additional interest: it shows how the arts matter.' Kevin Barry

ISBN: 978-1-904505-06-8 (2004) €20

The Power of Laughter: Comedy and Contemporary Irish Theatre

Ed. Eric Weitz

The collection draws on a wide range of perspectives and voices including critics, playwrights, directors and performers. The result is a series of fascinating and provocative debates about the myriad functions of comedy in contemporary Irish theatre. Anna McMullan

As Stan Laurel said, 'it takes only an onion to cry. Peel it and weep. Comedy is harder'. 'These essays listen to the power of laughter. They hear the tough heart of Irish theatre – hard and wicked and funny'. Frank McGuinness

ISBN: 978-1-904505-05-1 (2004) €20

Sacred Play: Soul-Journeys in contemporary Irish Theatre

Anne F. O'Reilly

'Theatre as a space or container for sacred play allows audiences to glimpse mystery and to experience transformation. This book charts how Irish playwrights negotiate the labyrinth of the Irish soul and shows how their plays contribute to a poetics of Irish culture that enables a new imagining. Playwrights discussed are: McGuinness, Murphy, Friel, Le Marquand Hartigan, Burke Brogan, Harding, Meehan, Carr, Parker, Devlin, and Barry.'

ISBN: 978-1-904505-07-5 (2004) €25

The Irish Harp Book

Sheila Larchet Cuthbert

This is a facsimile of the edition originally published by Mercier Press in 1993. There is a new preface by Sheila Larchet Cuthbert, and the biographical material has been updated. It is a collection of studies and exercises for the use of teachers and pupils of the Irish harp.

ISBN: 978-1-904505-08-2 (2004)   €35

The Drunkard

Tom Murphy

'The Drunkard is a wonderfully eloquent play. Murphy's ear is finely attuned to the glories and absurdities of melodramatic exclamation, and even while he is wringing out its ludicrous overstatement, he is also making it sing.' The Irish Times

ISBN: 978-1-90 05-09-9 (2004)   €10

Goethe: Musical Poet, Musical Catalyst

Ed. Lorraine Byrne

'Goethe was interested in, and acutely aware of, the place of music in human experience generally - and of its particular role in modern culture. Moreover, his own literary work - especially the poetry and Faust - inspired some of the major composers of the European tradition to produce some of their finest works.' Martin Swales

ISBN: 978-1-9045-10-5 (2004)   €40

The Theatre of Marina Carr: "Before rules was made"

Eds. Anna McMullan & Cathy Leeney

As the first published collection of articles on the theatre of Marina Carr, this volume explores the world of Carr's theatrical imagination, the place of her plays in contemporary theatre in Ireland and abroad and the significance of her highly individual voice.

ISBN: 978-0-9534257-7-8 (2003)   €20

Critical Moments: Fintan O'Toole on Modern Irish Theatre

Eds. Julia Furay & Redmond O'Hanlon

This new book on the work of Fintan O'Toole, the internationally acclaimed theatre critic and cultural commentator, offers percussive analyses and assessments of the major plays and playwrights in the canon of modern Irish theatre. Fearless and provocative in his judgements, O'Toole is essential reading for anyone interested in criticism or in the current state of Irish theatre.

ISBN: 978-1-904505-03-7 (2003)   €20

Goethe and Schubert: Across the Divide

Eds. Lorraine Byrne & Dan Farrelly

Proceedings of the International Conference, 'Goethe and Schubert in Perspective and Performance', Trinity College Dublin, 2003. This volume includes essays by leading scholars – Barkhoff, Boyle, Byrne, Canisius, Dürr, Fischer, Hill, Kramer, Lamport, Lund, Meikle, Newbould, Norman McKay, White, Whitton, Wright, Youens – on Goethe's musicality and his relationship to Schubert; Schubert's contribution to sacred music and the Lied and his setting of Goethe's Singspiel, Claudine. A companion volume of this Singspiel (with piano reduction and English translation) is also available.

ISBN: 978-1-904505-04-4 (2003) €25

Goethe's Singspiel, 'Claudine von Villa Bella'

Set by Franz Schubert

Goethe's Singspiel in three acts was set to music by Schubert in 1815. Only Act One of Schuberts's Claudine score is extant. The present volume makes Act One available for performance in English and German. It comprises both a piano reduction by Lorraine Byrne of the original Schubert orchestral score and a bilingual text translated for the modern stage by Dan Farrelly. This is a tale, wittily told, of lovers and vagabonds, romance, reconciliation, and resolution of family conflict.

ISBN: 978-0-9544290-0-3 (2002) €20

Theatre of Sound, Radio and the Dramatic Imagination

Dermot Rattigan

An innovative study of the challenges that radio drama poses to the creative imagination of the writer, the production team, and the listener.
"A remarkably fine study of radio drama – everywhere informed by the writer's professional experience of such drama in the making...A new theoretical and analytical approach – informative, illuminating and at all times readable." Richard Allen Cave

ISBN: 978- 0-9534-257-5-4 (2002) €20

Talking about Tom Murphy

Ed. Nicholas Grene

Talking About Tom Murphy is shaped around the six plays in the landmark Abbey Theatre Murphy Season of 2001, assembling some of the best-known commentators on his work: Fintan O'Toole, Chris Morash, Lionel Pilkington, Alexandra Poulain, Shaun Richards, Nicholas Grene and Declan Kiberd.

ISBN: 978-0-9534-257-9-2 (2002) €15

Hamlet: The Shakespearean Director

Mike Wilcock

"This study of the Shakespearean director as viewed through various interpretations of HAMLET is a welcome addition to our understanding of how essential it is for a director to have a clear vision of a great play. It is an important study from which all of us who love Shakespeare and who understand the importance of continuing contemporary exploration may gain new insights." From the Foreword, by Joe Dowling, Artistic Director, The Guthrie Theater, Minneapolis, MN

ISBN: 978-1-904505-00-6 (2002) €20

The Theatre of Frank Mc Guinness: Stages of Mutability

Ed. Helen Lojek

The first edited collection of essays about internationally renowned Irish playwright Frank McGuinness focuses on both performance and text. Interpreters come to diverse conclusions, creating a vigorous dialogue that enriches understanding and reflects a strong consensus about the value of McGuinness's complex work.

ISBN: 978-1904505-01-3. (2002) €20

Theatre Talk: Voices of Irish Theatre Practitioners

Eds Lilian Chambers, Ger Fitzgibbon and Eamonn Jordan

"This book is the right approach - asking practitioners what they feel." Sebastian Barry, Playwright "... an invaluable and informative collection of interviews with those who make and shape the landscape of Irish Theatre." Ben Barnes, Artistic Director of the Abbey Theatre

ISBN: 978-0-9534-257-6-1 (2001) €20

In Search of the South African Iphigenie

Erika von Wietersheim and Dan Farrelly

Discussions of Goethe's "Iphigenie auf Tauris" (Under the Curse) as relevant to women's issues in modern South Africa: women in family and public life; the force of women's spirituality; experience of personal relationships; attitudes to parents and ancestors; involvement with religion.

ISBN: 978-0-9534257-8-5 (2001) €10

'The Starving' and 'October Song':

Two contemporary Irish plays by Andrew Hinds

The Starving, set during and after the siege of Derry in 1689, is a moving and engrossing drama of the emotional journey of two men.

October Song, a superbly written family drama set in real time in pre-ceasefire Derry.

ISBN: 978-0-9534-257-4-7 (2001)   €10

Seen and Heard: Six new plays by Irish women

Ed. Cathy Leeney

A rich and funny, moving and theatrically exciting collection of plays by Mary Elizabeth Burke-Kennedy, Síofra Campbell, Emma Donoghue, Anne Le Marquand Hartigan, Michelle Read and Dolores Walshe.

ISBN: 978-0-9534-257-3-0 (2001)   €20

Theatre Stuff: Critical essays on contemporary Irish theatre

Ed. Eamonn Jordan

Best selling essays on the successes and debates of contemporary Irish theatre at home and abroad. Contributors include: Thomas Kilroy, Declan Hughes, Anna McMullan, Declan Kiberd, Deirdre Mulrooney, Fintan O'Toole, Christopher Murray, Caoimhe McAvinchey and Terry Eagleton.

ISBN: 978-0-9534-2571-1-6 (2000)   €20

Under the Curse. Goethe's "Iphigenie Auf Tauris", A New Version

Dan Farrelly

The Greek myth of Iphigenie grappling with the curse on the house of Atreus is brought vividly to life. This version is currently being used in Johannesburg to explore problems of ancestry, religion, and Black African women's spirituality.

ISBN: 978-09534-257-8-5 (2000)   €10

Urfaust, A New Version of Goethe's early "Faust" in Brechtian Mode

Dan Farrelly

This version is based on Brecht's irreverent and daring re-interpretation of the German classic. "Urfaust is a kind of well-spring for German theatre... The love-story is the most daring and the most profound in German dramatic literature." Brecht

ISBN: 978-0-9534-257-0-9 (1998)   €10

www.ingramcontent.com/pod-product-compliance
Lightning Source LLC
Chambersburg PA
CBHW070330230426
43663CB00011B/2272